Imaginative Bodies

Dialogues in Performance Practices

Guy Cools

Antennae
Valiz, Amsterdam

In Memory of Rosemary Butcher (1947–2016),
whose works and conversations inspired many of us.

Imaginative Bodies
Dialogues in Performance Practices

Guy Cools
Lisa Marie Bowler (ed.)

Guy Cools in Conversation with

Sue Buckmaster
Jonathan Burrows & Matteo Fargion
Rosemary Butcher
Dana Caspersen
Sidi Larbi Cherkaoui
Piet Defraeye
Tim Etchells
Antony Gormley
Jonzi D & Soweto Kinch
Akram Khan
Ruth Little
Russell Maliphant & Michael Hulls
Alain Platel
Hofesh Shechter

Contents

Introduction
The Body: Language Talks

The Art of Listening

To develop my work as a production dramaturg in dance, working with amongst others such highprofile artists as Akram Khan or Sidi Larbi Cherkaoui, my own interest shifted from the production side of the creative process to the receptive side: so as to continue to train one's perception or one's listening skills in a dialogical practice. And although writing always remained my own creative medium and output, I started to experiment with other forms of writing that were either more embodied and performative as in the *Rewriting Distance* performance practice, which I developed with the Canadian choreographer Lin Snelling. Miranda Tufnell, one of the gurus of British dance improvisation, with whom we started our *Rewriting Distance* research, defines a creative, improvisational practice as an essentially conversational practice.

> Creating becomes a conversation when we enter a dialogue with whatever we are doing. In this conversing we are drawn along in the moment-by-moment flow of sensation, interchange and choice, rather than following a predetermined intention or idea. Conversations grow as we listen and explore – a constantly shifting process of discovery that changes in momentum, rhythm, clarity or chaos as we work.[1]

In order to find different ways to embody my writing more, I also started to experiment with translating the dialogical or sometimes even polyphonic nature of oral practices onto paper. The conversations in this book are an example of the latter.

The Rebirth of Dialogue

> If we were apprentices of listening rather than masters of discourse we might perhaps promote a different sort of coexistence among humans: not so much in the form of a utopian ideal but rather as an incipient philosophical solidarity capable of envisaging the common destiny of the species.[2]

My own shift in interest from the active/production side of the creative process to the receptive/perceptive side seems to coincide with an ethical turn in the arts.[3] This ethical turn revalorises the act of listening in a dialogical practice that uses the sentient body to reconnect with its environment.

Since Bakhtin, there has been a re-evaluation and re-orientation of the importance of dialogue within the classical, rhetorical tradition dating from Socrates and Plato. In *The Rebirth of Dialogue*, James P. Zappen gives an overview of how 'the emergence of dialogue as a response to cultural values embedded within printed texts, beginning as early as Bakhtin and extending to recent discussion of the new digital media'[4] mirrors the way in which Socratic dialogue had been a response to an older, oral tradition. In order for dialogue – as an exchange of utterances – not to become cacophony, each participant in the dialogue also has to practice 'an active viewing of each utterance from the perspective of the other'. The dialogue is in opposition to monologic rhetoric. It proposes 'openness and incompleteness, becoming rather than being, the created rather than the given, the unfinished rather than the finished'.[5] This form of dialogue also clearly differentiates itself from the dialectic. Its purpose is not to persuade the other but to let new ideas emerge out of a creative interaction between many voices.

Gemma Corradi Fiumara is a contemporary philosopher who looks at the same Socratic tradition but through the lenses of such twentieth-century philosophers as Wittgenstein, Heidegger and Gadamer. In *The Other Side of Language: A Philosophy of Listening*, she pleads for a reappraisal of the receptive act of listening within a dialogical practice. Fiumara opens her book with the observation that in the history of Western thought, 'logos' is mainly aimed at 'saying', which is often the equivalent of 'defining' and has no 'recognisable references to the notion and capacity of listening'.[6] This lack of a practice of listening, according to Fiumara, is also responsible for the growing subdivision and fragmentation of our knowledge. As we institutionalise we tend to listen to and support only our own areas of interest and lose the ability to listen to the larger frames of life. For her, the lack of listening has severe ecological consequences (cf. the quote above) and she continues to argue that listening is the precondition of good research and of creative thinking itself.

Richard Sennett develops a similar argument to Fiumara In *Together: The Rituals, Pleasures and Politics of Cooperation* and discusses how the lack of dialogical practice and the failure to exercise one's listening skills is one of the main reasons for the diminishing social cohesion in the work place. As a sociologist, Sennett has been conducting extensive research on both the working conditions of back-office workers on Wall Street and those of computer programmers in Silicon Valley. His research provides both quantitative and qualitative data on how a short-time perspective has taken over on all levels of work, and how 'stability in the work has become a stigma' with 'project labour acting as an acid solvent, eating away at authority, trust and cooperation'.[7] Sennett describes several new pathologies such as anxiety and withdrawal, either into narcissism or complacency, which arise as a result of this process. He not only criticises, but also tries to offer a vision and strategies for reversing or transforming the current state of affairs. One of the main strategies he proposes, besides revaluing rituals, is to practice dialogic skills such as 'listening well', 'managing disagreement' or 'behaving tactfully'. He also underlines the importance of recognising the listener's share in a discussion, realising that receptivity means paying attention to both verbal and non-verbal concrete details in order to understand not only what is said but the underlying assumptions as well. Cooperation requires listening and only by doing so are we able to 'weave' the complexities, whether of society, of life in the city, of a group gathering or a choreography. Sennett, who himself also had a career as a professional musician, sees the professional performing arts as a particularly well suited laboratory for retraining our dialogical skills.

In a good conversation, neither of the participants knows in advance what the topics discussed will be or how the flow and structure of the conversation will connect and link these topics. It is only in the alternation of listening and speaking, of questions and answers, that an associative chain is established. The utterances of everybody participating are usually based on what people already know: their experiences and assumptions. But it is in the shifts of the conversation and in the spaces in between utterances that hopefully new insights arise that do not belong to one person specifically, but create a new shared collective consciousness. It is because of this intrinsic open quality of the conversation or dialogue that the scientist David Bohm proposed to practise dialogue in larger groups of people to recreate a sense of what is 'common' and recreate coherence where there is now mainly fragmentation. In *On Dialogue* Bohm follows a similar line of thinking to Sennett's. Social coherence in contemporary society is poor because there is a lack of 'shared meaning'.[8] This lack of shared meaning is the result of meaning being fixed in individually held positions. What we need to do, according to Bohm, is to restore 'the flow of meaning' by allowing different voices to co-exist. For this we have to practice dialogue. Bohm underlines the importance of listening skills for successful dialogue and acknowledges that new meaning can also arise out of mis-perception, as well as inevitable gaps in the flow.

In his book *Conversation Pieces: Community and Communication in Modern Art*, the art historian and critic Grant H. Kester introduces the term 'dialogical art practices' for contemporary art practices that 'share a concern with the creative facilitation of dialogue and exchange', where 'the conversation is an integral part of the work'.[9] As such, a dialogical art practice always 'unfolds through a process of performative interaction'[10] and again shifts its focus from the productive to the receptive side of the creative cycle.

The art of listening and a dialogical practice are fundamental to my work as a dance dramaturg. Out of the ongoing conversations I had with artists arose the desire to make some of these dialogues public and to offer them a stage to be 'performed' upon.

The *Body:Language Talks*

Imaginative Bodies: Dialogues in Performance Practices is the written record of a series of public talks that took place at Sadler's Wells in London between 2008 and 2013 under the title *Body: Language Talks*. We decided that the overall theme of the talks would be the body, both in relation to the place it took in the artist's work, and in relation to wider debates on the body in philosophy, science, medicine, anthropology, and the arts. Depending on the affinities of the artist, a more specific theme would be defined for each individual talk. Finally, it was very important to me to only invite artists whom I knew well personally, either through having collaborated with them as a dance dramaturg or curator or through a strong personal friendship, in order to be able to have a true and intimate 'correspondence' with them.

In *Making: Anthropology, Archaeology, Art and Architecture*, Tim Ingold offers a valuable semantic alternative to the term 'dialogue', by re-introducing the notion of 'correspondence', which takes place not only between humans but also between humans and their animate or inanimate environment, as well as between the craftsmen/artists and their materials. Ingold borrows the term 'correspondence' from the increasingly obsolete art of letter writing. He defines its two fundamental qualities. Firstly, it is always 'a movement in real time', which takes time and which 'may go back and forth, without a clear starting point or end point'. Secondly, this 'movement is sentient', giving rise to an exchange that manifests itself as

> lines of feeling, of sentience, evinced not – or not only – in the choice of words but in the manual gestures of the writing and their traces on the page. To read a letter is not just to read about one's respondent, but to read with him or her. It is as though the writer was speaking from the page, and you – the reader were there, listening.[11]

The first series of four talks took place on four consecutive Mondays and I spent the weeks leading up to each talk preparing it: revisiting the 'body of work' of the artists, rereading everything that had been written about it, and meeting up with the artists. For the first two talks, Sidi Larbi Cherkaoui and Akram Khan were the obvious choices. They were the artists I had collaborated with most intensely as a production dramaturg and they were both associate artists of Sadler's Wells.[12] Since Larbi's work is very much a contemporary form of storytelling with the body, I decided the overall theme for his talk would be *The Mythic Body*. We had collaborated very closely on a large group piece, *Myth*, in which we tried to (re)create mythical images. During this creation I had been highly inspired by the book *Myth and the Body: A Colloquy with Joseph Campbell*[13] by Stanley Keleman, whose main theme is that all myths are about the body: its birth, its death, and all the rites of transformation in between. With Akram, the obvious theme was the way in which he negotiates his position as an artist between different cultures, and how this negotiation takes place as much between different time perspectives and traditions as it does between places – hence *The Bi-temporal Body*.

For the next two talks I wanted to focus on more formal aspects of dance and choreography and chose as a theme the fundamental relationship with space on the one hand and music/

time on the other. The two exemplary British choreographers to research this with are Rosemary Butcher and Jonathan Burrows, the latter in close collaboration with the composer Matteo Fargion. I had worked intensely with all of them when I was still curating the dance programme at the Arts Centre Vooruit in Ghent in the nineties and had developed strong friendships out of this. Rosemary's talk, which was called *The Spatial Body*, was introduced by a quote by Gaston Bachelard, whose *The Poetics of Space*[14] is still the main philosophical reflection on space. During the talk, Rosemary reflected on questions such as how the two-dimensionality of the film screen dialogues with the three-dimensionality of a performance space, or how you can push the parameters of any experience to its very edges – spatially, not emotionally, speaking. For *The Musical Body*, Jonathan and Matteo's talk, I was inspired by Oliver Sacks' book *Musicophilia: Tales of Music and the Brain*.[15] As well as talking about the human brain's relationship with rhythm, Jonathan and Matteo also addressed the relationship between writing and a movement based practice, and how they translate the concept of using musical scores to dance.

For the second season, I decided to stick to the principle of only inviting artists I had a close relationship with, but I allowed myself to look beyond the disciplinary borders of dance. My first guest was Tim Etchells, the artistic director of the performance collective Forced Entertainment, whom I had befriended during their first visits to Belgium in the mid-eighties. In order to prepare the talk, I revisited Tim in Sheffield, his home base, and out of that visit came the theme of *The Imaginative Body*, or 'how language has the power to invoke other bodies'. The second guest that season was Dana Caspersen, William Forsythe's artistic and life partner, with whom I had also collaborated during my years in Vooruit. She is very articulate in her thinking and writing on the body and the collaborative processes within a contemporary dance company. *The Transformative Body* explored amongst others the 'ability to imagine multiple versions of the self, a proliferating, projective equation that moves out from where the body is to where the body might be.'[16] The last guest of the second season had to be Alain Platel, under the wings of whose company, les ballets C de la B, I had formed my own identity as a dance dramaturg. With Alain, the obvious choice was to talk about *The Political Body* or how 'the political potential of art lies only in its own aesthetic dimensions'.[17]

The third season continued to expand the range of artist and subjects. With Jonzi D, one of the founding fathers of hip hop culture in the UK, and Soweto Kinch, we explored *The Poetic Body* – how, in hip hop culture, dance, music, poetry and political engagement are intrinsically related. The latter reminded me of one of my favourite Foucault quotes: 'Noisy ear, unstable repetitions, passionate violence and desires – ... of intoxication and dance, of organic gesticulation: the flash of poetry and of abolished time, repeated.'[18] With the puppeteer Sue Buckmaster we explored *The Subversive Body* or how puppets and objects allow the body to be treated in an 'uncanny' way. One of the sources of inspiration was the book *Puppet: An Essay on Uncanny Life* by Kenneth Gross:

> The story of puppets becomes the story of embodied souls and ensouled objects; it insists that our souls are never perfectly our own, as our bodies are never our own.[19]

The final talk of this third season was with the London-based Israeli choreographer/composer Hofesh Shechter, who has established himself as one of the most successful contemporary choreographers of the moment, composing all the music for his own work. In *The Rhythmic Body* we continued to explore the essential nature of rhythm as the main formal principle of editing the work. Background readings were John Dewey, Walter Murch and Richard Shusterman. 'The resistance offered to immediate expression of emotion is precisely that which compels it to assume rhythmic form.'[20]

Finally, a fourth season was added with talks on *The Luminous Body*, with the choreographer Russell Maliphant and his long term collaborator, lighting designer Michael Hulls. In the talk we discussed their twenty-year collaboration, their work with Sylvie Guillem and the BalletBoyz, and their exploration of how movement and light can enter into a dialogue. 'Light is a landscape'; it is 'indivisible from the movement', and it can be made to move itself. In *The Metereological Body*, dance dramaturg Ruth Little and I talked about her work with Akram Khan and her interest in 'dramaturgical dialogue that goes beyond linear determinism – the orderly predictable world of classical physics and Aristotelian dramaturgical models – to an understanding of non-linear dynamics and living systems',[21] such as the weather. *The Energetic Body* with the British sculptor Antony Gormley was the ideal conclusion of the series. In it we discussed his life-long research into the relationship between body and space, as well as movement and stillness and the energetic qualities of the body as explored in his collaborations with choreographers such as Sidi Larbi Cherkaoui and Hofesh Shechter. 'In all these works the body has become a place in which mass has been released from its stable condensed form into a field of energy.'[22]

The experience of the *Body:Language Talks* has reinforced my growing interest and often even preference for oral forms of transmission over written forms. In *The Spell of the Sensuous* David Abram argues that we have lost our connection to the larger ecological environment – and the use of our own body as the memory bank of that connection – due to the overdevelopment of written culture. The alphabetisation and phonotisation of language and writing, which has replaced older pictographic systems in the Judeo-Greek tradition, have distanced language from the phenomenological reality it refers to. Abram gives a detailed overview and critique of this evolution, referring to the legend of the Egyptian King Thamus, as recorded in Plato's *Phaedrus*. Thamus is supposed to have refused the gift of writing offered to him by the god Thoth, arguing that writing also induces forgetfulness, since we no longer need to remember from within ourselves, but can do so 'by means of external marks'. As a counter-strategy to this distancing, Abram pleads for a revalorisation of oral cultures and of reading aloud, which is basically a 'synaesthetic' experience in which 'the eye and the ear are brought together at the surface of the text'.[23]

It is only when you are able 'to tell your story', as Ingold states, that you own it. It is how transmission of knowledge happens, and has long happened, in Eastern cultures and traditions such as the Buddhist or yogic one. What I also see in my work with a younger generation of artists, as well as the Internet and its phenomena such as the TED-lectures, is a similar re-evaluation of oral transmission without lacking the necessary rigour or depth. The dialogical nature of the *Body:Language Talks* would always vary in degrees, depending with whom I was 'corresponding' and how our interaction would develop, with me always practicing my listening skills. If successful, it would create openings for new insights to arise between the utterances.

In all of my recent critical reflection and writing on my work as a dance dramaturg, I talk about dance dramaturgy as a dialogical practice in which not only the dramaturg and choreographer are involved but anybody else who is part of a particular creative process. This dialogical practice is based on an oscillation between being receptive and being articulate, between listening and speaking. I allowed myself to add one more dialogue to the original series of *Body:Language Talks*, in which the Flemish-Canadian theatre scholar Piet Defraeye 'corresponds' with me about my work and my vision on dance dramaturgy.

In reading the transcripts of these dialogues, I hope the readers will experience the liveliness of the original talks and actively listen and participate in them, adding their own thoughts and reflections in the process.

Guy Cools
Vienna, 2016

Notes

1 Miranda Tufnell and Chris Crickmay, *A Widening Field: Journeys in Body and Imagination* (Alton: Dance Books, 2004), p. 41.
2 Gemma Corradi Fiumara, *The Other Side of Language: A Philosophy of Listening* (Oxon: Routledge, 1990), p. 57.
3 In 2012, I curated an international conference, 'Ethics in Aesthetics? For an Ecology of the Arts of both Environment and Body' and co-edited with Pascal Gielen a book, *The Ethics of Art: Ecological Turns in the Performing Arts* (Amsterdam: Valiz, 2014) on this theme.
4 James P. Zappen, *The Rebirth of Dialogue: Bakhtin, Socrates, and the Rhetorical Tradition* (New York: State University of New York Press, 2004), p. 3.
5 Ibid., pp. 42–43.
6 Fiumara, *The Other Side*, p. 1.
7 Richard Sennett, *Together: The Rituals, Pleasures and Politics of Cooperation* (London: Allan Lane, 2012), pp. 162–63.
8 David Bohm, *On Dialogue* (London: Routledge, 1996), p. 32.
9 Grant H. Kester, *Conversation Pieces: Community and Communication in Modern Art* (Los Angeles: University of California Press, 2004), p. 8.
10 Ibid., p. 10.
11 Tim Ingold, *Making: Anthropology, Archaeology, Art and Architecture* (London: Routledge, 2013), p. 105.
12 My previous book, *In-Between Dance Cultures: On the Migratory Artistic Identity of Sidi Larbi Cherkaoui and Akram Khan* (Amsterdam: Valiz, 2015), discusses at length their work and my collaboration with them.
13 Stanley Keleman, *Myth and the Body: A Colloquy with Joseph Campbell* (Berkeley: Center Press, 1999).
14 Gaston Bachelard, *The Poetics of Space*, trans. Maria Jolas (Boston: Beacon Press, 1994, 1957).
15 Olivier Sacks, *Musicophilia: Tales of Music and the Brain* (New York: Vintage Books, 2007-2008).
16 Dana Caspersen, 'Decreation: Fragmentation and Continuity', in *William Forsythe and the Practice of Choreography: It Starts from Any Point*, ed. Steven Spier (London and New York: Routledge, 2011), pp. 96–97.
17 Herbert Marcuse, *The Aesthetic Dimension: Towards a Critique of Marxist Aesthetics* (Boston: Beacon Press, 1978), xii–xiii.
18 Author's translation from French. Original in Michel Foucault,*Sept propos sur le septième Ange* (Montpellier: Fata Morgana, 1986), p. 52.
19 Kenneth Gross, *Puppet: An Essay on Uncanny Life* (Chicago: University of Chicago Press, 2011), p. 119.
20 John Dewey, *Art as Experience* (New York: Perigee Paperback, 2005 c1934), p. 162.
21 Ruth Little, speech at Kenneth Tynan Award ceremony (unpublished, 2012).
22 Richard Noble, 'The Utopian Body', in *Antony Gormley*, ed. Michael Mack (Göttingen: SteidlMack, 2007), p. 45.
23 David Abram, *The Spell of the Sensuous* (New York: Random House, 1996), p. 124.

The Mythic Body
A Conversation with Sidi Larbi Cherkaoui

Our body is our destiny.[1]

Guy Cools – I am very happy that Larbi is the first guest. I think we met at the very beginning – when he created his first dance piece, *Rien de Rien*, at the Arts Centre Vooruit in Ghent while I was still the curator there. That is where our relationship started, and then, when I decided to quit the job of curator to go back to the creative process, one of the very first productions that I was invited to support as a dramaturg was *zero degrees*, which was created here at Sadler's Wells.

For these talks I wanted to invite artists who I am close to and have a friendship with. But I also looked for an angle to frame the talk and from which to talk about the work. In Larbi's case it is a little book called *Myth and the Body*, which I discovered while we were collaborating on *Myth*. The book was published in 1999 and is a series of transcripts of talks that were held by Stanley Keleman, who is a specialist in somatic therapy, and Joseph Campbell, an eminent scholar in Western mythology. The talks were held from the late seventies to the late eighties, when Campbell died.

The main subject of these conversations was that mythology is about the body, and that all myths talk about the somatic evolution of the body – birth, growth, transformation, and death. It is a tiny book, but beautifully insightful.

Since *Myth* was the last production we worked on together, and since it was presented here at Sadler's Wells, I would like to start with *Myth*. Can you remind me what the whole genesis of that production was? You changed the title a number of times, which I think was important.

A mythic image is the shape of anatomy speaking about itself. The serpent of mythology is the spinal cord. ... The cortex is the thousand-petaled lotus, the crown of thorns. This makes mythic image incapable of being a reality apart from somatic reality. Mythic image is the body speaking to itself about itself. Myths are scripts of our genetic shape in social language. They are patterns of embodiment: they show us how to grow our inherited biological endowment into a personal form.[2]

Sidi Larbi Cherkaoui – Originally, *Myth* was supposed to be called *Trauma*, which is a very 'heavy' word. At that time I was thinking about how to deal with problems, 'childhood problems'. I was thirty and I felt, 'when am I ever going to get over these things?' I like my work to help me overcome personal issues, and, as I had been working with the dancers for a long time (with some of them for over eight years), I felt we could go into a theme like that. But then I felt the word was very negative, and to give that to the audience did not feel like much of a gift. People already have enough problems of their own.

As we were going into traumas, especially in a 'healing' way, we discovered that 'healing' can be a dangerous word as well. You always think 'healing' is positive, but as we were researching around it, we were finding that people wanted to heal people from things which were very normal, such as being gay. So to go from 'trauma' to 'healing' didn't feel right either.

Slowly, in a very natural way, we came to psychology, and then to mythology. What I like about mythology is that it doesn't have a real morality. It is more like cause and effect: 'If you do this, then this happens.' They are totally untrue stories – I mean, nobody believes them – but at the same time they create an image, and this image helps you to understand a psychological condition.

I like myths because they have been part of my life since early childhood. When I was studying Latin, the Greek and Roman myths were part of my education. At the same time I am a Muslim, so I have a lot of Islamic influences, and Catholic influences as well, because I grew up in Belgium. So all these things were already there.

And we were delving and searching. Trying to make sense of them and trying to see how we can recognise ourselves in these stories. We started to talk about the colours in mythologies and all the gods. A bit like Hinduism, because you have all the archetypes – so maybe the word 'archetype' is also important, because it helps to define all the colours of the rainbow.

Suddenly it wasn't black and white anymore, like in most religions – good or bad with nothing in between – but it felt like: there's red, there's yellow, there's blue. All these gods who have a different intensity. And all of them together created a sense of completeness. As I was finding the cast I had twenty-one characters on stage, which I liked as a number because it was very symbolic. Like the Tarot cards – I don't know if you know that there are twenty-one of them: The Arcane cards.[3] I like playing with numbers. At the same time we had scenes that were very concrete: for example Christine (one of the performers), who was a mother figure who rejects her newborn child.

What do we do with a situation like this? How do we deal with that? How does a child deal with it? How does a mother deal with it? It became a very complex piece because you never felt you knew what was the right thing to do. You didn't have a hero and a villain; it just constantly felt like, well, the hero is not so nice, and the villain is actually not so bad. It felt closer to reality.

Opposites are the tensions that are part of the formative process. When we can embody these tensions, we form our individuality. We are foolish and wise, wild and tame.[4]

GC – A lot of your work explores these binary opposites: male/female, earth/heaven. There is a book called *The Eye of Shiva*[5] by Amaury de Riencourt, which was recommended to me by Akram Khan (he used it as a source for *Kaash*), and I think he got it from Anish Kapoor, so there is a whole journey of collaborations and influences.

The essence of the book, which I think links to your work, is that originally man was living in a magical relationship with nature and the environment. And then, when mankind started to develop a scientific (or rational) consciousness, East and West developed in different directions. Where the West would think of these binary terms in opposition, Eastern thought would approach them in a more complementary way, without choosing between the two of them.

What is it that attracts you to Eastern forms of art, which you have been exploring more and more recently?

SLC – Well, there are many ways of explaining it. For instance, in the Japanese art form of Kabuki, a character can be many things at the same time. In a solo with a fan, the fan can be the bow and later become the arrow, or at the same time it can be a knife that stabs you. The actor too becomes many things. When you see Akram Khan's traditional work, you see him becoming as much Krishna as Shiva; he is all of them, all the gods.

That's what attracts me as an actor, as a dancer, as a human being: to allow yourself to be much more than just one thing. Not to be defined by what people see in you, or by what you see in yourself. No, you can suddenly be transformed. In a work like *zero degrees*, I definitely wanted not only to be the victim, but also be the other side, and understand that you are both, always.

GC – One of your most recent projects has been an exchange with Shantala Shivalingappa.

SLC – Shantala is a classical Indian Kuchipudi dancer. I went to India to work with her and she introduced me to that particular style of dancing – which is something between Bharata Natyam and Kathak (which is what Akram does). I have a million reasons why I wanted to work with her, but what was interesting for her, and made her want to work with me too, is that she had been doing a lot of singing and also a lot of dancing, but never the two together. This is something that I do a lot in *Myth*, and also in other pieces: I try to be the instrument as much as the one playing the instrument. She was interested in trying this. So suddenly we were trying to dance whilst singing the song, which was really very difficult. But in those little moments when it worked, it was uplifting. It is harmonising.

Both of us got attracted to each other and also our voices matched – we felt very in tune. We started playing around the theme of 'Adam and Eve', man and woman together, something very innocent like the beginning of a story. In my work with Akram there is something of a fight or union, but with Shantala there is no fight – just this sense of discovery.[6]

GC – I'm interested because you just mentioned it as her interest, but also as part of the essence of your work, that is the integration of the voice in the human body through singing. I remember that in *Rien de Rien* the discovery of that, through your collaboration with Damien Jalet, was something that you described as a somatic experience. Since then you have not only developed it for yourself, but you also ask all of your dancers to integrate that.

SLC – Maybe I should give you the history. In 1999 I started to work with Damien Jalet, who is a dancer but also a singer. He works on Italian traditional songs, which means that they are often not written down. They are songs that would be sung in certain villages in Italy during Easter – mostly religious songs. Religious in the popular sense, so not necessarily in church, but by villagers who just sing harmonies that are very powerful. In voices which are very nasal. I didn't know this kind of music at all; I didn't grow up with it and when Damien brought in this element in the creation of *Rien de Rien* – I got goose bumps. I was totally struck by the harmonies, it was like it was the first time that I understood harmony in music and what it meant. How one voice and another voice create something almost like a third voice. When I got that feeling, I didn't want to lose it ever again.

And so I started learning how to sing. He taught me how to go into the harmony, which is a very physical thing to do. First of all it was just based on memory – I have this fear of reading notes. It always feels like I can't do it; I don't have the training.

He started to teach me and would be using his own voice. Slowly we were harmonising, and then we were combining this with movements – he was dancing in front of me and I was behind him – a very simple image that is often used in choreography, four arms create a sense of a Shiva figure. This was in 2000. It felt necessary to do the movement whilst singing and necessary to sing while doing the movement.

That was my first experience of the voice. Then I was very lucky to meet very gifted people in music. I went from Italy to being interested in Corsican music, and then from Corsican back to Spanish music – whenever I feel or hear something that really matters to me or resonates with me, I will go and try to understand it. Shantala was using a lot of Ragas, using the voice in a very different way than I was used to. It felt very attractive, but not in an exotic way.

GC – Going back to *Myth* and its creation process: What I observed and what was so beautiful to see, is the way you work like a contemporary scientist, like a science lab, where all the dancers have a lot of autonomy. You give them subjects and ideas, but you also give them a lot of...

SLC – responsibility...

GC – ... and freedom to explore these ideas on their own. The first week of rehearsals – I remember we had two studios and maybe ten different groups of two or three people. It seemed that the way to keep these people together as a group were the yoga class in the morning and the singing class with Patricia Bovi[7] in the evening.

SLC – Dance classes never really spoke to me. I mean, I love dance, but the class was never something that I felt brought people together. Also, working with people who have such different styles, finding a movement that would fit everybody is impossible.

So it became obvious that we needed something else. I was really getting into yoga and understanding more about it – about the inside leg, about the spine, about how to be at one with gravity. Because really, standing up – what is it? I was trying to find a real physical straightness, which is not the straightness you get from the teacher in school (when they say, 'sit straight'), or in ballet, when they say 'stand straight'. The real straightness is something that is really effortless. It is like a feeling where suddenly your shoulders are not hunched up but opened up. You don't feel the weight of the world on your shoulders – you actually feel that it all glides off you – and you feel the only responsibility you have is to be.

I started to teach the dancers the little yoga I knew. It was about a kind of awareness and also just being very practical about how to get the body to be more flexible –

which also makes the mind more flexible. It is the same thing – the body, the mind – I hate this kind of separation. When I feel anger, my liver is angry. When I have an emotional problem, it is the stomach. When you want too many things, you have a problem around the neck; like when you have an existential crisis. And if somebody dies in your family, and you are afraid to die or be left behind, it is most of the times the lower back that gives you problems.

What was interesting is that as I was taking things from different cultures, the same things were always coming back. When I was in China I was doing a lot of acupuncture because it was a very stressful period there, and they were telling me the same things that I already heard when I was learning yoga, when I was learning kung fu, and in tai chi and in singing as well.

Singing and yoga were the two things that very logically brought the group together, when everything else divided it. Then, when we were putting together things slowly, they started understanding co-existence.

GC – (*He shows a video clip of the last 10 minutes of* Myth.)

I have chosen this fragment because I want to show another fragment of *Apocrifu* later, and somehow *Apocrifu* starts where this piece ends.

I am reminded that two of its main criticisms – and ones that made you angry – were the complexity and the overt religious symbolism, especially in this final section. But to me they are both very essential to the piece.

The complexity is something I remember us fighting about, and you being very stubborn, saying 'I'll keep everything in, and the challenge will be to compose it in such a way that all these images belong together'.

Why was it so important for you?

SLC – As we were making material, a lot of things got created and all of them made sense to the people involved. Then what most directors do is 'kill your darlings'; you have to cut, cut, cut, cut... I've been cutting all my life, and I like cleaning up, making it very pretty – and I thought, what if I don't; what if I keep everything, what if everything gets a place, what if I don't reject anything?

At the time, I was thinking about how to handle rejection; how to handle 'this is not going to have a space', and 'no, your solo is nice, but this one is better'. There is always a hierarchy. With this piece, I didn't want this. I wanted everything to get a space. Because that is what it was about: finding a space for everything, like in an encyclopaedia.

My image was a little bit like homeopathic science, where the active ingredient is always diluted in other stuff. It's not just pure vitamins, which are sometimes bad for the stomach because they are too harsh, too radical, too clean. Sometimes you need it coming from an apple. The body is very smart; it can take things. And I believe the audience is also very smart and can take out what it needs for itself.

The piece became more like a canvas. As a painting it was acceptable. I remember a journalist from Greece who had seen it once and told me: 'I think it is too much.' He was in Antwerp, so I brought him to the cathedral there, to see the sculpture at the entrance, which is really huge and full of apostles and all of that. You can't take it in, it is just too much. And I asked him, 'Do you think the artist is doing too much here?' He understood. When you really focus on the cathedral, you can see the story.

Also, I do like this kind of work when I am in the audience myself. Maybe it is my generation. We grew up with MTV – you know, watching MTV, being on the computer, doing your homework and listening to your mum at the same time – so I feel like it is also part of who I am. I like being very alert and awake, and able to take in a lot of stimuli at the same time. For *Myth* it was a choice more than a flaw.

One of the intentions of a mythological system is to present evocative images, images that touch and resonate in very deep centres of our impulse system, and then move us from these very deep centres into action.[8]

GC – We were trying to bring alive unconscious issues starting from the personal experience of the performers, and then we wanted the audience to be able to recognise themselves in it. This quote in the book made me understand that what we were possibly doing was creating myths. And then I got at least one personal, very subjective confirmation that we were able to do that. I think that it was not by accident that it was in Greece. After the performance there in Kalamata, I had to give an audience talk and I discussed some of the issues that we are dealing with today. After the talk, a woman who had seen the piece before came up to me and told me this personal and very touching story. She said that all of her life, in her dreams, she had an image coming to her, and then she had seen this image literally being recreated in the performance – in the midst of all these other images. Although she hadn't dreamt about it for rather a long time, it had come back to her the same night in a dream, but she felt that it had changed its quality. She was kind of unclear about what it meant for her as the experience was so recent, but it had deeply touched her. It was a very touching moment for me to understand, too.

SLC – It was a very interesting journey for us. In places like Greece they know about mythology. They recognised everything. Like the moment when three wolves come together and then suddenly they move together – they knew it was Cerberus, the dog with the three heads that guards the door to hell. We constantly felt they knew each image, grasping and appreciating every single symbol.

In Spain, it was more the Christian part that was appreciated. And the place that was the hardest was actually France, which also makes a lot of sense because in France they hate religion, and it felt like they did not want to talk about faith – they felt like, 'Are you here to convert me or something?'

The element of humour that is in the piece is, I think, a very Anglo-Saxon humour. So for instance in England I could feel that those elements were picked up, but in France, because people don't speak English, the balance was off.

With all the touring that I am doing now, I have realised how culture-specific countries can be, and how people, without knowing it, are very connected to their roots.

GC – I would like to introduce the next video fragment. In the end of *Myth* we have this librarian figure who is almost collapsing under the weight of the books, and in your next piece, *Apocrifu*, there was a lot of research about...

SLC – ... the book – the power of books...

GC – ... and the written word.

SLC – It was also about rejection. There are just three dancers, and I am one of them. I worked with the Bible, the Koran, and the Torah. We were juggling around as three dancers with these three books, and one of the things we discovered as we were doing research, was that some of the stories in the Koran are actually apocryphal.

I don't know if you know what the word apocryphal means. They are texts, or writings, that have not been accepted by, have not been introduced into, the Bible. So when the Bible was put together, certain texts were not selected. The selected ones are the canon and the non-selected ones are apocryphal texts. Because of this word, I felt like something had been rejected. I felt rejected.

I have always felt it in parts of my life: only half Moroccan, only half Belgian, I am gay. There are a lot of things that pushed me out of the system, like these apocrypha. Then I discovered that some of the apocrypha ended up in the Koran. The Koran, which is supposed to be the Angel Gabriel who came from God and whispered these words into Mohammed's ear!

Five hundred years earlier, the same texts were already in some apocrypha. I was totally amazed to find that there is a source of the source, and that by having been rejected out of the Bible, it became another religion – it became Islamic. It became part of something else.

What was also fascinating was one of the stories around Cain and Abel. The story is that Cain kills his brother and he sees a bird. A crow digging in the ground, so he thinks, oh, I should bury my brother like I saw the crow doing. It is a nice story that is not in the Bible, but it is in the Koran, and also, I think, it is in the Torah. In the Torah there is a comment on this, and it says, 'he who takes the blood of one, it is as if he takes the blood of all, and he who saves the blood of one, saves the blood of all'. It is about Cain. He wasn't supposed to kill Abel, so it tells people when they read it, 'know that you should not'. This extra comment became Sura 5 in the Koran. It used to be a comment, and then it became a real Sura, real teaching. I found that fascinating, to see where things come from, and how morality is being taken out of belief systems.

GC – Larbi actually also tells this story in the performance. (*He shows a clip of* Apocrifu.)

Whether we like it or not, we are incarnated. We are bodies on this planet, and all myth and all stories seek the origin and the end of our somatic structure. Myth as story is the life of our body in one or another of its forms. We are all making up stories, finding stories, finding facts to talk about our somatic origin, its growth and its end. ... In telling your story, look for the somatic shapes.[9]

GC – Death is a very important theme in all your productions, from the very first to the present one. Can you talk a little about that?

SLC – For instance for the solo, I was interested in old age or how to get heavier and heavier so the body gets harder and harder to control – there are very simple manipulations with which you can guide yourself very easily, so suddenly it becomes much more heavy, and you need more and more energy to be able to move the smallest thing.

I was inspired by an old lady who just had to cross the street, and the time it took her was like an eternity. I felt like it was a totally different life, a different way of dealing with distance, with getting there, and also the appreciation of life, or the appreciation of a goal.

When I work with differently-abled actors, they have another speed, another way, another perception, but you can get to the same place.

It teaches you patience – and you then think how to apply this patience to yourself in order to get somewhere. For instance, let's say kung fu. I wanted to learn kung fu, but when I started to learn, I thought, I will never accomplish it. Then I thought, if that old lady can get across the street, I can at least get to something that is close to kung fu.

But to come back to the subject of death – it was something that was always present in my family. My dad died when I was nineteen and this was a big shock. I did not have a good relationship with my dad at all. He was someone I did not like, I did not want to become like him at all. He was the total opposite of everything I wanted to become. And as I grew older I was more and more becoming like him, so I was like, how can I not become like him?, when, actually, I am a reincarnation of my mum and my dad. I am them, they made me, even if I am an individual. And I can go to my left hemisphere and think, I am an individual, but I also had to accept that shadow side, that father side.

It did not have anything to do with the culture, because the Arab culture was something that I accepted totally. I was proud of being an Arab, but I was not proud of being the son of my father. He was not really proud of me, either – there was this tension. But when he died, it changed everything. I could never prove him wrong.

He was someone who always told me: 'You will never make money by dancing'. I can tell you, I make money by dancing. It is possible as an artist to make a living. But I think today I am still not beyond that fact of proving him wrong.

And then, two years later, my grandmother died. It felt like death has always been a very natural thing for me. But not for my mum. I could feel that she was always really affected by it. When it happened, she got a hernia, her lower back – she could hardly move anymore.

When you lose someone it is very important in the family to restructure, to find out 'who does what?' Because if you don't restructure, you lose a function – you lose the father element, which can be an energy. It can be done by anybody. It does not have to be your father. It just has to be done. People always complain how they lose things. But they do not understand that it is not losing – it is transformation. You are changing, and gaining other things.

When you have a scar, it is new material. People always want them to heal, to become what they were. But I think, no, you have to go to what you have become. This scar tissue – it is really new tissue. When you go to indigenous cultures where youngsters scar themselves, or where they get tattoos – what are they doing? They are being reborn, by changing themselves. On their eighteenth birthday they are like the Phoenix who comes out of the ashes. They want to have new skin. And they do it consciously. We have lost this, but at the same time we have not lost the urge to do it. I had a tattoo on my back when I was twenty-three. Why did I need this?

I do not regret it because I feel that that was what I needed – this kind of ritual, this sensation of transformation, and it needed to be a very physical choice, something that I could choose, something that I could determine, that was part of my physical journey.

I think I will be a happy dead man. Because I think it is such a big transformation, and my whole life has been about wanting to change, to transform myself into something else. I think death is that ultimate transformation.

GC – Having been a privileged witness of your work, there is a huge transformation of how you deal with these things. If you look at *Rien de Rien*, there is an anger which is very much projected towards yourself, and in *zero degrees*[10] there is still this kind of fighting with yourself. But it is much lighter – fighting with the dummies and then it becomes a lamentation, so there is a sadness.

And in the last piece, *Apocrifu*,[11] it is about pulling yourself together. The message for me is that we are masters of ourselves, and that we do not need external things. It is very much about this maturity that you have personally gained, also as an artist.

SLC – It comes in waves. I think there are days when I feel totally in sync with the belief system I chose for myself, and then there are days when it makes no sense to me.

GC – Let us finish this talk with one last quote from *Myth and the Body*:

To be embodied is to participate in a migration from one body form to another. Each of us is a nomad, a wave that has duration for a time and then takes on a new somatic shape. This perpetual transformation is the subject of all myth.[12]

Notes

1 Stanley Keleman, *Myth and the Body: A Colloquy with Joseph Campbell* (Berkeley: Center Press, 1999).
2 Ibid., p. 3.
3 Arcane cards: The Major Arcane in the set of Tarot cards consist of 21 cards featuring archetypes or symbolic elements such as 'The Lovers', 'The Hanged Man', or 'The Wheel of Fortune'. In card games they serve as trump cards, while in fortune reading they are said to relate to matters of greater significance than those alluded to by the Minor Arcane cards.
4 Keleman, *Myth and the Body*, p. 64.
5 Amaury de Riencourt, *The Eye of Shiva: Eastern Mysticism and Science* (New York: Morrow, 1980).
6 Their collaboration resulted in the piece *Play*, which premiered in 2010.
7 Patricia Bovi: Singer and specialist in Italian medieval music. Founder of the group Ensemble Micrologus.
8 Keleman, *Myth and the Body*, p. 34.
9 Ibid., pp. 68-69.
10 *zero degrees* was filmed by Axiom Films and is available on DVD.
11 Information on all of Sidi Larbi Cherkaoui's works is available on www.east-man.be.
12 Keleman, *Myth and the Body*, p. 76.

The Bi-Temporal Body
A Conversation with Akram Khan

The memory is in the body.[1]

In my theory of the 'in-between-two-bodies', the body itself is a complex form, consisting of a body-being-present and a body-memory, each of which has another two levels: that of 'calling out' (appel) and that of 'recalling' (rappel).[2]

Guy Cools – Akram and I first met almost ten years ago. I was introduced to him by Jonathan Burrows, with whom he had done a choreographer/composer course and who had asked him to perform a duet with him for the fiftieth anniversary of the composer Kevin Volans at London's South Bank Centre.

As a programmer at the Arts Centre Vooruit in Ghent, I invited Akram with his Kathak work and his first contemporary dance solos. His first full-length company piece, *Kaash*, was partially created in residence in Ghent.

Since *zero degrees*, I have been collaborating with Akram as a dramaturg, and in my reflection on his work I am particularly interested in how intercultural issues are mainly a matter of bridging different times, such as the traditional with the contemporary. Again there is one major book that frames my thinking: *Le corps et sa danse* by the French philosopher Daniel Sibony, who defines dance as a movement between 'a body-memory' and a 'body being present'. Hence the bi-temporal body.

Akram, since our artistic collaboration started with *zero degrees*, I would like to start our talk with what the series of duets that you made with Sidi Larbi Cherkaoui, Sylvie Guillem and Juliette Binoche added to your knowledge as a choreographer and performer.

Akram Khan – Until *zero degrees*, I had never really explored any partner work. Even though I had done *Kaash* and *Ma*, somehow with every piece before *zero degrees* – even if it was a company of five or a company of ten – it would be a solo and nine dancers. And that was my own problem, or my education maybe, because Kathak is a solo art form (as a lot of the Indian classical dance forms are). When I related to people, it was for a choreographic reason; it was not necessarily a physical experience with another body, until I worked with Larbi. In a way that was the most important thing: there was a sharing of energy.

GC – When I was preparing the talk that I had with Sidi Larbi Cherkaoui last week, I was re-reading a lot of his interviews, and one of the things I remember him saying, was how much collaborating with you liberated the movement that was already in him. He was referring to the hand movements that were already very much part of his vocabulary, but which he needed to share with you in order to know how to continue to explore that very personal part of his own vocabulary.

AK – There are three directions in my artistic work.

As you said – there is the classical work, which is the solo dance form of Kathak. Then there is the company work; and then there are the collaborations. I was thinking of it recently, and I think for me the three directions relate to two people in my life, who each had very clear influences on one of those three.

The first one is my classical work and that relates very much to my father and my father's body – because growing up in front of my father's eyes there was something very classical about him. There was a huge amount of form around him. There were rules, there were regulations. Everything was almost mathematical with my father; he is an accountant, so that's not surprising. But I had a very strict relationship with him, and that comes from his own personal experience. He grew up in a family where he was the head; he had to run his family because his father lost his job. So there was some kind of authority about him. He built all these walls and rules and they were very precise, and so, in the way my father stands, when he turns his head the whole body turns. And his whole way of expressing himself, of course I was picking this up as a child – so in my classical work I relate to him.

And then there is the company work which I would say is much more my mother. With my mother's body everything is more circular; it is more huggable, if you like, and there is something exactly the opposite of my father's – very formless, very creative. She was a folk dancer; but she adapted, because her father did not allow her to dance. She would secretly go and learn classical dance, and when she wasn't allowed to do classical dance she would do pop dance, or she would do something else. She was constantly reinventing herself to survive, to stay connected to the arts in Bangladesh at a time when she was not allowed to, and so her body language is much more circular, much softer. That influence – her body influence – comes into my contemporary work. And the collaborations, I would say, is me.

GC – Again I am going back to last week's talk: In the discussion with Larbi I referred to a book that you suggested to me, which is *The Eye of Shiva*.[3] I think you read it when preparing for *Kaash*?

The book compares Eastern and Western religion, philosophy and science. The author says that in Western history binaries like female and male have always been put into opposition with each other, while in Eastern thought they are allowed to co-exist on an equal basis.

AK – Absolutely.

It is the dichotomy of the opposites. One place, which is the classical world, offers you tradition, history. It offers you discipline, something very sacred and spiritual, too. And the other place, the contemporary, offers you a science laboratory. It offers you your voice to be heard. It offers you numerous discoveries and possibilities. To be in a position where you can reach out to both, is the best place to be for me.[4]

GC – It is even demonstrated physically, in the performing arts: in Kathak you can go from the male to the female character just in the physicalisation of your body. The second duet with Sylvie Guillem was very different?

AK – Both of us were exploring not just each other's bodies (which was really another completely different experience to working with Larbi's body), but we were also somehow following a parallel journey. We are both classically trained – myself in Indian classical dance and Sylvie in Western ballet. We were trying to move out of it – but not move away. We wanted to take our experience of the classical with us.

With Larbi it was a male dancer who was very in touch with his feminine quality. With Sylvie it was a female dancer who was very strongly attached to a masculine quality. She has this kind of real masculine power, which interests me. The fact that she was much taller than me created interesting things and possibly new kinds of challenges for me. It was different, because when I was working with Larbi we were embodying each other's experiences – while with Sylvie, we did not necessarily share our material. With Larbi it was really a kind of breathe in and breathe out. What I would breathe out he would breathe in, and what he would breathe out I would breathe in. I remember that for three years before we even made the project, I was teaching him Kathak.

With Sylvie it wasn't like that because she does not recognise herself as a choreographer. She is very clear: she is the performer; the artist who executes the work. It was working with a body of someone who is actually very gifted, very sensitive, very creative – but it was really creating material *on* her body – and also together.

GC – I remember you worked with Nikoleta[5] as an understudy, and that if you had to change – doing partner work with Nikoleta and afterwards with Sylvie – it was a big shift.

AK – Because the body is not simple. I wish it was, but it is not. It comes with cultural background, it comes with political background, it comes with historical, religious background.

Each person is unique and so their experiences are unique. We thought of working with Nikoleta because she was one of my dancers and she had been a principal dancer with one of the ballet companies in Slovakia. Her body is similar to Sylvie's in some respects, and it is a classical body, but we had to shift everything. The whole rhythm, the whole energy would change because of Sylvie's background and her own identity, her own way of moving.

Even though the common denominator of these three works is my body in duet with another body, my body is changing because of them. Whether I want it to change or not is irrelevant because being in contact with someone who is so different brings out another side of you.

GC – And then Juliette Binoche also challenged you, or asked of you the biggest shift: to do a tango with her.

AK – It was the biggest shift – and it was also the biggest gain for me as an artist. Working with a non-dancer, I could not take things for granted the way I did with Sylvie and Larbi. With them, once we are on stage somehow I can trust that they are going to be OK. With Juliette it is not the case, and it is not because of her – it is just the fact that she has no dance experience. She did four months of serious training, but it is not the same as doing twenty years of training. On stage I have to be the one who is partnering, but I am also her shadow, so I play my own shadow in order to protect her.

For this particular project, I abandoned my own body and started with her body. I felt that if I had generated material for my own body for her to learn in four months, it would not have been possible, so I had to start with a blank canvas, which was her body. To abandon your own body, which you trust so much, means that you are already teaching your body something new.

GC – I would like to go back to *zero degrees*. You prepared it over a very long period – about a full three years. Before you actually started rehearsing you had regular meetings with Larbi, talking about the ideas but also going to the studio and trying out some of them. I was very privileged to witness this. I remember coming into the studio in Ghent and you were trying out Kathak rhythms on all fours at that particular time (which I am very happy you did not develop further).

In the end every section of the piece has a very clear identity, that was either initiated by yourself or by Larbi. The video clip that I would like to show is from the end of your story, which is a story of you going back to India. There is a whole story about identity and borders, but then at the end it becomes about death, because you discover a dead person on that journey.

First you tell the story in Larbi's hand movements, and then you retell the story in your language, which is a form of abhinaya.[6] Could you comment on how the abhinaya was developed in this particular piece – how much of it is traditional and how much of it is new? (*He shows a video clip of Akram Khan's classical solo from* zero degrees.[7])

AK – What is interesting for me, seeing it again, is the sense of questioning. It brings back the memory of why I am attracted to work with artists who are from different backgrounds.

I was asking myself why we decided to work together, and I think it was because we wanted change in our own body. Working with Larbi, with Sylvie, with Juliette, it was very much about that – it was about not just what work we can create, but how our bodies will change.

You see yourself in the other person – and I think that is what happened with Larbi, and vice versa. But the other very important thing you notice, is the fact that you see that they have something that you don't have. When I see this section it is very much like that. The root of it is the traditional language of Kathak, but it has been transformed completely through improvisation, because of me working with Larbi. It is a contemporary piece of work, not purely a classical piece of work.

Kathak has very particular dimensions, for instance the boundaries of how far the gestures should go. Of course it depends on the guru and what style it is, but underneath it, like Maharajee[8] said (Maharajee being my teacher's teacher, who is a torch bearer of Kathak) when he saw something of my work, funnily enough on YouTube apparently. They said, 'this is a contemporary piece of work', and he said, 'No, that is Kathak – that is a Kathak body for sure.' He could identify.

By working with Larbi, and by my own experience of venturing into contemporary vocabulary, the abhinaya is not in the framework of a Kathak repertoire, and so, in a way, it is very distorted.

GC – From an early stage in your career, you have been publicly and very consciously rejecting the notion that your work is about fusion.

AK – Yes.

GC – But you have been talking about 'confusion' – on the level of the body.

AK – 'Fusion' feels too much like perfection. It is a perfect thing, where two things fuse together to create something that becomes one. It is too much of a fantasy for me. I find it is much more complex. The word fusion feels trivial. I had been studying Kathak for some years, and then, when I went to university to get away from my community and my parents, my mother said I had to get a degree. So the contemporary dance started to infiltrate my body and my body started bringing up questions. Not consciously, but through the body. My teachers would notice it. My Kathak guru would say, 'that is not Kathak anymore. You are rerouting energy through a different way', and the same thing would happen with my Graham teacher or my Release teacher. The sense of chaos in the body, or the confusion, seemed a word that was much more relevant to the state I was in then, and the state I am in now, even more so.

To remain in that state seems important for me. I have a sense of real clarity in my Kathak. When I am doing Kathak I am at home. It is about wearing the costume, eating. I have to eat bann, because I have to feel like I am in India again. There is a whole ritual, because I feel so separated from it for most of the year.

GC – Fusion seems to be about blending and eliminating the differences. It is different from confusion. I mean, 'con' is also 'two', no? So it is like 'fusion' to a higher degree, where you keep the differences.

AK – Absolutely.

GC – To finish with *zero degrees*, I would like to quote from the beginning of a poem that was written about the piece by the Indian poet Karthika Nair, which has just been published in an anthology of contemporary Indian poets. It is a beautiful poem in a very classical form, especially in the way that she describes the relationship between you and Larbi. She calls you a warrior and him a monk. Are you happy with that?

I met them first in a land where borders
Get blurred; where day rises before night's end
And water morphs into high, brumal walls.
A warrior and a monk, two beings –
Flanked by shadows that grow and roam at will –
Cross-legged in thought, carving with four hands
Arabesques on force, loss, fear.[9]

AK – I am – but I think both are in both of us. I think that a warrior is only a warrior when he has the monk in him and vice versa. But for the piece I think it is a really nice way to describe the two characters.

GC – I would like to turn to the group work now. I have only been involved in the creative process of *bahok*, but I have seen the other ones several times, even during the rehearsal process, and it seems to me that there has also been a big shift there. Whereas in the earlier pieces – like *Kaash* for instance – it felt like a lot of the material was still developed on your own body and passed on to the dancers, in *bahok* you really use the dancers' own movement vocabulary as the building blocks of the piece. Is that true?

AK – Absolutely. In *bahok* I was putting my body aside and using only part of my body, which is the Kathak eye. Whereas with *Kaash* it was very much about using the Kathak material of my own body, in *bahok* I was exploring their bodies and each one was very different from mine. It was like a circus of different experiences.

GC – What you say now reminds me of an interview that you gave during the period of *zero degrees*. There was a special issue on the body, I think it was in *The Independent*, and they interviewed yourself and Antony Gormley.

You said something about the different experience of seeing it from the inside, and that you need to see it on other bodies too, to develop an understanding of it.

AK – The other day I was talking to the Artistic Director of the National Portrait Gallery about the portrait that Darvish Fakhr did of me, which is a series of portraits of me in nine different emotions. We were talking about the painting and how the painting does not change, whereas live performance does change every time. He said, 'no – that is not true', and I now agree with him. He said a painting does change, because when you first see a painting you think you have taken it in. But then you go away and when you come back you see it in a different way. You transform it, because you have gained a different experience. It is like the Indian time cycle, which is a circle, in a spiral effect.

GC – I just had a similar experience this week when I went to see the Rothko exhibition. You do not even have to go away: while you are there, it changes because of how your eye adapts to the space, to the changes in light. The painting becomes alive.

In *bahok* you worked with a group of dancers from very different backgrounds. There was the collaboration with the National Ballet of China, and you decided to bring this group together by exploring more theatrical devices.

AK – It was tough because we did not know how they would deal with the theatrical aspect. The ballet dancers hadn't ever done anything like it, even though they know narrative through their characters. But playing yourself is a different kind of theatre.

On the first day, I remember arriving late, and the National Ballet of China dancers were in one corner and I think Kim Young, the Korean dancer, Shanell, Lali and Sadju were in another corner, and Chia-Ying, who is Taiwanese, was in yet another corner.[10] I came in late on purpose, because I wanted to see what would happen without my input, without them having a reason to come together, and I was hoping that they would all be speaking to each other – but nobody was.

The Chinese dancers were in the corner talking among themselves, my dancers were talking among themselves, and so in a way they had created walls – because of culture, because of religion and because of the body, since the body has had a different education, physical education. It was difficult when we had to decide what class to give every morning, because the contemporary dancers were not sure whether they wanted us to do ballet; and the ballet dancers were not sure whether they wanted to do contemporary. As soon as I came in I decided that we were going to start not from moving, but from the most primal thing – which is to tell a story. I asked them to tell me a bit about themselves. We chose home, a dream, a nightmare as themes.

GC – Is it necessary for work to be autobiographical?

AK – No, not at all. I think it is maybe necessary for me at this moment – but I am thinking that the next few projects that I want to do should not be autobiographical. If I work with something that is not autobiographical, you still have to find something of yourself within the character that you are playing, or the piece.

GC – I do think that a work of art needs to have an autobiographical element. The fact that you start from their story and not your story means that they own it.

AK – If I do *Oedipus* or *Hamlet*, or something like that, it would not be an autobiographical thing, but I absolutely agree that you have to find something in your own life that relates to that story inorder for it to feel real, or to be, as you said,emotionally charged.

GC – Your work is being presented on all the world stages. In the reception of it, does it also change? It was a topic that came up last week, with Larbi. He is still very much surprised by how differently the same piece is received in a different country by a different audience.

AK – It is a whole subject in itself to understand why audiences react in the way they do – I remember when we did the *Mahabharata* with Peter Brook[11] – even as a child I noticed the differences. I remember there was a very dramatic, difficult scene with one of the main characters The wheels of his chariot got stuck in the mud and it was a very important moment because he was about to die. When we were playing in Japan, suddenly, the Japanese audience started to laugh at such a tragic moment. It was fantastic, we were just completely shocked. For me it was really a culture shock.

Does the work change? Yes – the work changes – but I feel more and more this is not because of the reaction of the audience. In the beginning I thought it was, but it may be more because of feedback from people that we trust as artists.

In the Théâtre de la Ville in Paris – one of the most prestigious theatre houses in the world – the audiences are unpredictable. They are a hard-core, classical Indian audience, funnily enough, and a hard-core contemporary audience. It is the most difficult audience in the world. We were doing *in-i* and maybe five to ten people were screaming and saying, 'this is crap, this is rubbish', and then the rest of the audience went crazy and started being positive and so you had this whole dialogue between them, and we were not involved. Suddenly they are having a fight amongst themselves. The more some booed – the more others would start cheering.

GC – Maybe it is cultural. I can imagine that the French want a subject to talk about, any kind of subject. You are offering them performances for them to talk about and disagree with.

AK – It is interesting. Talking with Nick Hytner, the Artistic Director of the National Theatre, he said that the British audience at the National are more content-based, while the French audience – I am generalising – are more emotional.

This slippage between the lived body and its cultural representation, between what I call a somatic identity (the experience of one's physicality) and a cultural one (how one's body – skin, gender, ability, age, etc – renders meaning in society) is the basis for what I consider some of the most interesting explorations of cultural identity in dance.[12]

GC – Going back to *bahok*: Bringing all these diversities into the piece – how did the audiences in different places react to it? The dancers and performers came from all these different places and you kept some of their vocabulary and their own very clearly recognisable cultural identity.

AK – This is difficult to say, because I haven't been on tour with them. In India and China particularly, there is this very interesting revolution of contemporary dance going on at the moment, and it is still being discovered. There is a strong sense of their cultural identity in the work, but I always feel that we have to be careful with the 'Green Card', you know, 'this is a cultural thing, we will get attention for that'. It has to be deeper than that.

It can't just be the effect of bringing together different bodies – there has to be an internal reason for me. This subject of these different people coming together in a station was because of my own experience of working, of being in Japan, where I was in a lift – did I tell you this story?

I was in a lift and well, that is where the idea came from, an elevator. There was this huge world conference happening, and I got on the lift, and as I was going up, just before the doors closed, a Japanese woman came in who was wearing this very traditional Japanese outfit, and also an African gentleman in a very traditional African outfit. There was an American guy in a suit and two Europeans, but it was difficult to say where they were from. So we were in this tiny lift, and there was an awkward silence, and everybody was trying to find a space to look at. We were all either looking at the ceiling or the doors. The kimono dress was phenomenal, and I wanted to ask so many questions, but there was this fear. We were in close proximity and I didn't know what she would think if I asked her, and anyway there would be a language problem – lots of walls being created in such a tiny space.

In the silence we were going up in this lift – and the lift gets stuck. The first minute nobody says anything, everybody is very calm. Zen. When we realised that nothing was going to happen, everybody started talking, at the same time, and it was interesting that in a moment of crisis everybody comes together regardless of language, culture, or how you look. I am trying to explain to the Japanese woman that there is an alarm – 'we can ring the alarm' – and at the same time 'but can I also ask you about the colour of your kimono?'

It was so fascinating that at the moment of crisis suddenly we felt that we were the only people left in the world. That experience was always in me, and I felt that somehow it came back in the company work when we were stuck. And out of being stuck in that certain place, we all realised that we had something in common: we all wanted to go home. There was a reason why I wanted to work with these different nationalities – it was not just the fact that there were different nationalities, but there was also a personal story that I experienced.

GC – I propose we look at a fragment of the final result, and I have chosen the first really big group section of *bahok*. What amazes me is that the piece introduces all the individuals and their stories, their movement language, and how these are connected. And then you have added into it some of your own signature – which is a sense of rhythm and of speed that comes from the Kathak – so I think it is very rich. (*He shows a video clip of the first group section in* bahok.)

Do you think you will re-work some of it when the dancers from the National Ballet of China leave?

AK – For sure – the essence of it will be there, but with three new dancers... even one dancer will change the whole work. The new dancers will not contribute necessarily as much as the original dancers because those dancers' bodies and minds all contributed completely to the work. They will have to find a compromise.

Sometimes that is a very interesting process: to find yourself imprisoned, if you like, in a structure, and then to find your own freedom within that. That is what I have always tried to find in my own work. For me Kathak became a prison, and at a certain stage in my life I felt, well, how do I continue to find freedom in it? How do I find Akram within that?

Notes

1 Akram Khan in *Letters on the Bridge*, a documentary film by Gilles Delmas, following the creation period of *bahok* in 2008.
2 Daniel Sibony, *Le corps et sa danse* (Paris: Editions du Seuil, 1995), pp. 89–90, translation by Guy Cools.
3 Amaury de Riencourt, *The Eye of Shiva: Eastern Mysticism and Science* (New York: Morrow, 1980).
4 Akram Khan, programme text for *Sacred Monsters*, 2006.
5 Nikoleta Rafaelisova, Akram Khan's choreographic assistant and understudy for Sylvie Guillem's role in *Sacred Monsters.*
6 Abhinaya: the art of expression in Indian dance. First mentioned in the 2,000 year-old text of the Natya Shastra, abhinaya encompasses movement of the body and hands as well as facial expressions, and can be naturalistic as well as abstract and stylised.
7 *zero degrees* was filmed by Axiom Films and is available on DVD.
8 Pandit Birju Maharajee, born 1938 into an ancient Kathak dynasty, is a celebrated dancer, teacher and. choreographer of Kathak. His disciple Sri Pratap Pawar, known as 'India's Divine Dancer', is Akram Khan's teacher.
9 Karthika Nair, 'Zero Degrees: Between Borders', in *The Bloodaxe Book of Contemporary Indian Poets*, ed. Jeet Thayil (Tarset: Bloodaxe, 2008), p. 315.
10 Members of the Akram Khan Company: Young Jin Kim, Shanell Winlock, Eulalia Ayguade Farro, Sadju, Sun Chia Ying.
11 As a 14-year-old, Akram Khan played the role of Ekalavya in Peter Brook's stage production of the *Mahabharata*, which toured all over the world.
12 Ann Cooper Albright, 'Moving Contexts', in: *Dance: Distinct language and cross-cultural influences* ed. Chantal Pontbriand (Montreal: Parachute, 2001), p. 47.

The Spatial Body
A Conversation with Rosemary Butcher

Grandeur progresses in the world in proportion to the deepening of intimacy.[1]

Guy Cools – In the next two talks, it seems that we are addressing the two big formal subjects: 'Space' and 'Time'. They are so connected that we will navigate from one to the other, of course.

I am very, very honoured and pleased to do this with Rosemary, because she is one of the choreographers in Britain who has been doing really fundamental research on Space, and on the relationship between the body and space.

Rosemary, we met at the end of the nineties, when I was still working in Ghent, Belgium, where I presented *Scan*. Since then we have met quite frequently in London, in Belgium, in Munich and in Montreal – where we have also presented some of your work. I always enjoyed the long conversations we had about life, and about dance in particular.

When we met here in London earlier today, one of the first things you told me is that you had been asked to put together a selection of dance films for the BBC.

Rosemary Butcher – Yes. It is curated through South-East Dance and the British Council, and there may be an offshoot into the BBC – but this was asking choreographers working with film to talk about their own work, and also asking them to relate to and speak about artists who had influenced them, or particular films that they felt were really interesting and influential.

GC – They asked you what your favourite dance film was and you chose Douglas Gordon's *Feature Film* installation – which is a magnificent installation of the hands of a conductor conducting all through the score of a Hitchcock film. Why did you choose that particular film?

RB – I had quite a lot of difficulty trying to actually locate a dance film that I felt was particularly relevant to my practice. Not that I couldn't appreciate dance on film, but I had been working and researching for quite a long time to try and differentiate between dance on film, and film and the moving image, and how to choreograph through film. These were all the things that I was battling with in my own mind to try and present in a film, which is what I really wanted to do. And in my research I had gone to a Douglas Gordon retrospective in Edinburgh – and I was very impressed by the fact that I could identify with the piece itself without actually knowing necessarily what was going on. This sort of ambience was what I related very much to; I felt it was immediately very choreographic, because it was on its own time-based meaning. It lasted for an hour and forty minutes if you stayed, but you also had the choice to go in and out of it, and that did not take away from the presence. The direction of the movement was actually also relating to other things. The orchestra was hidden. There was no orchestra.

I felt hugely influenced by the idea that this was possible, and by its very particular history and background; I also knew that the work had come from a huge amount of investigation and sourcing. That has always been of great interest to me – that things haven't just arrived; there has to be a source that relates to the whole concept of the work itself.

GC – The question is how to research this two-dimensionality of a canvas and the three-dimensionality of a performance space.

RB – I have only recently started thinking of the work that I am interested in as research-based – I think it always was, but as the time goes on, I realise that everything pertains to it. As far as the actual performing of it – how do you explore the sensitivity and the thinking and the philosophy of an idea through the performance – gestural, spatially, physically? You are looking at one set of things happening, but actually how do you then allow something else to be going on without actually describing it or telling people?

I think that in dance it is very hard. It doesn't deal with time in terms of progression, and it doesn't deal with the past in terms of knowing the past – you have no knowledge of where someone is, or of where they have come from, unless it is described. It is actually impossible to make that happen through the physicality.

GC – I am also interested in this movement between the screen and live performance. In some of the conversations we had recently, you were saying that maybe you wanted to make a film version of this live piece, or this installation piece should have a live version of it.

Can you comment on this dialogue between the live performance and the screen, which is so different spatially?

RB – I always envisaged that if you place the two things together, then that will actually make sense of the whole idea. I think the complexity is that I don't actually know about the side on the film, but as far as I am concerned, I sort of really understand the nature of the live performance. But live performance in itself is not sufficient to me now – it does not go to the places that I want to explore, so I have to learn about another medium. I have been so influenced by moving image on film that I am actually borrowing from other mediums, but also processing from the medium I understand. I am just on the edge, I think, now, of trying to allow the balance to shift.

GC – Could you give some concrete example?

RB – The last piece, *Episodes of Flight*, was always a struggle to work on the edge of film; it was always going to be the combination of two things happening simultaneously, because of my interest in duration and synchronicity – how things can come together and depart from each other; all these areas of collision and spreading of scale. They can all be manifest by the idea of actually making things meet and part again. First of all, the work was going to be submerged by the top coming towards the bottom gradually – but then there was great difficulty in getting the bottom to rise – the top could fall but the bottom could not rise – so how do you bring space together? These were my questions: How could I bring two bodies together to collide, seemingly over a period of time, and then go back?

I spent ages exploring that. I could not get it to work. So then I took it the other way: I had the two sides trying to reflect the map on the floor. The sides were an exaggeration of what was going on, on the ground. So there was a synchronicity, as this figure was progressing – a complete duality between the existence of what is in space and what is outside. Both I think would make very interesting films once I get to how that will technically and philosophically work in another medium.

The other thing is, there is very little editing. It is not about taking sections of movement and choosing. It is about allowing the thing itself to exist in its own time and space.

GC – You mentioned that a lot of your work is about basic oppositions, like spatial oppositions. There has also been much research about flying and falling in several productions.

RB – Flying and falling and long journeys – either condensed to a short period of time that actually means a long period of time, or a linear journey that is full of treacherous adventure. The question is, how do you push the parameters of any human experience, but done spatially not emotionally – so you are not giving all the information. If you push something to a point where you are feeling the extent of the time limit, then in a way you are exploring a long distance. Spatially the edges really interest me – going to the edge of things – falling, as in *Scan*, but being picked up. Recovery is another ongoing theme. Nothing actually stays within its own space, but it falls within its own space – and it is recovered within its own space.

GC – As an introduction to the video fragments that you selected to show, your most recent work – *Episodes of Flight* – is about the experience of going back to New York. One of the things I remember very well you described was that it was about the edges of the space; space being curved as a physical experience of re-visiting this city, which made a lot of sense.

RB – Yes – it was a very abstract version of it. I have now probably almost an abstract archive of a period of time in my life. It was explored by a return visit, but the actual memory of the visit was explored in the sense of just the state the city was in; of the way the city set itself up and how the journey itself was an exploration that kept turning around on itself. The decision not to go to the centre was always there, because there was always a sense of being on the peripheral.

The functionality of the movement was because there was nothing ornate, nothing extra. Yet still to have the idea of the form reliving itself – it was totally about the form taking itself on. If one thing altered, everything altered – no single thing altered without being informed by the thing before or the thing after it.

GC – You chose a fragment of the last piece, and then, for the second fragment you chose a piece which is almost twenty years old or even older?

RB – It is thirty years...

GC – ... thirty years old and you said that it is basically the same thing. As an introduction to the video fragment, can you explain how it researches the same theme?

RB – There is no direct back and forward, but there is a strange feeling that the last piece that I have just completed has huge references to a piece made in 1978-1979 for very different reasons. Both about edges, both about the nature of entering and exiting – coming into a space or leaving a space. Also, the second piece, called *Spaces 4*, is totally improvised, something that I was experimenting with in the eighties.

I found it fascinating to put the two things together – I only have a short fragment of the early piece because I had to get it off the reel, and it is really quite old, an early video. I am talking across it because I was being interviewed; I am describing what is going on – but it was actually in silence. (*He shows an excerpt of the video of* Episodes of Flight*, and then a fragment from* Spaces 4.)

I was provided with situations, the improvisations of which could then move Heinz Dieter Pietsch, the visual artist, on to make objects. Then we would improvise again with the objects, and then we gradually – with discussion and watching – found an end result.

The movement picked up on how the sculptures were made. The dancers leaned or rested up against them, and actually formulated a sculpture in themselves. They were picking up on the shape of the sculptures and then taking that initial movement and moving into other movements, linking up again with the shape and the texture. It was very much concerned with edges and not with completely finished objects, which allowed the dancers to fill in the points that were empty.

Finding holes, that is what interests me.[2]

GC – Both pieces refer to the edges, and there is also much about the empty space in between. There are other pieces where the desert or Antarctica[3] are starting points. A lot of your work creates a sense of silence and also looks at how the body relates to this.

RB – So much has changed in terms of how work can be described or what kind of work people are making about those issues. But the eighties were a very interesting time, very free – in fact you could make a piece about space. I am far more interested in the space than I am in the movement. And what is interesting now, is that I am far more interested in the absolute detail of the body – like seeing Elena Giannotti come full close up. The film hasn't been edited, and so it is very raw – but it is interesting just to see that body full scale on screen. If you go back to the seventies and eighties, work then actually was quite untidy. But I love that. I have been criticised heavily for it – it was never finished – but then, it wasn't about completion.

GC – Can you say more about this shift from the space to the body? Was that a kind of gradual thing, or was it moving forwards and backwards?

RB – I always wondered whether it was because I wasn't technically very informed. Or I was informed, but it did not interest me very much. So it was a way of getting off the hook, but not in a bad way. Visual art changed the way I thought about how movement could be seen in its closest form, and also the sense that because I was processing movement, it could be what it is. I tried to do that, but it did not work, and then I realised that in order to get it very close to being – say, for example, in Bill Viola's work – of the sense of states being caught, then the body had to be very accurate in whatever small way it could be. And that is when I think my focus changed to getting detail absolutely right. Precision, detail, and the sense that the body belonged to itself. The idea belonged to the body within itself.

Scan came from trying to look outside and inside of the body, at the bright and dark extremes of radiographic images.[4]

GC – In the fantastic monograph that has been published about your work, *Choreography, Collisions and Collaborations*, *Scan* takes a very important place. Having seen *Scan* myself on different occasions, it also feels like an iconic piece to me. Do you like that, in relationship to what you were mentioning?

RB – Yes, I think it is the last piece where I was using the technical expertise of the performers – but trying to get them to lose the technique, while keeping the accuracy and performance quality. It was a piece that was informed by seeing X-rays – very early X-rays – in particular ones where we were seeing women who were talking about the sense that they had seen that their wedding ring had also been X-rayed.

The idea was that people were looking in themselves, and the piece was looking in, but being pushed to the out – the inner, the out; the negative, the positive.

To structure it, I worked with the articulation of bones and weight and texture – and also the relationship between two figures that were totally dependent on one another. There were two couples; four people, each relating to each other, and every performer only moves because of the instigation of the other performer, so wherever the impulse was, it was taken, so it was full of rhythm energy. And it was lit in a way where it was half hidden and half seen, and the philosophy was that it was seen on four sides – everybody saw everything but not in the same order – and everybody experienced everything but not in the same order.

There has been a lot written about it because I think there were a lot of things to read into it – both in the sense of how it had grown, but also because people could see a strong sense of it coming from a female – coming from the sense of the exploration of the woman.

I had worked it in such a way that the space gradually tilted so at the last minute one side of the space was higher, and for about ten seconds the whole space was disoriented, and then it shifted back again. Which also happens in *Episodes of Flight* – when in the third section the space tilts – and in your mind everything is moving towards the centre, so it speeds up. It was very risky and very physical, but it was the last sort of piece of that kind that I made, and was interested in making, and therefore I think it does have quite an interesting place.

GC – Yes, and also the way that again the live performance ends and then the video takes over.

RB – Well, the video was the second half and it went backwards. The filmmaker actually decided to go from the end of the piece to the beginning of the piece, so it ends up with a rehearsal and it is in the centre of the floor. It was a strange collaboration because it would not have necessarily been how I would have resolved it. But it was one of those occasions where I accepted the proposal from the collaborator. Actually in the end there were only twenty-five minutes of material and there was only one way to go and that was back down into the floor again, away into the distance.

GC – We will show a fragment of *Scan*, but it is framed by two versions of another piece – why?

RB – Yes, there is a reason for that. Probably this other piece, *White*, is more driven – *Scan* in a way was better resolved than the piece that comes after it but the piece before it is the piece that I cite as moving into a piece that in itself is a film. It is a solo from the end of a piece, but it was always going to be on twenty-four screens, and the dancer would move through the twenty-four screens all the way along. It progresses over about an hour as an installation.

In real time it lasts twenty-five minutes. But as a little bit of an example of that idea – of taking a particular movement and pushing it into a different place and medium by just in fact slowing it down slightly – it belongs somewhere else, which is quite interesting. It belongs to another piece, so I sandwiched these two just because then *Scan* does look extremely central, physically, to a special time. (*He shows three video clips of* White, Scan, *and* White, *the film version.*)

RB – I realise I haven't credited people. Anise Smith and Anna Holter are the German dancers, with Elena Giannotti, performing *White*. In *Scan* it was Jonathan Burrows, Lauren Potter, Henry Montes and Rachel Vonmoos, and it was Elena in the journey of the film.

GC – One of the authors who has inspired me in my recent thinking about dance is the French philosopher and psychiatrist Daniel Sibony. In his psychiatry practice he developed the notion of the in-between: that being a human being is about negotiating between the two parental lineages that determine our identity.

He was also passionate about dance, and he wrote this beautiful book called *Le corps et sa danse*[5] – 'The body and its dance' – a definition of dance as being a movement between the 'body memory' and the 'body present'.

Now looking at these fragments and also knowing – as you just described – how the film was used in *Scan* as a memory of the process, it feels as if film has this memory quality in relation to the present and the live performers. Would you agree to that? Is it something that you are conscious of?

Memory is the residing place of life-experience, the collection that reveals and/or fabricates order and meaning.[6]

RB – It is actually refreshing my mind again. The images are quite ghostly, which I don't think was exactly meant like that. It happened because the camera was also recording from behind, so it was a mixture of live and recorded image. But because, again, it was a very long journey going round and round and round, the element of the film was always about the nature of the past being remembered. And also about the power of amplification of something that was seen one way, but remembered another.

Because of the huge extent of the journey that everyone was on, there had to be a way to notate it. You almost have to be your own archive. Somehow you are writing and thinking and recording as well as doing. What interested me when I started to work with the space being exaggerated, and the memory coming back in another form, was that there was much more room for the concept. That the movement was much more a signature to something else, rather than the thing itself.

GC – In your last couple of pieces the performer has become very important as an artistic collaborator – in particular Elena Giannotti. Can you expand a little bit on this? Did it happen by accident, or did you just find the right person?

RB – I don't know – but it wasn't by accident. It was the only audition I ever did, and she had travelled from Italy to Germany. I think it was a collision again (I use this word quite a lot). I had a sense of wanting to not explain everything anymore about a piece of work, that somehow it could be felt by another person but belong to a human being as well. It was, 'how do you translate a personal involvement to another person without actually giving them the information?'

So instead of solos belonging to one person, they were very special solos because they encompassed a wide range of ideas belonging to a person. So it might be like a book you might be writing about them; ideas were being expressed through them but they were coming from me.

GC – For instance, you mentioned that for *Episodes of Flight* it was very much about the process of layering.

RB – Well, yes – everything that started off in the piece was highly elaborated, and then I cut out anything that actually seemed to say more. I cut down to very few ideas that ended up being quite functional.

But in a way everything had to be contained within that space through that movement. The other elements of the collaboration were things that would not be described in any other way, but in fact just existed within their own physicality. The information came from the sound and from the visual to give a sense of the space relating to a whole identity, and a person's identity within a space.

GC – How much of this identity is yours, and how much is hers and where do you meet?

RB – She would probably have to talk about that. She does not become me – she is her. But she reads all the things that are given and all the books and influences. She wants to be part of the structure. I talked earlier about the accuracy that you get once you get rid of all the other things pertaining to emotion – whatever emotion is there. If you don't direct emotionally, then the precision and accuracy has to be so strong. And I think it is one of her greatest performance qualities. I mean, if she was improvising it would be her. But she is not improvising, and so, yes, truly, it is a collaboration. But it is conceptually still driven by a single idea.

GC – The last video fragment that we have to show is from *Hidden Voices*. It is a film version.

RB – Yes, it was originally a live piece that was split over four nights. And for Channel 4's *3 Minute Wonder* they asked if I would do it. I thought, well, I will split this piece – the same piece every night, divided into four. I have chosen the last three and a half minutes as an example of this piece – again a journey, a journey on the spot but spatially everywhere, moving through a life – in fact Elena's words are, she felt she 'had gone through a life', doing it for Channel 4. A life in four minutes.

GC – (*He shows a video clip of the last 3 minutes of* Hidden Voices, *the film version.*)[7]

I chose the next quote because I think that it describes what the dancer is about, and also it relates to how, as you yourself mentioned earlier, you felt the exploration moved from space to the body being a space, and then to the architecture of the body.

What a dancer makes available to choreography is particulate, mediated by energy production and use, rather more than it is solid or hard edged, or monolithic. The expert dancer is gifted in this offering of potential – and aspires, in turn, to qualitative transformation.[8]

RB – It is the cutting, dividing the space – and what makes sense of it is the inner division. It is in the very small details of how the body itself is subdividing itself, although the body is in one place.

GC – We think of rhythm as being about time, but it is also about spatial elements. Meaning that the space has a rhythm of its own.

RB – I often think in this piece that it is happening in one place, but you are guided to all the other places by light. A bit more dramatic in a sense. But there was the sense that the emergence and disappearance of the figure also engaged in a spatial dialogue with itself between light and dark, between being seen and emerging, coming up into the light of something and then disappearing. And it is all happening, although the movement is – if you see it in the studio and in daylight – it is rigorous, and it is the same, and it never stops. The intensity is drawn out by the nature of the repetition, the absolute accuracy of that foot, being exactly the same distance – always one foot in front of the other.

GC – Where do you want to go next? Is there already a vision?

RB – In work?

GC – Yes.

RB – I am trying. I want to make an installation. I want to be able to pull all these things that I am interested in into something that really works. So that I can hold on to it for longer, be with it longer. It is more about fulfilling several compartments, trying to let them rest together. It interests me more than actually making more pieces. I feel in some ways that it has been explored to a certain degree, where you would repeat – it is inevitable that you would repeat. But I think there are a lot of angles that I am interested in, and I want to spend the time to really do it – really invest.

GC – But you have already made installation pieces?

RB – I am not sure whether they are truly installations. I use that term 'installation performance', but, you know, I'm not sure whether I really fully understand the nature of that. I think it is much, much more complicated than just letting a figure exist in a particular space and saying, well, this is what they are doing. It is time-based.

I think it is about how a viewer perceives, and is informed by the nature of the elements, that I am interested in going on with, which means understanding film more. More, more...

Notes

1 Gaston Bachelard, *The Poetics of Space* (Boston: Beacon Press, 1994), p. 195.
2 Rosemarie Trockel in: Rosemary Butcher and Susan Melrose, eds., *Choreography, Collisions and Collaborations* (Middlesex: Middlesex University Press, 2005), p. 73.
3 The pieces he refers to are *White* (2003), which was inspired by Ernest Shackleton's journey to the South Pole, and *Vanishing Point* (2004), set in the desert in Andalucia.
4 Rosemary Butcher in: Butcher and Melrose, *Choreography, Collisions and Collaborations*, p. 69.
5 Daniel Sibony, *Le corps et sa danse* (Paris: Editions du Seuil, 1995).
6 Bill Viola in: Butcher and Melrose, *Choreography, Collisions and Collaborations*, p. 73.
7 A clip of the film version of *Hidden Voices* is available on Rosemary Butcher's website: www.rosemarybutcher.com.
8 Susan Melrose in Butcher and Melrose, *Choreography, Collisions and Collaborations*, p. 179.

The Musical Body
A Conversation with Jonathan Burrows & Matteo Fargion

Rhythm can restore our sense of embodiment.[1]

Guy Cools – I am very pleased to speak with both Jonathan Burrows and Matteo Fargion, because they were my introduction to British dance when I started as a very young curator in the early nineties. Being very generous artists, they also introduced me to Rosemary Butcher and to Akram Khan, who I have both now interviewed as part of this series, so it feels like things have come full circle.

In any other art form, people tend to look at a body of work as a whole journey, whereas in the performing arts – because of the temporality of it – we always look at the most recent piece. I appreciate that in these talks the conversation is not connected to one particular piece, but that we are going through the whole body of work. I have enjoyed preparing for each talk, looking at all the old work and re-reading things written about it, also by myself.

The two of you have been working together for almost fifteen years now; a relationship that has changed and become more and more intimate. You also recently revisited *The Stop Quartet*, which is like an iconic piece half way through that journey. You were mentioning earlier that when you look back at some of your older work, it does still feel like there are elements that are still very valuable for you.

Jonathan Burrows – The temporality of dance is of course a fantastic quality, and very liberating because it means that to a large degree, as dance artists, we are not surrounded by the constant presence of the history of the art form. There are many ways to record it, on film or video or computer, but they are a representation of the performance, they are not the performance itself. So it seems to me that this is something that has allowed dance to go on reinventing itself with each new generation, so that ideas recycle but by the time they have recycled they seem to have already shifted. I think that is why dance remains one of the most experimental of art forms.

On the other hand, I think every artist inevitably has a longing, that at a certain point they might look and say, 'well, here are four or five volumes of poetry that exist, as tangible objects'. But poets rewrite also. Wordsworth was notorious for constantly trying to revise his earlier work, so that with *The Prelude* – the poem about his childhood in the Lake District and his travels to France – when you buy a copy of the Penguin edition, there are two parallel versions, because the final version was so different to the first. Choreographers don't have that problem – we can revise our performance every night if we want to.

Matteo Fargion – People say it is different every time anyway, even if we do not change anything.

JB – We performed *Both Sitting Duet* last Friday in Berlin, and there was a lady who has written about it, so she had really watched it a lot. 'Oh', she said, 'I have analysed this performance, and you didn't do the same piece tonight.'

MF – She seemed quite cross!

JB – And actually we had done exactly the same piece.

GC – Somehow it is related to why I brought in Oliver Sacks. There seems to be a very strong element of memory: our memory immediately changes reality. At my university there was a brilliant teacher who wanted to research the memory of audiences after performances. They set up an experiment where they made a show specifically for the test, and they were going to interview audiences. His original idea was to interview them immediately afterwards, again six months later, and then again a year later, to find out if the memory gets less and less clear. That was his hypothesis. But the first questions, immediately after the performance, showed that people already remembered things completely differently than what they had just seen, and when they were confronted with the video material of the actual performance, they said the video had been manipulated. They trusted their memory more.

For me, what has been so fascinating about you, is that there seem to be underlying themes that you have been researching very rigidly, over and over and over again, in different forms.

JB – I was going to say one more thing about audience memory: there is a fantastic book called *Rites of Spring*,[2] which is a discussion of the ideas of *Le Sacre du printemps* and what the piece meant, but also what the very strong reactions to the piece were when it was first shown; what it meant in parallel with the awful violence of the First World War. The author tracked down all the people who claimed to have been at the first performance, where there was this famous reaction from the audience, and he showed that it was actually impossible for a number of them to have been there. There was strong evidence that some of these people were in fact somewhere else that night, and that what they had seen was a later performance, but they had genuinely come to believe that they had been at the iconic first performance.

But yes, there is no doubt that the perception of an audience changes. It is a thing that is as much alive as the piece itself in performance.

GC – Do you have a memory of the original desire to collaborate, the original kind of subjects that you wanted to explore together?

MF – My memory is that we met through a mutual friend, who was a composer. He took me along to see *Hymns*, and apart from finding it very funny, I could see already an interest in structure, musical structure, which I liked. In fact I think I said to Jonathan straight away that I liked it because I found it very abstract, which I was surprised at, because it was very personal material; but somehow the way it was presented seemed to be very abstract.

So that was that, and I remember then playing some music to Jonathan when he came for dinner, after having charmed him with food. It was a short piece that I had written called *Five Frugal Pieces*, which was very reduced and for me quite similar to *Hymns* in the way that the structure and very personal material co-existed.

JB – Do you remember the piece?

MF – I remember that you really liked it and then commissioned me to write the first piece we did.

JB – What I know is that during the Mozart Bicentennial I came out of the closet and realised that I didn't like Mozart yet (and my fear is that when I am seventy-five or eighty I am suddenly going to get it and there is not going to be enough time to listen to it all). But the person that I do love is Haydn, and in Matteo's household I have never been allowed to listen to him. And then, finally, because I bullied him into listening to Haydn's *The Seasons*, Matteo said, 'But you just like very flat music' – because I like Haydn, reggae music, English folk music, hymn tunes and so forth – but the awful truth is, it is partly what attracts me to the music that Matteo writes.

MF – No comment.

GC – You just re-lived *The Stop Quartet* (1996-2008). Was this also an exercise in revisiting, like you mentioned that Wordsworth revised?

JB – There were a few reasons why I wanted to re-do it. I had always thought that I should do it again while there was a chance that physically I could still manage it. And even then I wasn't going to be in it, but Henry Montes bullied me into doing it because he said, 'I won't do it unless you do it', and I said, 'I'm too old and very stiff, and it will hurt.' But I trusted him and actually it did not hurt, and it was a fantastic piece of research for me to re-investigate a previously occupied body, as it were. But the reason I wanted to do it again was because from time to time there have been a number of people who have lamented the fact that while *The Stop Quartet* is a dance piece, what Matteo and I do has moved in a different direction – and I wanted to show, to myself and to them, that actually *The Stop Quartet* is the same work.

It was very interesting for me performing it, because when I walked on stage, and when I came off stage at the end, I felt exactly like Matteo and I had been performing any of the three duets that we have made. The inner life of it felt the same, the rhythmic relationship between performers felt the same, and the play in it felt the same.

I am not sure that you can always control the trajectory of the work that you go forwards with. I found a fantastic quote by Francis Crick the other day, who, along with James Watson, discovered the double helix form of DNA, for which they won the Nobel Prize in Physiology or Medicine in 1962. Francis Crick said, 'It is true that by blundering about we stumbled on gold, but the fact remains that we were looking for gold.'

I thought this is such a joyous description of the actual process of an artist working, because it is very easy to reframe your work with greater clarity after the event. I am an obsessive reader of interviews with artists, and I always come away thinking: but they knew what they were doing and I don't know what I am doing. But I suspect that actually none of us knows what we are doing, and we do just blunder about, and the only thing is to have an image of the gold that you are looking for; somewhere out there.

GC – How was *The Stop Quartet* for you, Matteo? You worked with Kevin Volans[3] to compose the music.

MF – How was it to re-see it? I recognised a lot of the material and that was quite interesting. I mean, from the pieces we have made since or if not the material, then maybe the tricks of the trade. I was able to see the choreography in a very different way now. When I was watching it as a composer, I had no idea how it was made and I could not imagine the complexity of it. Now I just thought, yeah, I know that, I know how to do all that. It did not seem like a museum piece. But I agree with Jonathan that the relationship between it and, say, *Both Sitting Duet* is very close, or with *The Quiet Dance*.

JB – I have been trying to write a book for choreographers,[4] reflecting the multiplicity of means which we are now using. I had been leading a series of discussion workshops and I had written down a huge amount of material from many, many different artists, to use as a resource. And I asked Matteo one day, 'Could you give me a quote for the book?' It was quite amazing, he did not even hesitate or blink his eyes, and said, 'Stealing from yourself is good, but stealing from others is even better.'

But now he is upset because I did not put it in the book – it was too good. It was very clear when we saw and when I danced *The Stop Quartet* that the amount of stealing from ourselves was huge. There is a movement which comes from *Hymns*, which I made in 1988 (*he shows the movement*), and I have used it in every single piece I have ever made. Not in the kind of 'this is my signature' way; it is just out of pure laziness, because the movement does something that at a certain point I always want a movement to do, and then I think, well, what is the point of making a new one, I have that old one. And the truth is that not one single person has ever noticed that I do it in every piece.

MF – Except me.

GC – Do you remember when we had this public talk in 2000 at the Royal Opera House, as part of the *Catalytic Conversations* with Antony Gormley?

JB – Yes.

GC – And you came to that talk with a very long list of questions, which were all very pertinent, and I feel like you have answered a lot of them, but still you are asking the same questions. So I would like to put the whole list up on the screen. (*He shows and reads out the questions.*)

- *What age am I when I perform? Can I dance the age that I am?*
- *Where does the image of my dancing-self come from? What part is mine and what part is still trying to please the people who taught me?*
- *Is it sometimes humiliating to dance?*
- *Can I use the useful information my body has absorbed and separate myself from what is no longer appropriate?*
- *Can I use the language of ballet, ignoring the fact that it transforms the body into a site for the representation of wealth and privilege, of the colonial?*

What other bodies possess me from the past?

- *Since the search for perfection has been so much a part of my training, can I ever let it go?*
- *How do I translate the physicality of another person onto and into my own body? How and when might I repossess my own body, my own dance?*
- *How would I move if I dared?*
- *How do I move when I don't question how I'm moving?*
- *Do I have to be a virtuoso? Do I want to be a virtuoso?*
- *Why do I want to perform?*
- *How is performance different from life? How is it similar?*
- *What is extremity in performance?*
- *How is technology changing my relationship to my body?*
- *Is this a personal journey?*
- *If this is shared then what am I inviting people to share?*
- *What can the audience take from or give to a performance?*
- *What is the performing space?*
- *How do I bring the performing space into focus?*
- *Is it more eloquent not to speak?*
- *What does 'too meaningful' mean?*
- *What is repetition?*
- *How shall I keep notes?*
- *Am I asking questions that have already been asked?*
- *Can I accept the contradictions?*
- *How can I simplify all of this?*

For me it was amazing that you articulated all of this in such a particular way in 2000, because it seems to me that it was a kind of program for the duets that the two of you have made together, right?

JB – Yes. I found in a notebook from about that same period that I had done an exercise that was called 'Ask yourself ten questions a day for ten days and don't answer them.' So I thought I would try it again.

GC – And you have probably come up with the same questions?

JB – Well, it was a mixture: some questions circled back and some questions appeared to have moved on. But there certainly is a carrying forward of thoughts, although for that talk in 2000 I was trying to do something slightly less personal, that I thought might be more universal.

MF – How do you mean, *Weak Dance*?

JB – *Weak Dance Strong Questions* was a piece that I made with the theatre director Jan Ritsema, where we moved for fifty minutes in silence: two bald, middle-aged men moving as though we would ask a question. And we thought that we would do it just a few times for our colleagues, but then it kind of became a success and we performed it a lot – and eventually I stopped it because I felt that I would go mad if I asked any more questions, and that I wanted to go back to making the kind of work that makes statements, which is what *Both Sitting Duet* became.

But I think also that this list of questions reflected something across the field of dance, which is about the crisis as to whether movement can be valid as a subject matter in itself.

GC – Matteo, let's step into the performance aspect of it. You have always been performing as a musician. How was the step into the movement part of it?

MF – It came about by seeing *Weak Dance Strong Questions* and thinking that I was missing being on stage and performing. It is as simple as that. We talked again about how we could work together, and I suggested that maybe I could be on stage again. I am a musician, but I have never really had an instrument that I could perform with. From being a teenager I had played the bass guitar, but nothing that would give me the satisfaction that I get from these pieces, so it was a purely selfish request to start with. And then there was the desire to find a way that we would be more equal, if you like. 'Let's do a piece in which you don't just write music and I move – let's both make this piece, let's both perform.'

At first the only way I could think of it was treating it like music, tricking myself into thinking I was playing a percussion piece, which is a trick I sometimes still use.

Depending on the performance, the accuracy of the movements comes very much from the musicality: the score is written musically and I am just performing that. The fact that it is bigger movement and does not actually produce sound is immaterial.

JB – I think there has been a much greater acceptance and interest in untrained people dancing and performing. It has partly to do with this question about movement. For myself I had reached a point where I had become obsessed by virtuosity in the body – and I am not even particularly virtuosic which made it worse – and I felt like I was searching to find more and more complex detail in the body, and yet I could never make it as articulate as William Forsythe.

I felt like I had reached a dead end, both personally in my own body, but also working with dancers. By working with people who were not trained dancers, I suddenly saw movement again freshly. It has to do with the efficiency of the body, the way the body makes a movement more and more smooth, which starts at a certain point to render it invisible. The analogy I always give if I am talking to people in workshops, is that if you are cleaning your teeth with your right hand, you are hardly aware of what you are doing (if you are right-handed) – but if you clean your teeth with your left hand, it suddenly becomes an evident activity.

And when Matteo first started performing movement, that was what I felt. It was like a re-training in movement for me, but not from the direction of technique. Matteo's body was spontaneously negotiating patterns which were actually very difficult for him, and by me watching him negotiate those patterns, my own body was reminding itself of its own negotiation at a certain point, and therefore being refreshed. Having said that, Matteo has been on the road now for six years, and he has done 170 performances, so he cannot really be called an untrained dancer anymore.

GC – How much of it was consciously inspired by *Hands*? There is a huge resemblance.

JB – You mean with *Both Sitting Duet*? Yes, we always wanted to do something with *Hands* and we tried to make a video installation with multiple screens. The original film of *Hands* was very short (to fit the format of the BBC's *Dance for Camera* series for which it was made). It was four minutes thirty-seven seconds.

We did not know much about the medium of installation, and so it was quite poor, but the idea remained somehow unfinished business. We have tried to liberate ourselves from the thought that we always have to make something new, because I am not really a very imaginative or creative person. I just like working: I have my moments, but it is not like I live in a wonderful dream of ideas; I have hardly any ideas.

We like the thought that we don't have to reinvent ourselves, but rather to re-invest, so to us it is about, 'What did we not do that we wanted to do, and why did we not do it?' Usually it is because we think somebody else has already done the idea, but if it keeps coming back, like with the walking in *The Quiet Dance*, we just say, 'Well, let's do it anyway.'

So *Hands* was part of a pattern of re-investing in things that we had tried and abandoned. We abandon a lot, we throw away a lot. We have thrown away whole pieces. We even at one point threw away three whole pieces in a row, which is partly why we live in a strange kind of funding void, because we are unable to frame what we do in a way that makes sense in a funding context. We never know what we are doing. We don't start something new until we finish the thing before, and even then we cannot do that straight away, because we are still processing what we have just done.

GC – I have a strong memory of a dinner at your apartment, where Matteo said, 'We have made a piece, but we decided to throw it away and start something new tomorrow.'

Shall we have a look at *Hands*? (*He shows the video of* Hands.[5])

JB – The first minute and a half was choreographed by Matteo, not by me. I had given him six gestures and asked him, 'Can you write these as music, so that a musician could sight-read it as gestures?' I thought that they would be very rapid, like a piece of Bach keyboard music, but he turned up a week later and then did this kind of incredibly plodding slow...

MF – Flat music!

JB – Flat music, yes, and it never changed. I still have the original score of *Hands* that Matteo wrote. In a way that process of translating, of squeezing movement into musical structures, was already there then.

GC – Because *Hands* was made for film, it took a long time before you decided to also do a live performance of it.

MF – I forgot about that.

GC – I remember when you were preparing for it, that somehow it didn't work as you wanted it to, as a live version, until you came up with a solution, which was to amplify very gently the hand movements.

MF – Did we do that?

JB – Yes, I remember.

GC – And I also have memories of discussions about how the visual and the auditory function together in that way, and it seems to me that a lot of your work has been an exploration of this.

JB – We have become very aware that visual rhythm is much weaker than auditory rhythm. That is why physical performance can either be really held up and shifted by sound, or it can be crushed by sound. So, for instance, if we amplify the sound of the hands, it is just so that you notice the rhythm of them, because otherwise, even if what Matteo was doing was very delicate on the piano, the rhythm of the movement would easily become something muddy. A little bit of amplification really helps to equal the weight of the two parts.

GC – The other thing that you mentioned was the idea of researching scores, and that is really what you have been doing with the three recent works. Can you comment a little bit on this?

MF – *Both Sitting Duet* was made as a translation of a score, which for me seemed to follow on exactly from *Hands*, which is also written from a score. Only *Both Sitting Duet* was somebody else's much more elaborate score – Morton Feldman's[6] in that case, as opposed to my plodding flat music.

JB – You are never going to let up on that, are you?

MF – No.

JB – Well, I am going to play Haydn all the time.

MF – But the other two duets were not researching scores; they were not made with the same idea of translating a score.

Rhythm turns listeners into participants, makes listening active and motoric, and synchronises the brains and minds of all who participate.[7]

JB – There was a certain point when I thought that a lot of the dance that I was seeing and experiencing, apart from ballet, had let go of pulse. I understood that this was perhaps to do with the dance needing to assert itself as an art form in its own right, because for many years it was seen as a sister art form to music.

What I also saw was that there was a particular time of dance pieces, which had become very familiar to me, and it has to do with weight-based contemporary dance, whether that be Limón technique or even contact improvisation, where the time of the body that you are dealing with is the time of the body falling. So there is quite a similar time across different pieces. The only person who was doing something different from that, was Anne Teresa De Keersmaeker.

The thing about trying to work with rhythm... When I was working with hymn tunes, there was a sentimentality around them and an irony that I could pull out of it, but there was also something about the full squareness of it that I could push against rhythmically in dance. But when I took away that kind of music and tried to work in silence, I found it very difficult to find my way through the rhythm: I had no scaffolding.

So the scores thing started with Matteo suggesting a way to notate rhythm on graph paper. The only other person that I know who did that was Shobana Jeyasingh. I had seen one of the scores, which Kevin Volans had shown me, which was for a piece he had written the music for. He was so astonished because before he had written a note, Shobana had already sent him the score of the dance.

And the other thing that comes out of it has been made clear to me this year: I taught a workshop in Berlin, and we were in a room in the former Berlin Bus Depot, which was in the process of closing. They had given a studio to the dance course, but the swing band of the Berlin bus drivers still met there to rehearse, playing Bert Kaempfert medleys, which I like, and they were in the next room with only a thin partition between, and it was impossible to hold a choreographic workshop because I just wanted to sing along. So I had to take the students into a dilapidated kitchen, and we had a whole day ahead of us in there, and I didn't know what to do, so I got them to write scores for pieces that they could not practice because we did not have enough room.

I think they hated me by the end of the day; they must have thought the exercise was so academic and arbitrary. And yet even I was astonished when they worked out and performed the scores the next day, because the level of choreographic thinking was extraordinary. I was surprised, because in some way I had always associated choreographic thinking with a certain sensory experience within the body, but it was interesting to see that, of course, there is a sensory world that you work with physically, but there is also this other thing which is more abstract.

MF – Patterns?

JB – To do with patterns, but what these students did, seemed more than pattern; it was a kind of abstraction that could also appear deeply personal. It reminded me why I like working with scores, and it has to do with quieting the sensory experience of the body, which can often draw you back into a place that is familiar. Body patterning is so powerful that it will draw you back to what you always do. The graphic experience – something to do with the act of writing or drawing – seems to release an imagination different to the imagination released by moving or researching movement.

MF – The composer Morton Feldman often talked about notating music in order to slow him down, because of course you go to a piano and your fingers will play the chord you are familiar with playing, and it is very hard to break those patterns. I have even tried things like playing the piano backwards. Feldman worked very much at the piano, but notating as he went along, in order to avoid those habits. So even for musicians I think the act of notating, and thinking about how to notate something clearly, gives them ideas of how to go on.

JB – I think in dance we tend to think a lot about going into a room and researching movement, and Matteo taught me to risk that you don't go in and research, you just go in and make something – and then leave.

MF – As soon as possible!

JB – I have slowly built up a trust in the fact that you can make a good decision quickly, and the thing that takes you hours and hours to find is not necessarily richer. I was reading Allen Ginsberg's essays recently and he talks about 'First thought, best thought', which came from his Buddhist training.

When we work we are quite old fashioned, in that we start at the beginning and go forwards, and we make one thing a day. A 'thing' is whatever we want a 'thing' to be. And then we try to have the discipline to stop. Sometimes we have stopped after one hour. Deep down we want to go on, because we think we ought to, but when we have the discipline to go home, we actually continue working unconsciously in a much better way; and we can't wait to get back together again to continue the next morning. It stops being an exhaustive process.

I find that when I am making a piece, there are a number of levels of working. One is that there is the smell, or atmosphere, of the thing, and you don't know what it is, but you sense it. Then there is some kind of visual image, which you should not trust, but nevertheless you store it away some place. And finally, there are all sorts of activities which you do not know whether they are useful or not, but you do them anyway. Before we had made *Speaking Dance*, I spent three months reading only contemporary playwrights, but I did not know why I was doing it.

The dance is synchronous, not literally with regard to the movements, but in the way in which the dancers divide time, run through it and let it converge in stops. Even if real contact is rare, the dancers are intimate partners in rhythm.[8]

GC – I would like to show the next video: a fragment of *The Stop Quartet*, the last part of the piece. (*He shows a video of the final section of* The Stop Quartet.[9])

I have this memory of you telling me that you only set the footwork, and that the rest of the body movements were kept very free.

JB – Yes, the upper body movements were often – William Forsythe has a nice name for it – 'residual movement'; the accidental movement that happens by going from one place to the next place.

The footsteps came from a technique like ballroom dancing manuals, where you have boxes with numbers in and you put your foot here on number one, and then on number two and so forth. Every section of the piece has a different pulse and even a tiny change of pulse completely alters the body. With *The Stop Quartet* it started out with Henry Montes doing something very slow, and it was very awkward, but then I asked him to do it four times faster, and he couldn't help but make that flow of residual movement. He is a New Yorker of Colombian extraction, so there is a certain dancing body present there already that somehow resurfaced. As soon as I had seen what he was doing, I copied it.

It is an example of something that I think Matteo and I have worked with a lot, which is to set up a very formal structure against which you push. And from this, then many very informal possibilities and freedoms arise, sometimes to an extreme degree, but often unspoken. I found in performances of *Speaking Dance*, that there is very fast alternation between us, and we can actually change the speed of it, for instance radically slow it down and then speed it up again within seconds, without prior negotiation.

GC – It seems to me that it has been a long journey, a long desire, to go into language like that?

MF – Musically I have always enjoyed setting text and been very frustrated with finding the right text. When I was much younger I became disillusioned with the fact that poetry is too heavy, it has too much there. But at the same time that Jonathan was secretly writing what turned out to be the first text for *Speaking Dance*, I was writing something for Siobhan Davies where I was also using language in a not too dissimilar way. I was looking for language that was very plain and did not have too much meaning in it, so I took Italian folk songs and translated them very badly into English, and somehow that gave me permission to do what I wanted to with it. And it was after I played them to Jonathan that his writing came out and we kind of – I don't know – was that at the end of your writing?

JB – Yes, after he played me the music I said, 'Why don't you come round to my flat tomorrow, and I will show you what I have been doing, because it is the same.'

MF – It was the same, but we honestly had not discussed it at all – it just seemed the right time to introduce language in a different way into the work.

JB – When we made *Speaking Dance* we thought we were making a piece about language, but we realised afterwards that we were trying to move towards making a music piece, which was what we wanted to make after we had made two movement pieces. And somehow the language is not the primary thing in *Speaking Dance*, but rather the thing that mediates between the movement and the music, with rhythm and counterpoint remaining the common denominator.

MF – It always seems to me that rhythm of speech produces rather boring music, whereas the musicality or the tone of speech might be more the clue. Like Debussy for instance, in the opera *Pelléas et Mélisande*, it is the tone of the French language, the melody of it – that seems to be much more apparent.

GC – If you go through the three duets and use similar research principles or the knowledge that you have about structure, do you find that *Speaking Dance* was different from the other ones, and if so, in what ways? In the musicality of it? Or the composition?

JB – It is not so different in how we made it, it still has a lot of quite simple counterpoint, very fast alternation and things like that, and it is rhythmically not dissimilar to the other pieces. But the big leap, I think, was how the piece went from A to B, which was a more unexpected journey than with the first two duets.

GC – Can you expand a little bit on that?

MF – We ran out of words and I panicked, I felt we should throw away the piece. But Jonathan persuaded me that we could actually do something else with it. He suggested that we could drop the fast patterning of words and sing instead, for instance, or get up from the chair and wave our arms about.

JB – I said, 'What are we good at?', which is not very much, but we scraped together some things that we knew we could do. That was our principle for how to continue: If we run out of words keep going by whatever means necessary.

MF – Yes, so having got over that first obstacle of 'You have broken the surface of this piece' – it took me a long time to accept that – but once that was absorbed, it seemed like anything was possible. At lot of it was actually found material that we already had, which we reworked or kind of slotted into place quite quickly, you see – unlike *The Quiet Dance*, which was agonising, very slow, detailed work from beginning to end.

JB – But there was a performance of *Both Sitting Duet* in Leuven, where somebody who had seen it before came backstage afterwards and said, 'There is something wrong; the first time I saw it, I felt that each part seemed to freshen itself and draw my attention back in, and now it all seems to pass in a blur.' And we realised that we were not fulfilling an idea that we had had about performing it, which was that every part must have its own energy and start fresh, as though it was the beginning. And we weren't doing that because it had gone well in performance, so we had been seduced by the rhythm of the whole piece.

But after that, with *Speaking Dance*, Jérôme Bel came to see it and he said, 'There is something wrong, it is not connecting for me, this sectional thing, I can't make sense of it.' And he was right, and it was exactly the same as *Both Sitting Duet*, but in reverse, in that we realised that as we had become more confident with performing *Speaking Dance* we were taking longer and longer pauses between sections. We felt that it was nice and relaxed, but in fact when we had first performed it, we had had a really sharp timing in the gaps, so that one section ran invisibly on into the next.

MF – We were struggling with the continuity of it.

JB – Yes, so then we went back to that sharper timing in the gaps, and the sense of the piece reappeared. But it was interesting to discover that what worked for a through-written piece, which was to be absolutely sectional, didn't work for a piece that was already in sections. With a piece already in sections you had to run one thing into the next in a very smooth and rhythmic way, otherwise you lost the continuity and the audience couldn't make sense of it – they couldn't connect the separate parts.

GC – I think this is a good place to round it up. We have covered a lot, and it has been an amazing journey – fifteen years in this hour and a half. Thank you to Jonathan and Matteo.

Notes

1 Oliver Sacks, *Musicophilia: Tales of Music and the Brain* (New York: Vintage Books, 2008), p. 382.
2 Modris Eksteins, *Rites of Spring: The Great War and the Birth of the Modern Age* (Boston: Mariner, 1999).
3 Kevin Volans: South African composer who studied with Karlheinz Stockhausen and is associated with the musical movements of 'New Simplicity' and post-minimalism.
4 Jonathan Burrows, *A Choreographer's Handbook* (London and New York: Routledge, 2010).
5 The video of *Hands* is available to watch on Jonathan Burrows' website: www.jonathanburrows.info.
6 Morton Feldman: American composer (1926–1987), associated with the *indeterminate music* movement of the sixties. He experimented with alternative methods of musical notation, such as grids and graphic symbols.
7 Sacks, *Musicophilia*, p. 266.
8 Myriam Van Imschoot on *The Stop Quartet*, 1996.
9 *The Stop Quartet* is available to watch on Jonathan Burrows' website: www.jonathanburrows.info.

The Imaginative Body

A Conversation with Tim Etchells

The voice summons the body.[1]

Guy Cools – Tim and I go back to the mid-eighties, when Forced Entertainment came to Belgium for the first time with a piece called *(Let the Water Run its Course) to the Sea That Made the Promise.* During the entire next decade I kept travelling to England to see more of their work, because it touched me so deeply. I even remember spending a summer holiday in Sheffield with Tim.

Then I left theatre to work more exclusively in the dance field, and Tim's career became more international and his work also diversified into writing and visual arts. We grew apart a little bit. This talk is therefore also an opportunity to reconnect.

I would like to start with one of your most recent experiences, a performance visual art work in a gallery in Japan.

Tim Etchells – We did two things in Japan: We presented a Forced Entertainment performance called *Quizoola!*, which is a six-hour improvised marathon of questions and answers in which the performers kind of play – in a very live context – and the audience can come and go. It is very much based in language. To present it in Japan, we used simultaneous translation.

The trip was part of an arts triennial in Aichi Arts Centre in Nagoya, and my partner and I, Vlatka Horvat, a visual artist, created a piece in which we spent five hours in a gallery for five consecutive days. Each day was broken down into one-hour long sessions – five sessions each day. Each hour was constructed according to a system of rules, very simple rules. They weren't about language; they were about composition and about using a table to construct a dialogue between the two of us. For example, the first hour each day was a kind of choreographic piece that came out of Vladka's work, based on hands on the table and positions and gestures and abstract arrangements across the table. It was a kind of call and response, pairing and mirroring and so on.

We filmed the work from above, and each day we presented the live hour of the piece but also the documentation of the previous days, so that over the five days of the performance there was a kind of accrual of material in the space. You would see different versions of the same activity. The camera shot on the table meant that the rest of our bodies were cut off, so you really did have this sense of the hands as slightly disembodied creatures that have their own lives. It refers a little bit to animation.

The second hour each day was about arranging items on a table, and the third was spent making drawings. There was a sheet of paper on the table, again filmed from above. We made a rule that we would have only one pen, which we would hold together, so controlling or moving or manipulating the pen was a collaborative effort between the two of us. It was again a dialogue and a kind of call and response, but the interesting thing about this hour was that it was much more blurry than the hands hour – instead of A B A B A B you had this continuum of impulse-encounter-impulse.

Can we see a clip of that?

(*Guy Cools shows a split-screen video clip of the installation.*)

The recognition of the body's pulsatory movement generates images and perceptions that are the alpha and omega of myths.[2]

GC – Language and the body are both triggers of memory and sources for storytelling and imagination. It seems that in your work you are trying to explore how you can evoke the presence of 'the other' with 'the other' being absent. The project in Japan happened in silence, so it was just about this physical presence. You mentioned that originally you had an idea of using language, but in the end it was not appropriate to do so.

TE – One of the sections had the feel of a chess game – you could really see one of us making a move and the other thinking, and there was a lot of intentionality and psychology to it. But the drawing section wasn't actually a psychological game, more a set of mechanical propositions and counter-propositions. Often one of us would start to do a movement, in a way refusing to hold the pen still, and the other would be forced into the role of trapping it, which would result in this skidding movement on the page.

I was thinking about a couple of things. One was about the mechanics of the hands on the page as they control the pen, almost like some broken piece of machinery, like a seismograph. I was also thinking about those spiritualist modes of trying to cause marks to be generated from somewhere else. So it didn't feel hugely relevant to personally be there. There were no witty exchanges of looks while we were doing it, but a certain tendency to zone out and to just really let something happen on a page. Our hands felt like scurrying creatures, and it was never clear who was leading, who was following, or where the impulse was coming from. Often, when discussing it afterwards, one would say, 'Wow you were controlling it way too much', and the other would say, 'What? That was you!'

The first drawing we did was like arm-wrestling. By the time we got to the fourth one, it all became much more delicate and sort of provisional in its hold on the activity. The first one was all about will, and it became less and less about will, and much more about – I'm not sure I've got the right language yet to talk about it – something about mechanics.

GC – Impulses?

TE – Yes, impulses, but in a neuronic, mechanical way. It wasn't about desire.

GC – What kind of thoughts would you have while you were doing it?

TE – Sometimes I would think, it's great that we haven't covered the paper in the top part, or we haven't gone over to that corner, let's try and stay away from it, and then I would feel her going over there and think, nooooo!

My favourite parts were when we were making incredibly delicate adjustments and the pen was almost having a little life of its own.

GC – There was no language involved at all?

TE – For the fifth hour each day we had imagined this structure where we would describe the situation in the room verbally, and play off each other's descriptions. But we both sensed quite quickly that as a game to play in a country where not so many people are focused on speaking English, it wasn't very smart. So instead we made an hour which was about copying texts from an English-to-Japanese dictionary and using the Japanese words that we were teaching ourselves to draw pictures on little cards. One of us would draw the character for road, the other would draw the character for horse, and the other would draw the character for rain, or car, or vending machine. And over five days we built up a vocabulary of characters that we had learned to draw. It was as close to language as we got.

But all of them were done in silence. People were very free to be very close to us while we were performing. Some came right up to the table. It was interesting for me, because most of the time my performances happen in theatre spaces, where you know where people are and how to address them. And in gallery spaces it all goes to shit because people are all over the place and there are little kids down there with their eyes level to the edge of the table and so on.

GC – Some of your visual art does the opposite to this project. It is just language, but the language always invokes situations and people. I am thinking especially about the neon lights that you have been making.

TE – I think my interest is in liveness, the moment of encounter – whether that is the moment of encounter in a theatre, or in a gallery or public site (when I am working in visual art), or the moment of encounter with the written word on a page. In particular I look for the way that an encounter with a work of art animates the space between the viewer and the object. One idea that is recurrent in my work is this idea of the co-opting of the spectator – inviting or forcing them to partly assume ownership over what you are doing.

It works particularly in terms of language. One of the video pieces from 2001-2002 is called *Starfucker*; it is basically a white text on a black screen that unfolds line by line. As the spectator you are watching a film, but really you are just reading. Each line is a description of an image which you are invited, or forced, to unpack. The first line in the video is 'Bruce Willis and Sylvester Stallone sharing a shower'. It's a picture, and you are the one who has made it. It is a weird experience.

What is amazing about it is how tremendously vivid those pictures can be. An earlier performance work which I made with Forced Entertainment, called *Dirty Work*, is a description of a theatre performance that couldn't happen. It is done by two people who sit on stage, side-by-side on two chairs, with a third performer behind them who occasionally plays some music on a little record player. And all they do is describe a show. The first line is something like, 'Act One begins with five great nuclear explosions. Spot the mechanical dog is presented. Spot barks. Spot fetches a newspaper. Spot rolls over. Spot plays dead.'

It is about the writing being simple and very clean, very pictureable. It interests me that you can make bodies that way – you can summon bodies that aren't present and that in fact don't exist. I very much like real bodies. Why would you work in performance if you weren't fascinated with the materiality and presence of bodies in space?

But the possibility that language gives you to invoke another body is an abiding interest, partly because it does this weird performative manoeuvre on the spectator. Those pieces – *Starfucker* and *Dirty Work* – have a habit of getting you to picture relatively benign things, but as time goes on they will ask you to picture things that perhaps you might not want to picture, and then it gets into very interesting territory: because you've read it, or heard it, you have already pictured it, but you kind of wish you hadn't. It tests the relationship between the viewer and the work.

The body organises sensations that arise out of tissue metabolism, and this is what we call consciousness. This somatic process is the matrix for the stories and images of myth.[3]

GC – You say that language has the capacity to make non-existing realities present. Does it also work the other way round – is the physicality of the body also a source for stories and imagination? I am particularly thinking about some of the autobiographical elements in your earlier work.

TE – Yes, even though the work with Forced Entertainment has its conceptual basis, it is essentially made by a bunch of people being in a room together for very long periods of time – five months' worth of rehearsals. So the focus becomes less about your idea, but more about concrete things like how many chairs, how many people, all of those things. What interests me is the actuality of things – learning to pay attention to what is really there in front of you, people, bodies, juxtapositions, space.

Elizabeth LeCompte, the director of the Wooster Group, said that she has to go to the rehearsal studio in order to see how it doesn't work. She might have a great idea in her mind, but when she goes to the studio she finds out that it's crap. That is truth. You spend an awful lot of time looking at stuff that doesn't work.

Maybe we can show a piece of one of my video works. It is twelve minutes, but I won't say too much about it now. It is about the relation between what you can see and interiority. (*Guy Cools shows the video work* Downtime.)

GC – Can you explain how you made this video?

TE – I set myself the task to think about a particular topic, in the case of this video it was goodbyes, and I just sat in front of the camera for twelve minutes doing that. And after I had done it I tried to make notes on what I had thought about, and then went back over the tape and tried to map the notes to what I could see on the tape.

What was interesting to me was that it reinforced my sense that spoken language can't communicate experience or thought – you can't say what went through your head in twelve minutes. It is a doomed project. But I am interested in language *because* it is a doomed project. What was also interesting was this sort of speculative mapping of spoken language to the movement of the face, the codes that happen on the face. It has a relation to a number of other artists and works, particularly the Warhol screen tests. They are the length of what used to be a 16mm film reel, maybe twelve minutes or so, and for each of them he basically parked an actor or celebrity or person in front of a camera to make their portrait, set the camera going and then walked off, leaving them there. It is about how these people cope with the gaze of the camera, the task of spending twelve minutes in their own company with no instructions. They are hugely revealing, in every case. Some decide to stare at the camera but after about six minutes just can't keep it going; others seem anxious from the first moment – every variety is there. There is something about the sheer delight in the registration of that level of detail.[4]

What you were watching in my video was true, because I did think about goodbyes and these really are some of the things that went through my head while I was doing it. But you could totally take that commentary off it, and you could say I was thinking about what I was going to have for lunch or whatever. The human face is an amazing screen, and spoken language is a very interesting way of projecting on top of it.

GC – I have been doing performance research with the Canadian choreographer Lin Snelling, where we disconnect physicality and spoken language and kind of explore them as parallel tracks. You can just play one track without the other, or, as you do in the video, put them back together. They are connected, but the disconnection seems to be more evocative for the imagination.

TE – One of the very few principles that I always return to is the idea of disconnection. E.M. Forster advises novelists to 'only connect'.[5] Those are his two words of advice, 'only connect', and it makes a lot of sense. But I always try and disconnect things from each other. Often my temptation is to bring disparate kinds of materials into the space: text, images, costumes, materials of space and so on. And there is a general tendency for those things to fall into each other and stick to each other and become a new, hybridised and slightly gluttonous object. That is of no interest to me.

For me there is a desire to keep stuff separated out, so that as a viewer you have an active and fecund job of reading between separated objects. The work of combining hasn't quite been done for you. These days there is a big premium on interaction, which is great, but I never felt that performance or cinema or the novel are at all passive. There is a huge action in reading, not just in books. To look is an active thing, to watch, to understand, to make connections. It is almost as though in the rhetoric around the interactive and the participatory, there is a general forgetting of the fact that spectatorship is a hugely authorial and choice-making thing.

GC – The last Forced Entertainment piece, which recently premiered, starts with a long dance section.

TE – That is down to me. For one reason or another I have been invited into collaborations with different choreographers. I have worked quite a few times with Meg Stuart, contributing text to projects of hers and being present in parts of the rehearsal process. I worked with and without Forced Entertainment with Wendy Houston, and most recently with Fumiyo Ikeda. In tandem with that, within the work with Forced Entertainment, there has always been a pull towards the ridiculous dance, the vaudeville or the cabaret or the private dance that has kind of gone wrong. For us it always turned to an idea of failure, of the absurd, the sort of theatrical ambition that crashes.

In the new piece we work a lot with movement, but I am reluctant to use the word dance. It is referring to the kind of dances that you might see on a cruise ship or something, even though they are performed by people who are old in their years, at least for the amount of energy required, and there is a certain falling-apart quality. But of course there is a big comic potential – Morecambe & Wise being the masters of the show dance that goes wrong. In my cultural heritage that is a big thing, and then there is also something about energy, about physical commitment, about throwing yourself into something. That has been there in the work of the company since the very beginning. I am very interested in it now, when most of the company are in their mid to late forties, exactly when we have made the most gruelling physical piece ever for us! There is an awful lot of sweat in the room, and a lot of very red faces. We were laughing at ourselves, saying we could have saved ourselves somewhat by making this when we were twenty. But it is much more interesting watching them doing it now.

GC – Maybe we can have a look at the video of the collaboration with Fumiyo Ikeda, *in pieces*. Would you like to introduce it?

TE – I should say that this was shot before we finished the piece – it is just a fragment of material that we were working on. Stuff of the kind that made it into the final version of the show. (*Guy Cools shows a video clip of* in pieces.)

Some of the principles that we were working on were back-cataloguing, memory and narrative, and the fragment. When you put one fragment next to another fragment, then it has exactly this relationship of speaking across a gap – there is a fracture. We were playing with that in terms of listing text, and listing movements, so there were a lot of very short phrases, both in terms of text and movement. A list really.

What you hear in the beginning of the video is part of what in the performance is quite a lot longer; a list of yes-es, which are all qualitatively different from each other. What is interesting is that they all summon a context and a narrative – some are nebulous or unclear and others you recognise immediately. So one of Fumiyo's yes-es instantly unpacks to produce the school classroom, or the scenario that one wants to imagine there.

I am very fascinated by the transforming capacity that somebody like Fumiyo has; that the temperature and the texture of her movement and her presence can be very hard and angular one moment, and very soft and dissolved another. That moving from state to state has a very fecund, energetic capacity to produce thoughts and speculation on my part – what is it, what is it?

It is generative, especially when it is chopped very small. A lot of what we did, was to work on very short things, just flashes really. What interests me about Meg Stuart's work, her solo pieces, is the sense that her body can change its hardness or softness, or the amount of space it seems to occupy, or the age it seems to be. Meg uses all of that language that comes from computer technology to describe the processes that she is interested in. It is morphing. And I was so interested in this morphing quality, that I didn't want the text to come in and explain anything. I couldn't think of anything more horrible, because it was so open and fluid, and rich for that. So the text is just lists; there is no overwhelming narrative.

Fumiyo finally breaks off from the listing and speaks, but she does it in Japanese, for fifteen or twenty minutes. What is great is that she occupies the language. When Fumiyo works in English, you can tell there is a sort of battle, but when she speaks Japanese, it is really like a different person entering the room. And for those in the audience who don't speak Japanese, it becomes again this kind of screen upon which you project, like a face or a body that is not speaking.

What I mean is that the theatre must take account of how technology (from the phone and the Walkman upwards) has rewritten and is rewriting bodies, changing our understanding of narratives and places, changing our relationships to culture, changing our understanding of presence.[6]

GC – You were referring to Meg Stuart earlier on, and her use of computer technology. In your own thinking and writing, you have been reflecting on how technology influences our bodies. In your novel, the main character is in between this virtual world of computer games and reality.[7] Where does your fascination with this idea come from?

TE – I am fascinated by how technology changes how we are as human beings. I used to say that the work I was making with Forced Entertainment back in the eighties was understandable by anybody brought up in a house with the television always on. For me, certainly, there was a long time when television felt like it was a constant background noise.

Interestingly, now I never watch television. But the interest I think is in the way that exposure to technology changes the way we are able to think and feel. With television it felt like it was something about the fragment and about simultaneousness. In a room with the TV on, there are two stories happening, the one that is happening in the real world and the one that is happening in the telly. And that kind of dance between the two things is interesting to me.

GC – Is the virtual reality of the computer game a link that lets you step over from one to the other?

TE – I am not very utopian about all of that interactive stuff. I am not a 'Oh dear the internet is ruining the English language or the brains of young people' kind of person, but I find it interesting how people can occupy more than one realm at the same moment. It is sort of in and out of fiction – it changes the co-ordinates of what we are.

GC – To finish, I would like to give you this last quote, which has always been at the back of all the old Forced Entertainment programmes. Are you still doing that?

'We hope you enjoyed our show.'

TE – Probably. I think if we didn't play in England, we probably wouldn't do it, but politeness and political pragmatism make you add this line to your programme. If we played in Berlin, we wouldn't need to write it, but here it seems necessary somehow.

GC – Do you think it is Victorian?

TE – Yes, frankly, the whole programme note. England is a real problem, because it demands explanation. It is timid, especially now: art is frightened; cultural institutions are frightened. That is a difficult context to negotiate. Cheery note to end on!

Notes

1 Tim Etchells, in a pre-show talk with Guy Cools.
2 Stanley Keleman, *Myth and the Body: Acolloquy with Joseph Campbell* (Berkeley: Center Press, 1999), p. 79.
3 Ibid., p. 5.
4 Andy Warhol's *Screen Tests* were made in the Factory Studio in New York City between 1964 and 1966. In total there were more than 500, however not all of them were kept. Some of the most famous subjects include Salvador Dalí, Edie Sedgwick, Allen Ginsberg, Bob Dylan and Yoko Ono.
5 E.M. Forster (1879–1970): English novelist and essayist. 'Only connect' is the epigraph to his novel *Howard's End.*
6 Tim Etchells, *Certain Fragments: Contemporary Performance and Forced Entertainment* (London: Routledge, 1999), p. 97.
7 Tim Etchells, *The Broken World* (London: Heinemann, 2008).

The Transformative Body
A Conversation with Dana Caspersen

The body of a piece is a confluence of energies, and the body of the individual dancer is similarly a complex system of energetic counterpoint.[1]

Guy Cools – Dana and I met ten years ago, when I was still working in Ghent. We produced one of her choreographies while she was working there in residence, and we also had some great conversations outside of work. The present talk gave us the opportunity to reconnect after a gap of almost ten years. Dana, it was a great pleasure to visit you in Frankfurt last year to prepare for this, and also to see The Forsythe Company rehearse.

I would like to tackle three subjects that we talked about then: your experience as a dancer and performer, and how that shifted through your long career – more than thirty years, and more than twenty of them with William Forsythe's company; how The Forsythe Company work as a group and their very particular way of creating and developing work together, and, finally, a more philosophical subject, which I know you are very articulate upon – reflecting what the body means in contemporary society.

I am curious as to how, with the hindsight of these thirty years of your career, your thinking about being a dancer-performer has shifted. Were there any pivotal performances or experiences that opened up new ideas and experiences for you?

Dana Caspersen – I never went to a dance academy. I learned to dance in a haphazard way – first a theatre school where there was a renegade dance teacher who didn't give much in the way of technique. He was kind of a contrarian, and I learned as a kid how to scurry around the edges of the large chunks of dance.

I was fortunate in the end to get some good training in New York from Maggie Black,[2] and I spent several years with the North Carolina Dance Theater where I worked with lots of different choreographers and started practising what it means to articulate and become a clear expression of particular kinds of emotions.

Eventually I came over to Europe and started working with Bill (William Forsythe), which was a big shift. The way that he has taken the classical and uses it as a field of information has been a big influence on my life. It has helped me to start to see the components of things; how the whole is composed of these very articulated and differentiated parts, and how these parts become a whole not by being a collection of things, but by being in relationship to each other. When I am moving into something, whether it is a type of situation or a particular motion or a certain type of language, I need to practice. I am a person who spends a lot of time in the studio, always checking, 'how is this? yes? no? is that?'

I have come to understand that this obsessive interest in detail doesn't get in the way of freedom. Sometimes that can be confused: when young dancers come up against details that are hard to do, it may seem like these get in the way of freedom, where the larger patterns come alive. I have learned that in order to dive into these details, I need to allow them to remain differentiated within themselves so that the larger whole can emerge. That is probably what I have spent the middle part of my career learning how to do: how to remain free, to be able to access power from a lot of different situations – from weakness, from strength, from sorrow, from joy, and within that to remain articulate on what it means to connect to people on stage and in the audience.

Some of the questions that I have been steadily preoccupied with:

- How are the details and fragments of complex motion and patterns shaped by the whole?
- How is the whole shaped by details and fragments?
- How does detailed articulation emerge in the body?
- Of what is the wholeness of the dancing body composed?[3]

GC – You already mention that there is so much practicing. In one of the texts that you sent me in preparation for the talk, you had this beautiful definition, calling it 'relational practice, less positional practice'. Can you comment on that?

DC – Let me demonstrate, it's easier! (*demonstrates fourth position from classical ballet*) The way I relate my gaze, my head, my feet, my shoulders, my hips, my feet to my head is called épaulement. What I understand it to be is a pattern of relationships throughout the body that not only coordinates me within myself, but directs your attention geometrically in the room. Something we did in the eighties, was to say 'this is fourth position classically, but this (*inverts position*) is also fourth position because I have taken these two things and turned them inside out, deciding to make my legs my arms'.

When people learn épaulement, there is a big difference between learning it as a position and learning it as a series of relationships. You begin to understand that a complex relational situation, as opposed to a complex form, can be changed while still remaining in the same relationship (*changes position again while maintaining the essential oppositional quality of fourth position*). The relationship itself is like a thought-object. I learn how to feel it so I can let the thing change through the room, but it can stay the same in my mind as an idea.

For *The Room As It Was* we had made three entire ballets, but decided to chuck them out on the day of the show, as I recall. Instead we went back to a series of duets that we had worked on earlier. We started out with exercises – applying this kind of pressure to make the other person change (*demonstrates on Guy Cools*), and then applied this motion to the memory of the duets we had. So I would take this relationship with you (*to GC*), and at the same time I would be thinking about the duet that we had done. That is what I am doing in the video clip which we will see in a moment – trying to mirror where you are, thinking of our relationship, and still do the duet on some level. That is relational practice. There are the kinds of dances that have to do with simple energetic motions, there are the kinds that have to do with complex formal relationships, and then there are kinds that have to do with states. Did you see *Angoloscuro?*

GC – Yes, I saw the rehearsal.

DC – Yes, so *Angoloscuro* is composed of states. I am some kind of terrible baby who is rhaaaa.

Over the last few years we started doing stuff that is very much based in these energetic states that come into relationships – juxtapositions of different balances of energy. The company has become adept at working in this way; we have been doing a lot of improvisational stuff, which doesn't mean freely dancing around, but rather having specific tasks, like for example, 'I am going to use my right elbow to draw you guys while I think about tracing the fruit on the table with my head and flipping it all upside down.'

And now we are doing things like trying to do two characters at the same time; recently I did one where I was an evil neighbour and at the same time a very prissy nervous person, and I would flip back and forth between the two of them.

This ability to imagine multiple versions of the self, a proliferating, projective equation that moves out from where the body is to where the body might be, creates a situation where space seems to be inhabited by a complex, fluid matrix of potential motion and form, of which the body is part. ... This quality of being in multiple states at the same time is one that is often present in Bill's work.[4]

GC – One of the most inspirational writers on dance for me is Daniel Sibony, a French psychiatrist/philosopher who wrote about the concept of the in-between. As people we are always in between two identities – the mother image and the father image, but it then gets more complicated. In his book *Le corps et sa danse*[5] he defines dance as a movement between a body memory and a body present, and he also uses the concept of remembering – taking apart the elements and putting them together in new combinations. There was something in what you were saying that reminded me of this.

Shall we look at the two fragments you just mentioned? (*He shows two video clips: a section of* Workwithinwork *and then a fragment from* The Room As It Was.)

Could you contextualise these two pieces? Where are they in the repertoire of the company?

DC – I think *Workwithinwork* was a bit prior to *The Room As It Was*. It is pretty much set choreography which really is part of all that research into the classical and the question of how the classical can remain intact while still becoming what it can also be. *The Room As It Was* is the piece I was talking about earlier, where we were remembering the duet. It was a piece that we did right before the Ballet Frankfurt closed, and it was kind of transitional, working a lot with improvisation. It was the first time we relied in a larger way on memory and extraction from memory – and then, as the writer said, remembering while at the same time also being in the current moment. We called it *The Room As It Was* because we would say, 'let's be in this room, and let's also be in the room as it was yesterday or five years ago, or will be tomorrow'.

GC – This notion of creating different states, different times, and to live them all, trying to represent them simultaneously, is a signature of Bill's work. In one of the texts you sent me it said that on the one hand dance is very much a down-to-earth practice, and on the other hand there is also an ecstatic dimension to it.

DC – He is not the kind of choreographer who will say, 'and now you are feeling really sad'. He brings in things from a lot of angles, which he senses are the right direction. He doesn't necessarily explain them or know what they are.

What I have discovered is that part of the work of the performer is to be a person who can feel a piece coming and move towards it themselves. Bill won't tell you exactly what to do all the time. Oliver Sacks, I think, says that we are always dreaming, even while we are awake, and I think as dancers we need to be conscious of the fact that we are doing something particular but are at the same time inhabited by all the people we know, all the fears and loves we have, our past and our hopes. To ride that and not to decide is what I think is one of the most interesting practices. Get ready, as far as you can, and then let it go. Try to allow it all to be present at the same time.

GC – What you are now describing is a way of breaking down the conditionings by society; the expectation to behave in a particular way.

DC – I have been thinking a lot about framing recently. Becoming conscious of how we frame things ourselves, and how society frames things, is a way of breaking it down. How you have come to believe that what you believe is true determines what you decide you are capable of doing. For example you don't do what you don't think you can do. In the last few years, I have been studying to become a conflict mediator, and it is very interesting. It circled back to performance in a way that I wasn't anticipating.

If someone says to you, 'Look, here is a way for you to learn how to understand larger patterns and to figure out how to be able to drive them and enter into patterns that are larger than you; patterns that are moving through a larger group', then you can become conscious. The more things you try, the more conscious you become of what you already think. We already always think our body, even if we are not conscious of what we are doing. We already have an idea about what our body is in space, how our relationships to others work, what we are capable of, what our dynamic is, what we can be for others – these are all learned things. They are not necessarily true, but we believe them to be true. I think a dancer benefits from being put in very confusing situations where you try to do several things at the same time, or you try to be – of course that is what acting is – something other than what you normally believe yourself to be.

GC – You just mentioned the conflict mediation in connection with dancing and performing – the project you are working on at the moment has a social dimension because you are working with youngsters from different backgrounds and also with immigrants in Germany. Can you comment on this transfer of experiences, the knowledge that you built up through dance, and how you take it into this new territory?

DC – I started studying a couple of years ago. It is a university programme and my teachers there said, 'Great, you can mix dance and conflict studies.' I said, 'The last thing I'm going to do is to get involved in some terrible performance' and completely refused to have anything to do with it for two years. I also had a hip replacement so I was really out for a while.

When I got back to work I suddenly became very aware of how we as dancers and artists are constantly engaging in transformative processes that say, 'Here is this. What is it also? What haven't we seen that is actually there?' We do this in a very practical way, but a lot of the time I find that we are not conscious of the fact that these processes are transferable across fields.

For example in conflict work it is very important to transform the space of conflict so that people have the chance to come back to it and maybe find a new way out for themselves. Yesterday I tried to involve some people in a project that brought together very conservative people with some non-conservative people, immigrants who don't speak German, people who really wish there were a lot less immigrants, all kinds of people. It is very much like walking into a room with forty dancers and getting something going. I was thinking it really is exactly the same thing, which is to create new types of pressure, energetic pressure between people within the room so that something shifts by itself, or brings something up so that the people themselves shift.

My project currently is to think about what it means for performers to become conscious of what they already know, the transformative processes that they're engaged in, and for them to use it. A lot of dancers hit forty and then that's it, they need to move on and figure out what to do. Most don't have university training so they feel like they're starting from zero, when in fact they have this phenomenal experience and ability to transform within themselves, to transform their relationships with others, to transform the space.

A company of performers and creators can be seen as a kind of body, and the work that a company creates can be viewed in the same way; as a body that is composed of our thoughts and the different ways that our individual bodies are thinking.[6]

GC – When I came to watch the rehearsal in June, having myself worked with a lot of choreographers and large groups of dancers, I was amazed how organic and flowing the whole process was. Bill was guiding, but all these other voices of performers and supporting staff were very audible in the room, asking questions, making suggestions. It seems that the company has developed a way of working with each other that has a very fluent quality. Also, referring to one of your own quotes, the group itself functions as a body.

DC – It doesn't mean that it is harmonious, or that we even really know what is happening. Sometimes it will be a giant struggle and a nightmare, and sometimes it will happen just like that (*snaps fingers*). But there is always a point when I suddenly feel like the piece itself comes down into the room. A lot of us have been working together for a really long time, and there are also some brand new people who are fantastic. Bill is very fluid, almost maddeningly fluid sometimes, but it makes a place where you can stay for a long time, change, and you can come back and have your own ideas. The people who come are people who are interested in thinking about things on their own and having people to bounce stuff off of. Dancers are accustomed to being critical, to having people go, 'No that doesn't work at all', or 'That's fantastic', or 'What if you guys try this?' Every day we spend four, six hours watching each other, having people watch us, commenting, seeing what works better, endlessly working on tiny details – for weeks – and then just throwing the whole thing out. So you become accustomed to it as not being goal-oriented, more a process of developing a discerning attention about motion and energetic states and relationships. I think that is what keeps the company alive over the years. There is not much of an interest in re-creation, although it doesn't mean that we don't keep working on stuff we have been working on before.

GC – Would it kind of resemble a contemporary science lab where there are...

DC – ... different stations and stuff? Yes!

GC – Where things happen simultaneously.

DC – Sometimes we work on stuff in separate groups, developing a ridiculous amount of material that you could never put into one piece. Hours of it. Somehow it seems to be necessary. Performers have to be prepared to let stuff go, stuff they've worked on for a really long time.

GC – Shall we look at the two group pieces? The next two fragments are *Artifact II* and *The Loss of Small Detail*. (*He shows a video clip of each work.*)

DC – *The Loss of Small Detail* is a piece where we worked on what we call 'disfocus', which is a kind of inversion of épaulement. Where épaulement is a way of moving geometries out into space in linear ways, disfocus is taking the whole thing backwards – when I think of moving forward, I have an equal tension behind me, so it becomes a circular motion backwards and inwards (*gets up to demonstrate*).

Bill said, 'What is the inverse of this type of very linear outward motion that defines the classical?' and the result is that you can tell I have energy moving backwards while at the same time allowing what is normally linear to become collapsed without becoming mushy. What I find important in this kind of work is that it doesn't become simplified in the streams that compose it. There is another part in there where there are these kind of breakings that fall through the body (*demonstrates a rippling breaking movement*).

GC – In any creative process there is a transformational dialogue between perception and articulation – perception being the more receptive state and articulation the active state. When you start changing your perception, it influences the articulation; it transforms it. Is this focus something you have consciously been researching as well?

DC – I am trying to think about what it means to maintain the ability to have speed and detailed articulation without force. There will be a dynamic motion but it won't be forceful, which comes through this feeling of letting things collapse internally without blending, maintaining their discreet components. It has a lot to do with gaze. In general I find that different states of performance have to do with how you literally look with your eyes and your face.

Experiencing fragmentation is another way of experiencing connection.[7]

GC – The other main research project within the company and within your own choreographic work is this connection between fragmentation and unity. When you start researching fragmentation and deconstructing, you also discover unity.

DC – What I have discovered is that wholeness in the body, in an energetic state in general as a performer, is not contingent on the absence of problems, or the absence of break. You can be broken and still be whole, actually. I naturally have an interest in detailed motion, and I am interested in what makes the whole for a dancer, for a group, for a society. What happens when we focus on the details?

One of the next video clips is of a solo with Homer, a dancer who only has one leg, which I choreographed. I became interested in working with him partly because I was born with cancer and had surgery very young, which caused some problems later in my life with my spine. I became very conscious of what it means to have things be unstable, tending to fall apart, and to think of what it means to have the body vanish. Obviously all of our bodies will vanish, and a little tiny part of my body vanished very early on. Homer had just had cancer and had his leg removed, and we decided to work on a piece. We ended up working on what it means to face death, the absence of the body – what it means to be alive in the face of death and all the articulations that are required to remain present and in motion in the face of the fact that it will all stop.

GC – Shall we have a look at the next three fragments? (*He shows video clips of* The The, Prelude 17 *and* Solo for One Man.)

DC – The first one, *The The* is a piece that Bill Forsythe and I made together. It is Jone San Martin and Christina Buerkle. It is a very structured improvisation.

The next one, *Prelude 17* is a piece I made: I took a fugue of Bach and analysed the structure. For example, there is a theme and sometimes he inverts it; and there is a rising and a descending theme which I translated into a score and then used to create the structure of the piece and also the motion. There were originally four voices in the Bach fugue, so I had the women reading what happened to each voice. For example at zero second, for Voice 1 it said 'nothing', so I had them say 'nothing', 'theme A, B'. That is what the soundtrack is.

The last clip is of Homer Davila, *Solo for One Man*.

GC – How did you meet him?

DC – I met him in New York – he was a friend of a friend and showed up at BAM (Brooklyn Academy of Music). I kept thinking about it and called him and asked him if he wanted to do something.

GC – When was this? Is it recent?

DC – No, it was five years ago. Homer died two years ago, the cancer came back.

GC – Thinking about the video clip before that – the voice has been very important both in your own trajectory and in the company's work in this last period.

DC – Yes, I have been doing voice work for the whole period that I have been with the company, and particularly in the years when my hip was so problematic. I have written a lot of the text that we use in pieces, and I'm speaking.

We think about the voice itself as an expression of the body. It can be about actual language and text, but most of the time it rides a line between song, normal spoken language, or sounds like 'swoosh' – for example in *The Room As It Was* we used the sound of the breath as the score for the piece.

There is a piece we are doing at the moment called *Theatrical Arsenal* where I and four guys are performing text that is very musical, but based on actual words that form a comprehensible text. They are doing a foley soundtrack alongside it, using their bodies and their voices. The second part of the piece is made up of very structured group improvisations. They are creating, in time, the landscape of the piece, and we are creating the same type of landscape with sound and language. The two have become really intermixed for me – I don't really think about them as separate now.

GC – It reminds me of something that we talked about when met for the first time, in Ghent in 2000: I had just done this research in Greece about lamentation – the *moiroloi* – and it was a real discovery how through the voice you can go deep into these visceral emotional states.

DC – I was watching dancers work the other day and was thinking about how indescribable dance actually is when it is effective – something happens that you literally can't describe. Similarly, the voice – when it is a pure voice – has this quality that allows you to connect to the way we vibrate.

You sent me a quote from Oliver Sacks, I think, saying that a person who listens to music is automatically a participant in the music.[8] I was thinking about how often I watch dance and don't feel like a participant, because there isn't that same kind of connection that you feel when you are one with the music. When dance does somehow make me a participant, it is because it has accessed a very visceral level by some kind of extreme virtuosity. I value virtuosity, and I think sometimes it is undervalued. The ability to be virtuosic in a variety of arenas lets you access states that allow you to connect to the public.

GC – Which reminds me of one of my strongest experiences as an audience member; it was one of The Forsythe Company's early pieces, I don't remember the title, but I remember that throughout the piece I actually felt it in my spine!

You have been exploring neuroscience and the mirror neurons – can you comment a little bit on that?

DC – Yes, the article that I sent you. On the one hand I think (*laughs*) it doesn't really matter, but on the other hand I am very interested in this research that has been going on about what motion does, what particular kinds of thinking do to the brain, and how you create these neurological patterns. To me épaulement for example is a way someone can learn how to become conscious of and master complex relational patterns. But I think it has to do with *how* we teach young dancers, not what we teach them.

It takes years to become conscious of what you already believe, because so much of what we believe our body to be has been learned very early on. And it affects how we choose to act and stand and sit later on – the subtleties of stance have to do with what we believe.

I was doing a workshop with a lot of people on different levels of dance ability, so I asked each one to stand as they felt. I said, 'Look, the work you are doing as performers is to become conscious', and I asked everyone to mimic each other – we went from one person to the next and the changes were very subtle because everyone was just standing still. The room would shift in this radical way as people became conscious of what they were, and why they were like that.

The mirror neuron thing means that what you have already learned how to do you can see, and what you haven't learnt how to do is much harder to see. If I watch you doing something that I have done, my brain does it with you even if I am sitting still. But if I have never done it, my brain won't be able to do it. We lay down those neural networks through doing it, and through repetition they become more permanent in the brain.

I think that I personally value classical ballet technique because I think it allows people to develop a very differentiated use of the limbs, but often, because of the way it is taught – particularly to women – women come to believe they are trying to do something they can't really do and they will never get there. So when I am working with young dancers, I am constantly saying, 'What are you deciding to do?', so that they are moving towards creating something that is not external to them, but alive.

I think we have to teach kids to keep stepping out of where they are and see things categorically rather than as objects like 'This is a dance'. Yes, this is a dance, but what is it? What are the categories we have chosen to engage with here? What if we step back another category: can we see that, 'oh god, I didn't even realise I am doing the same thing again, let me see if I can find another way to do that!'

An unmade piece is a question in the collective mind of the group.[9]

GC – Final question: although both you and the company as a whole have been cultivating this state of not knowing where to go next, is there a desire where to go next?

DC – For me there is. I am very interested in how we engage with each other in different situations and what that means for the stage as well. I would like to become more and more conscious of how the patterns that we are all involved in have been created, what is driving them, what values are important to us and also drive the theatre. To think about how society is built and how we choose to interact with each other. Are strategies effective, are they damaging? What other strategies could we choose? That is what I am interested in.

GC – Thank you, I think this is a nice way to conclude it.

Notes

1 Dana Caspersen, 'Decreation: Fragmentation and Continuity', in: *William Forsythe and the Practice of Choreography: It Starts from Any Point*, ed. Steven Spier (London and New York: Routledge, 2011), p. 95.
2 Maggie Black was a legendary ballet teacher in New York City from the seventies to the nineties. Dancers from all the big companies came to her studio to benefit from her anatomically focused approach.
3 Caspersen, 'Decreation', p. 93.
4 Ibid., pp. 96-97.
5 Daniel Sibony, *Le corps et sa danse* (Paris: Editions du Seuil, 1995).
6 Caspersen, 'Decreation', p. 94.
7 Ibid., p. 99.
8 Oliver Sacks, *Musicophilia: Tales of Music and the Brain* (New York: Vintage Books, 2008).
9 Caspersen, 'Decreation', p. 94.

The Political Body
A Conversation with Alain Platel

The political potential of art lies only in its own aesthetic dimensions.[1]

Guy Cools – It has always been very clear to me that all these conversations would be both professional and intimate, with artists whom I admire, but have also collaborated with in various ways and became friends with. We have had some amazing guests, such as Akram Khan, Sidi Larbi Cherkaoui, Jonathan Burrows, Rosemary Butcher and Dana Caspersen, and I am very happy that Alain is the next one, as in my personal journey into dance and performance he was actually the first.

In the nineties, I was partly responsible for the artistic programme of the arts centre Vooruit in Ghent where Alain and les ballets C de la B were the resident company for a long time. And when I left there and started working as a freelance dramaturg, it was again with les ballets C de la B.

Each talk so far has had a kind of sub-theme. With Akram it was the notion of the intercultural, with Jonathan and Matteo it was about musicality and rhythm, and I think that today we will touch upon the political, both within the work but also outside, in the way that les ballets C de la B is organised as a company.

I read in a recent interview with you in one of the national newspapers in Belgium that you said 2010 was a special year for you. Can you tell us why?

Alain Platel – Yes, it was a special year for me as an artist. I was happy to make two very different pieces, which in very different ways fucked up my mind in a way that I liked very much. One of them was *Out of Context*, which we showed here at Sadler's Wells – a continuation of the work I have been doing with the same group of people.

This is in itself quite new for me because I used to change the cast for each new piece I made, but since *vsprs* we have been working with the same group. *Out of Context* is quite nude, and also very confronting. It asks, 'If you don't have anything left, what is left?' It was beautiful, on a human level, with these people.

When they started the tour, I had to leave them for a while, because I had decided to do another work: *Gardenia*. The subjects of the piece were older transsexual and transvestite people, all between sixty and seventy years old, who all knew each other from a long time ago when they worked in cabarets. Since they all now have their own lives, only a few stayed in this cabaret world, but they wanted to meet each other again and make a piece with me and another director.

It was huge for me – it is a world that I, like many people, knew from pictures but had never worked with and on many levels it was difficult. It really is a different world, and another psychology. It taught me a lot about how to cope with yourself and your image of yourself, because in that world you meet people who in fact will never really accept themselves. It was confronting. Everybody has these moments when they think, am I OK?, but for the majority of people the range between the extremes is quite narrow, while most of the people we worked with for *Gardenia* have never quite accepted themselves. It was different from the image I had of these people who party a lot.

Poverty is a metaphor for people's bareness in their own lives. It's raw, cruel. The characters are less camouflaged, perhaps because they don't have much left to hide.[2]

GC – For me there was something very similar in the way that *Out of Context* is being set up – the performers walking on stage in their own identity, their own clothes, then taking them off in that process to the nudity, the underwear, the blankets, with it all being reversed at the end of the performance – and *Gardenia*. There, too, you have this transformative process and unveiling of identity between male/female, dressing/undressing.

AP – I did realise at the end of 2010 that these two pieces are linked in a certain way, it's true. But only in a formal sense. The other things that happen are much more important for me – the psychology and the way that you meet people, collaborate with them, and what kind of dialogue you find with them. In these respects the pieces were completely different.

In *Gardenia* I worked with a group of amateurs, which I like to do and have done before. They were people who stood at a certain point in their experience of life, quite far in – most of them in fact were ready to stay at home and knit because they were all on retirement.

In *Out of Context*, these are people at the beginning of their lives, trying to discover, being very curious, while the *Gardenia* people were in many ways already burnt out. I mean, they are people who have lived 'a problem' – their homosexuality, coming out, transforming sex and gender – which in the seventies was much more problematic than today. To be confronted with their story, the sadness and the disappointments, is totally unlike what happens in *Out of Context.*

GC – Maybe we should go back in time and jump to the beginning of your work, which is often inspired by difference – the physical language of psychiatric patients or people with mental illnesses or disorders. Can you comment a little on this thread of your work?

AP – I noticed you are going to show some images – maybe I should introduce them? Because in fact these images were a real turning point. When I found them it was such a relief, because they showed something that I had been looking for for many years.

I had been studying psychology and pedagogy and had ended up in theatre more or less by accident. But I was absolutely obsessed by and passionate about these worlds that I discovered when I studied psychology and pedagogy and worked in children's psychiatric hospitals and a centre for children with cerebral palsy. Talking to and working with people with extreme physical problems, I found something that I hadn't been aware of before, something specific that for me had to do with sensibility, and with the fact that the body takes over when you are not able to talk about certain things anymore.

When I was working on performance pieces, I was always looking for these elements, and finding the images changed everything; I could suddenly be more explicit. I found them in one of my favourite spots in Ghent; Museum Dr. Guislain, a museum linked to a psychiatric hospital. They have amazing exhibitions there, where they show not only the whole history of psychiatry, very visually, but also create links to contemporary arts, and art made by people in need or people who live in psychiatric hospitals. I think it is the most beautiful art that exists in the world.

Every time they have a new exhibition, I go and see it. And in one of these exhibitions a film was projected on a wall; it was not the centre of the exhibition but it drew my attention for some reason. It was a film made by a psychiatrist who lived more than hundred years ago, at the beginning of the twentieth century, so these are very old images. He lived in Leuven and he had filmed how his patients behaved.[3] The images were used in the context of a medical documentary that is now shown in schools and at universities to illustrate certain things. When I saw them, I wanted to show them to the dancers, to see how they would react. I was very embarrassed, shy, and afraid to show them because these images are quite extreme, but it was the beginning of something that I still continue to work on.

GC – Shall we have a look at them? (*He shows an excerpt of the video documentary.*)

You used these images as part of the rehearsal process of *vsprs*, but you had already been exploring similar things in previous productions, right?

AP – Yes, I had been looking for a physical language that I would explain as being my contemporary vision of how to express deeper feelings. I think it has always been one of the aims of dance: how to express in movement things like love or despair. How do you translate that into something contemporary, something of today?

With this group of people I suddenly wanted to know how they interpret those images. The people in the images are described as sick people, but for me that was the last thing I was thinking about. I don't see them as such. I see them as people who are extremely sensitive. When you are very sensitive to life, to things that are happening around you, and you don't know how to express your feelings, I can imagine that you would go into these kinds of extreme behaviours.

To my surprise the dancers loved it. They thought it was inspiring, and they recognised something that corresponded to their own vocabulary, their own physical language and their own way of expressing things. But it was also awkward at first, and they had to see it again and again and even had to imitate movements from the film before they could go deeper. What was very surprising for me was that they felt much more exposed than when they had used their own identity, name and background, as we had done in earlier pieces where I had focused more on the cultural and social body. They felt that working with these images – as we did for *vsprs*, *Out of Context* and *pitié!* – was deeper, more personal, and more exposing.

Physical pain does not simply resist language but actively destroys it, bringing about an immediate reversion to a state anterior to language, to the sounds and cries a human being makes before language is learned.[4]

GC – I introduced this quote from the book *The Body in Pain* by the American scholar Elaine Scarry. Its main thesis is that there is a state before language, before civilisation and culture, and that when we experience pain physically or mentally, we reverse to this state. Is this something you can relate to?

AP – I think that solidarity can grow from this experience. We are equal in sorrow, pain, despair, when we are confronted with death. For me it is not a surprise that one of the major themes in the whole history of art is indeed pain.

When I worked in the centres for kids with cerebral palsy, I felt that maybe people who are confronted with this kind of difficulty from very early on in their life are often a step ahead of us in terms of sensing the essence of life. Maybe it sounds a bit big, but I found that the people there knew very quickly the difference between what was important and what was not important in life. I discovered in their way of perceiving and living life a kind of poetry that we sometimes have forgotten, or lost, or never even experienced.

GC – In your work there has always been a balance between performers being invited to make a solo for themselves, and the group sections. But it seems that in the recent works, since *vsprs*, the group has become more important.

AP – It's true. I think that because of these themes we are working on, we tend to look for the links between us more, the things that connect us as human beings.

And there is something else. I don't think it is a coincidence that the moment when I was confronted with this idea of community, of being together, happened when I visited an occupied territory. In 2001, I decided to go to Palestine – I was invited – and it was a very shocking experience, which made me decide to go back almost every year. The second time I went, I took some dancers with me to see how we could work together with the Palestinian dancers. Beforehand I asked my dancers and the Palestinian dancers, by email, to prepare something so that when we would meet on the first day we could start by showing some work to each other. What was weird, and quite confronting, was that the Palestinians had only prepared group things, and the Europeans only solo elements. And not just solos, but most of them were also improvised – while the Palestinians' group dances were very fixed.

After working with this group for two weeks, I discovered that the Europeans were fascinated by the Palestinians, and especially by their group dances, so they asked them to teach them some of the dances that were based on the folkloric tradition, particularly the dabkeh, which is a typical Palestinian folkloric dance. They loved it! Some of these people continued to work with me on *vsprs* and *pitié!* and they always refer to these moments as being extremely important.

GC – Shall we look at a fragment of *vsprs* to illustrate the connection with the previous images and the group sections? I selected the beginning of the final part, which I think shows a very clear link. (*He shows a clip from the final section of* vsprs.)

AP – The dancers loved this part, they absolutely adored it. Recently Rosalba talked about it in a public discussion, and all of a sudden she started to cry; she missed this moment so much.

For dances like *La Tristeza Complice* ask the audience to be willing to stay with the performance, even when the situation becomes disturbing or uncomfortable. For me, this is when the act of watching transforms into the act of witnessing.[5]

GC – Audience response to your work has always been very mixed. I personally experienced this when I led a post-show discussion after you presented *Out of Context* at the festival in Kalamata, in Greece. You referred to Rosalba (Torres Guerrero) and how the dancers enjoyed doing this, but there was also a part of the audience for whom it felt like the suffering was real, and that you were pushing the dancers to extremes where they didn't want to go. How do you deal with these very different receptions?

AP – I have often been confronted with the question, 'Do you want to shock people?' I find this disturbing, because the answer is, 'Of course not'. I don't know many artists who really want to shock, especially in the performing arts. But to confront myself and an audience with images that are sometimes difficult to cope with – yes! I am on equal footing with the audience in this sense, because I feel as uncomfortable as the people who are watching it.

In the rehearsal space I am dealing with something special: with performers who want to perform – to expose themselves on stage, which is a very strong thing to do. I personally don't understand, I would never have the courage. What I try to do is create an atmosphere where people feel safe to expose themselves, to show us what they want to show. I think they sense very quickly that I would never abuse them – I would never use an image just because it is interesting or shocking or whatever. I will only do it when, first of all, there is a need to, and also if they want to do it, and they are not suffering. You can't perform a piece 150 times knowing that someone is suffering.

Sometimes it is surprising how you arrive at a certain situation where all of a sudden something very touching happens. In the scene in *vsprs* that we just saw, it has something to do with ecstatic states, very simple movement linked to this religious music.[6] They connected to each other by doing something extremely individual that was surrounded and supported by the music and the whole atmosphere. The audience also plays a role here – it is a question of deciding, 'OK, try me! Whatever happens on stage, I'm here to share.' But you can also decide not to, and then it can become very violent.

GC – My personal experience, when I saw it for the first time at the Théâtre de la Ville in Paris, was that by the end of the piece there was a real sense of community and solidarity, on stage and also with the audience.

AP – I am looking for that when I make pieces. How do we connect?

GC – Can you maybe illustrate this by giving one very negative and one very positive example of how the work has been received?

AP – I recently heard from somebody – somebody I don't know, an email that was sent on by someone – and she said, 'I'm in a huge discussion with some people because I loved the performance, and there was a group of people who hated it.' I am shocked when I hear this, because I can understand not liking a performance, but to hate it? Hate is something that affects you extremely deeply. But it happens, apparently.

Out of Context I think is a very warm piece. But the way the dancers move is also inspired by those pictures of people in the psychiatric hospital, which for some people is difficult to watch. It may create a feeling of disgust – it is a reaction that we get from time to time.

At the same time, something happened with *Out of Context* that really overwhelmed me in the positive sense: At the end of the performance one of the performers always asks the audience to raise their hands, and you see

– whoosh! – all these people who raise their hands, which is already very touching. When they do it, he then asks, 'Who wants to dance with me?' Usually, nobody comes forward, but there are places where people do. I think it is an extremely courageous thing to do, to come to the front of the stage not knowing what is going to happen. Once, in Portugal, not just one person came but forty!

But there was one moment that I will never forget, at the Théâtre de la Ville in Paris. When Romeu [Runa] asked, 'Who wants to dance with me?' nobody answered, and all of a sudden there was a guy, twenty years old or so, and he shouted, 'Of course I want to dance, why do you sit there? How is it possible that you remain in your seats? I am from Iran, I'm a refugee from Iran, I've just arrived in France and in my country it is forbidden to dance!' All of a sudden this performance, which was not meant to be directly political at all, became extremely political. The guy came on stage and he cried a lot. Romeu took him in his arms, danced with him a little bit and then put him back in the audience. Afterwards, when it was finished, I looked for Romeu but couldn't find him – he had disappeared, until I found him behind the curtain crying his heart out. It is confronting when something like that happens, a magic moment.

I remember talking with Pina Bausch one evening and she told me something similar. It gave me the shivers. Her company were in Turkey for the first time, a long time ago, and there was a moment in the piece when the dancers would go into the audience and show little pictures of their relatives, and normally they then went back onto the stage. In Turkey there was one evening where they started showing these pictures, and people began to take out their wallets: 'This is my niece, and here's my grandson.' For the next fifteen minutes there was an exchange between the dancers and the audience, and then they got back up on stage and continued. These are amazing moments.

GC – The story of your experience in Palestine shows how you quite explicitly look for ways to hold a dialogue with what happens in the world when you are working in the studio. You also, I think in the last couple of years more and more consciously, find ways to make the work speak with the world once the creation process has finished. You made two documentaries, one about the history of the company and one about the last performances of *pitié!* in Kinshasa. Shall we have a look at a short fragment of this documentary about the Passion, and can you talk a little bit about the experience of bringing the piece to Kinshasa? (*He shows a clip from the documentary film* Passion – Last Stop Kinshasa.)

AP – The counter tenor Serge Kakudji, whom you just saw, is from Kinshasa. Before we did this project, our Musical Director Fabrizio Cassol said to me, 'I've seen this young man singing baroque music in Kinshasa, you wouldn't believe it.' I said, 'It's impossible, I mean, how can somebody who lives there be interested in Baroque music and sing Händel and Bach?' Just by describing this guy – who was only seventeen years old at the time – Fabrizio and I decided that we had to invite him to this project. We managed to arrange that he could come to Europe and join the project and at the same time fulfil his dream, which was to study Baroque music here. He couldn't study it in Kinshasa, he had just learned it by listening to tapes. Serge became the Jesus figure in this project.

Our dream was to take the piece to Kinshasa so that his family could see him perform. But there were a lot of people in the company who, for ethical reasons, thought we should not go. It was a huge financial investment and the question was, 'Could we not use the money for better things than just go there and perform?' In the end we decided to go, and the agreement was that those who wanted could donate their fee to a Congo fund that would be used for projects that we would do there. When we were there we also asked people, 'Do you think it is right in an ethical way for us to come here and perform', and they explained to us that it was so important for them that we would come and show this work and work with them. Much more important than to give money or be engaged in social projects. This cultural event for them was – I use this word very often – food.

As far as I am concerned politics concerns the way things come into being. Politics is how you at Les Ballets make productions. The consensus model by which you operate as an organisation. The way you give everyone in the working process a voice. And how you handle all these voices without your work looking like something produced by opinion polls.[7]

GC – I wanted to show this quote from Hildegard De Vuyst, who has been your dramaturg for more than twenty years. She said that there is also a political dimension to your work that has to do with how the company is organised. From very early on you have opened up the company to support and develop the choreographic careers of many artists – Koen Augustijnen, Christine de Smedt, Sidi Larbi Cherkaoui, to name a few. What where the motives behind that? I think there are very few companies in the world that work like this.

AP – I think in the beginning it was based on embarrassment. We were a group of friends making small pieces just for fun, and nobody wanted to be the leader of the gang. We wanted to be a very democratic group of people, because everybody was aware that we were absolutely not good dancers, not good actors, and nobody was able to direct. So we embraced the idea that anybody could participate in the way that he or she thought best. Gradually it then also became an ideology, as we felt it was not a good idea to link the company to one person. We thought it would be better to stimulate each other to try and figure out the things that we could do, either alone or with people. There were moments when it became difficult, for example when you are confronted with four choreographers or directors who want to make pieces but there is not enough money, or you have to wait for each other because the logistics are not available. It can lead to tensions for people who are ambitious. But I think we have now found some sort of balance. I have to fight against the conception that the company is linked to me and to my name, but the idea of sharing makes me happy and I think it has become a political choice.

GC – Can you reveal some of the ideas you are working on for the future?

AP – Yes. We are living in exciting times in Europe – but don't worry, it will come to you too!

What is going on in Belgium at the moment is quite extreme; it is overwhelming and a challenge for us. I was invited to do a project by Gerard Mortier, who used to be the director of the Paris Opera and is now working in Madrid. He wanted me to work with the music of Verdi, which is the kind of music I absolutely do not like, so I said yes!

It is actually fantastic, and I have even started to love the music – very ambiguous music. I discovered two major themes in it: one has to do with Verdi's aim to reunite people, because Italy was not a unified country when he wrote it and all of his operas somehow mention this. 'People, we should unite to become one country', but in a very positive way. Now something similar is happening, but in a more dangerous and extreme way, which I really find very curious. The other theme, which many people who love opera believe in, is the power of love. I am going to try and put these two things together.

In fact the starting point was to work with a huge mass of people – 100 to 150 people – who are going to be used as one body, showing how a mass can become extremely frightening but also extremely seductive.

GC – I would like to thank you for sharing all of this with us.

AP – Thank you very much.

Notes

1 Herbert Marcuse, *The Aesthetic Dimension: Towards a Critique of Marxist Aesthetics* (Boston: Beacon Press, 1978), xii-xiii.
2 Alain Platel, interview in *Le Monde*, 1996.
3 Arthur Van Gehuchten, 1861-1914 was a professor of medicine in Leuven and later Cambridge. He began filming neurologic patients in 1905, and used the films for teaching purposes as well as diagnosis and documentation.
4 Elaine Scarry, *The Body in Pain* (New York: Oxford University Press, 1985), p. 4.
5 Ann Cooper Albright, *Choreographing Difference: The Body and Identity in Contemporary Dance* (Middletown: Wesleyan University Press, 1997), xxii.
6 The music in *vsprs* is an adaptation of Claudio Monteverdi's *Maria Vespers* by the saxophonist and composer Fabrizio Cassol. It is played, and partly improvised, live on stage by his band Aka Moon, who bring an element of jazz and gypsy music to the Baroque score.
7 Hildegard De Vuyst in conversation with Alain Platel, in: Alain Platel and Gregory Ball, *les ballets C. de la B.* (Tielt: Lanoo, 2006), p. 136.

The Poetic Body
A Conversation with
Jonzi D &
Soweto Kinch

Noisy ear, unstable
repetitions passionate
violence and desires –
... of intoxication and dance,
of organic gesticulation:
the flash of poetry and of
abolished time, repeated.[1]

Guy Cools – I remember very well the first time that Jonzi and I met. It was at the first *Big Intensive*[2] that Sadler's Wells organised, in 2006. We immediately got into a conversation and I was struck by Jonzi's curiosity – always questioning people and himself. I am very happy to continue this dialogue in a more formal way, in front of an audience.

We are going to talk about the body in his work, from the past to the present, and also try to look into the future.

Jonzi, you just produced a retrospective where you showed a piece from seventeen years ago together with a new piece. In both you embody and perform your own work. How does that feel for you?

Jonzi D – It feels slightly more painful. I made that piece in my mid-twenties, it was my physical prime, six-pack, clang-clang-clang, you know what I mean. It is a little bit harder now. But what feels richer is the experience I've had over the last few years, the amount of work that I've seen, the amazing developments in the work, and how I can apply that to this work. It is not so much about the physicality of it anymore but more about the intention behind characters, and the way I amplify elements – EQ basically; the way I equalise the show is very different to when it was originally produced.

GC – What struck me when I was watching the retrospective last week, and what I hadn't realised before, is that the spoken word is as important as the movement and the dance, or even more so. Can you comment on that? And I think it is also where the relationship between you and Soweto comes in?

JD – When I was in my final year at the London Contemporary Dance School, I struggled with being a rapper and being a contemporary dancer at the same time; they are two very different contexts. During the day I was studying dance, running around with tights on, all like, 'ah, we're dancers' – and then in the evening the complete opposite, being the rapper, wearing your baggy clothes.

I am both those people, but it was really difficult for me.

Lyrikal Fearta was created within the spoken-word rap community. I wanted movement to help illustrate the words, so it was a very clear relationship. The first two pieces in *Lyrikal Fearta* were *Silence the Bitchin'*, which is basically a random battle rap in which I graphically illustrated each line of rhyme with a movement and then took the rap away, and *Aeroplane Man*. Both of these pieces were text-led. The only other piece that was not text-based, but movement-based, was *Safe*, which equally had lots and lots of text, but the initial reason for the piece was a movement.

GC – The two of you met on *Aeroplane Man*.

Soweto Kinch – That's correct, we first worked together on *Aeroplane Man*. I remember seeing an excerpt of it on Channel 4, thinking, this is great! And then, soon after I left Uni I was brought in as a deputy for Jason Yarde who was MD [musical director] on the stage show. When was that, probably like 2003?

JD – 2001 I think, let's say 2002.

SK – Quite a long time ago.

I grew up in a theatrical environment. My father is a director and a playwright and my mother is an actor, and I'd seen the power of theatre and dance to change perception, but I hadn't seen anybody yet to embody that using hip hop as a tool. It is interesting because hip hop and theatre share this multi-disciplinary interplay of different forms. If you are a hip hop artist you have to understand the five elements – the visual language of graffiti, b-boying and movement, emcee-ing and turntablism.

One isn't divorced from the other. It has increasingly become that way, but at its inception there was an interplay of these forms, the same actually as in jazz. Jazz music at its inception was integrally linked to dance. The jive bands of the thirties, the great big band leaders, from Ben Goodman to Chick Webb, all improvised – they would look at what was going on in the crowd of lindy-hoppers and dancers and adjust their set depending on the energy in the room. Jazz has become a far more intensely cerebral pastime now, divorced from dance.

Hip hop began explicitly as dance music to be appreciated through movement, not mere listening.[3]

GC – Shall we have a look at the Channel 4 version of *Aeroplane Man*? There was the original solo that you reworked for last week's retrospective, then there was the film version, and also a bigger stage version, wasn't there?

JD – There was. It started with the solo, it became a two-and-a-half hour musical opera, and then it got squeezed into a five-minute TV show. (*Guy Cools shows the short film version of* Aeroplane Man.[4])

Jonzi's use of parody, irony and comedy helps to multi-layer the stereotypical images. *Aeroplane Man* is a fantastic example of hip hop as a functional art form, as recreation, entertainment, and a political tool.[5]

GC – I brought in this quote, referring to *Aeroplane Man*, because it characterises two things that I think are typical of your work: A political dimension that you keep very much alive, and also a kind of self-humour and self-relativism. Why are those two things so important to the work?

JD – I think that as someone who is greatly influenced not only by hip hop, but by people who really challenge the status quo head on – speakers like Malcolm X, artists such as Bob Marley, Fela Kuti, Isaac Hayes. There were so many of them, particularly in the seventies, that just had something to say! – I find that motivation to create attractive and it is what makes me feel relevant. It would be really difficult for me to make work that doesn't have a political resonance or a personal resonance.

Hip hop as a culture, when I first saw it, it just reminded me of my life. Seeing early images in the movie *Wild Style*,[6] of rubble, you know – I grew up around that;

I pretty much grew up on a building site. There wasn't anywhere to play, officially, but we just used to climb into this building site and run on things and paint on walls and stuff, so I completely related to the marginalisation of 'how to have fun'. I think the self-relativism in my work comes from hip hop's desire to represent who you are, to show your uniqueness. One of the things that is important in hip hop is that YOU DON'T BITE, you have to present what makes YOU special. Without that, hip hop would not exist.

SK – I think humour, when I have used it in my work, is one of the most acerbic and underhand ways to convey very powerful political ideals and principles. You have a laugh, and only later do you consider the content of what I am actually saying.

Maybe we as a generation are quite disdainful as well – guards go up immediately when somebody appears on the pulpit, preaching from the lectern, 'You should live like this'. We are kind of averse to that style of delivering raps now; it has perhaps had its high point.

GC – You both already mentioned how the origins of hip hop – spoken word, music, movement – are all like one. So I am curious how you start composing in a collaborative process. Is there always a source, or a point of instigation?

JD – For me the term hip hop theatre means always thinking about how the elements of hip hop can help to contribute to one message or one point. To use the piece *Safe* as an example: the story was about repression, about holding things in, and the technique of popping was what was used to show that. Meaning and motivation kind of came on top of that, afterwards. To get the sense of this thing travelling along the body that needs to come out, I used a scratch pattern, and at a different point in the piece I used another piece of music, by Raekwon, produced by RZA, that I think really touches...

SK – ... *Glaciers of Ice*, that's dope.

JD – *Glaciers of Ice* – anybody who is into hip hop here knows the tune *Glaciers of Ice*, there is a quality to it that is just aaahhhhrgh – like something peeling off your skin ...

SK – ... attacked by mosquitoes!

JD – Yeah! I always thought that that piece of music would go really well in the piece.

When it comes to sound devices, movement devices, text-based devices and visual devices, I tend to look first what hip hop can offer.

Artistic appropriation is the historical source of hip hop music and still remains the core of its technique and a central figure of its aesthetic form and message.[7]

SK – For my part, the narrative is always prime, even when there isn't a script. That initial bit of inspiration can just be a feeling. I might have watched a bit of political discourse on television that has left me feeling incensed, and then I try to put that feeling, as nebulous as it might be, into sound or lyrical form.

Especially when we collaborate, the thing that links the otherwise disparate forms of communication is the narrative, the story, the text.

GC – How do you then develop the text together – is it through improvisation? Or scripted? You collaborated on the piece *Markus the Sadist*, which we will show a fragment of. Again the lyrics are a very important part of that piece and its narrative, and I wonder how you went about developing that together?

SK – It was brilliant. Jonzi assembled in a room seven, eight, I don't know how many lyricists, actors, myself as a musician as well, to come up with the lyrics. Something very natural happens when you have a group of emcees together in what we call a cipher – even if there isn't officially a cipher set up with beats and people rapping continuously, just the energy in the room when there are so many rappers together means that stuff happens. We had different assignments, 'OK, I'd like you to look at sixteen bars that describe this character's state of mind.'

Because I was aware that Rob Broderick was there, and Jonzi was there, when I had to write or bring something to the table of course I wanted to really raise my game and convey emotion.

JD – The emcee is ALWAYS battling, it doesn't matter what the context is. If there are eight emcees in the room and we've got to write sixteen bars – I'm going to write the nicest shit right now! There's a natural kind of...

SK – ... iron, sharpened iron kind of thing, in the freshest possible way. That sense of wanting to trump each other lyrically but being aware of what the story needed as well, I think created a very powerful dynamic. The script came very quickly.

JD – It really did, man. I also knew what the story was, pretty much. I had done a lot of stuff with a dramaturg who works at the Royal Court Theatre, who helped me find the direction of the piece – and you did as well (*to Guy Cools*), maybe you don't remember, but we had a little conversation. I don't know if you realised I was fishing! I got the clarity of what each scene meant, and then I was able to give that information to them, and they just flowed with it, it was absolutely incredible. I really loved that project and I so want to bring it back.

GC – Shall we look at a fragment of it? (*He shows a video clip of* Markus the Sadist.) This part of your message is also a strong reaction against the commercialisation of hip hop culture. Can you comment on that?

JD – Yeah. Chuck D. He quoted – I was going to say famously, but obviously I don't remember the quote – 'I do rap music 'cause I never dug disco.'

Does that sound right? Something like that. The point is, I remember that hip hop, when it first came out, was something only a few people did. It was a form that was only for a certain type of mind-state. Commercialism was on one side, and hip hop was for people who weren't into commercialism. So to see hip hop erode into this vacuous form, where the form is there, but the content is lacking... All you've got is the beats – well, just about, you haven't even got the beats now! We'll comment on that side of it, but basically all that is still there is the form of delivering text rhythmically over a beat, whereas the motivation for the lyrical content is now so often really questionable.

I don't think that this is as the result of emcees; I think it is as a result of the people who are promoting music and promoting these ideas. Because I know there is a bundle of excellent emcees out there – I'm sitting next to one right now – who are just struggling to get what they think said out there, whereas you got people singing 'black and yellow, black and yellow' and oh, it's no problem for them, getting heard.

I got a real problem with the commercialisation of it; I think that this culture came from a marginal perspective, and the argument is that we are losing this perspective because a lot of rappers are now making money, yeah, and those one percent are the ones that are speaking the loudest. But my question is: where are the ninety-nine percent of emcees that ain't on that?

Rap's complex attitude toward mass circulation and commercialization reflects another central feature of postmodernism: its fascinated and overwhelming absorption of contemporary technology, particularly that of the mass media.[8]

SK – The oppositional qualities of hip hop, the fact that it did question the status quo, inspired a lot of people – even many who didn't have the same urban background in the Bronx or wherever; who weren't black – but it gave them a sense of empowerment and identity. Look at the effect that Public Enemy had in middle-class suburbs right up and down the world.

That oppositional element has been severely diluted. A comment that I was just making before this discussion was that all the 'other' dissenting voices in hip hop are now classed as 'political rap'. Leftfield, bohemian, quirky, intelligent, rap. As if the other stuff isn't political. It is even more insidious and political when it's promulgating a lifestyle – that is the right-wing equivalent of political rap!

GC – This dilution that Soweto is referring to – is it also happening in the way that hip hop as a dance form is now often incorporated into contemporary dance?

JD – I think I am less suspicious of the context of contemporary dance, because contemporary dance has always been marginal. It has always looked for new ways and new perspectives. My main worry is *Got to Dance*, *Britain's Got Talent* and what they are doing to hip hop dance. Aaahhhaargh. It's killing me!

I actually think that what contemporary dance can offer to the form is exciting and can actually open up the form, and I guess I'm talking personally: My training at The Place is, in a way, the creative foundation on which I built hip hop dance theatre and my own approach to it. If it wasn't for my studying at The Place I don't think I would have thought of doing hip hop in this way.

GC – I remember when we met six months ago and I invited you to do this talk, you were reversing this thought. You said, 'Maybe release technique is an unsophisticated form of breaking.'

JD – Yeah, totally! I mean, on a technical level, a lot of the stuff that we explore in contemporary dance training, Feldenkrais and all that, is the same stuff that we do in hip hop anyway, just not broken down so much and less academic.

When you look at how b-boys use momentum – I don't think that release technique ever got to the level at which b-boys explore the way in which movement is sequential around the body, allowing it to literally fly.

GC – Contemporary philosophy has been describing hip hop culture as one of the most contemporary cultures because of the way that you use appropriation, new technologies, and also because of its self-consciousness. In a way this is again an appropriation, a claiming of your art. How do you deal with that?

JD – I think it has always been the case, to be honest with you. I think some of the most extreme developments in art happen through a sense of marginalisation, and a feeling that you've got to force this thing out.

I'd like to talk about crump dance as a form. It comes as a direct result of a social context and the way in which L.A. gangbangers have a choice; they either shoot, or they dance. This was literally the case in early seventies hip hop culture. Contemporary visions of art are being made against a socio-economic background, from a place of cultural and economic marginalisation, and I don't think you can ever discount this context.

SK – I agree with you, but there is also a danger that you pander to this almost Van Gogh-like fantasy of how the artist creates, as if tension and material hardship were necessary to create great work. I think actually what has allowed art to flower in these communities is just being away from the commercial eye, having some free space to incubate ideas and try things out before they become a global phenomenon and then get sold on to someone else and invariably watered down. Actually, creative autonomy is what we need – not just tension.

GC – How important is the oral culture? The spoken word, but also graffiti? One of the contemporary philosophers that I am really wild about at the moment is David Abram, who wrote a book called *The Spell of the Sensuous*.[9] One of his theories is that a lot of the problems in our society are caused by the fact that we have disembodied knowledge, and that this is partly because of the written word – the abstraction that is the Western alphabet. He thinks that we need to re-evaluate oral culture and find a way to write so that the writing has a symbolic value again, not just an abstract value. Which I think happens in graffiti.

JD – When you look at a lot of text back in the day, the nature of hieroglyphics for example, they were pictures of activities which had a direct relationship to meaning. I'd like to think that graffiti touches on these ideas.

The roots of it is just someone's name. But how someone's name can be looked at in so many different ways, I find that just brilliant.

SK – Our normal alphabet is about being able to make the sounds, not what the symbols look like. One thing I would like to add to that is that hip hop has added a new kind of vitality to poetry as a form. Anybody who has studied poetry at school knows that trying to take in the vitality of the poem just through the words on the page is one thing, saying them out loud is something different. As an emcee, when you listen to poetry on the track it's not just about what they say, it's the way that they say it and how they can convey so much meaning and experience, attitude and personality in the timbre of their voice and the context in which they use those words. You're right, you need a whole new system of conveyance to describe this interplay of words and music and symbols on the page.

GC – What you refer to here reminds me of my own training in literature – I was lucky to have a class with one of the great Irish poets, Brendan Kennelly, who is up there with Seamus Heaney, and his way of teaching poetry was to take us to the pub, where we had to sing our poems out loud. According to him, it was the only way that you would really understand the written word.

Going back to graffiti – you made a piece about it where the graphics literally come alive through the bodies of the dancers. Maybe you could introduce it before we watch a clip?

JD – Yeah, I'd like to. What was really great for me doing this piece was that there wasn't an overwhelmingly sharp political point to it, other than that we were going to tell a story about graffiti artists, using all of the elements of hip hop – rap, turntablism and hip hop dance styles. I wanted to shine a light on one of the lesser spoken about aspects of hip hop culture, which is graffiti.

GC – The piece is called...

JD – *TAG.*

GC – Your retrospective ends with a battle between old-school and new-school hip hop, and you publicly make the statement that 'hip hop is not youth culture anymore, it is a culture.' We have been looking at the past, but if we look to the future, where should hip hop as a culture go to next?

JD – That's a huge question and I really struggle for the answer. I worry that it is the end!

And the reason that I say that, when I first discovered hip hop, it wasn't bastardised. There was a sense of pureness to it. I hate that term, but there was. And I think that since the media and capitalism have realised that hip hop is a great vehicle for selling things, it has been impossible for us to return to those roots. I wonder if maybe there is a new next thing about to happen.

Rap highlights the artwork's temporality and likely impermanence: not only by appropriative deconstructions but by explicitly thematizing its own temporality in its lyrics.[10]

SK – I'm not quite as pessimistic myself, because I think there is such a specific system of aesthetics and quality control within the culture. What the industry is doing out there will vary – whether people get interested in selling or identifying the Olympics with it, whatever. There'll be peaks and troughs. But the art form itself is consistent.

There is a very powerful analogy with jazz, where, if you can play, you can play. You are either improvising, you understand the idiom, or you don't. Poseurs pop up in the public eye every couple of years, but for anybody who has studied the idiom, you know if someone is real or not.

It is the same with hip hop. There will always be a sub-culture or a consistent base within it that produces solid people – who will perhaps go on to great commercial acclaim.

You only have to look at the online battle community. There is tremendous hunger and thirst for skills, for freestyling ability, and suddenly these rappers are getting millions of views on YouTube, and then that engenders a new kind of popularity.

GC – In Holland I teach at a vocational dance school, the Fontys Dance Academy, and they were one of the first in Holland to open a whole profile for hip hop dance, with some of the best teachers and practitioners in the field. But inside this new department there is now a huge discussion going on about 'What are the basics of it?', 'How pure do we keep it?', 'Do we call it hip hop, or do we call it Urban Dance and open it up more?', 'Do we include Asian cultures, or is it the Afro-American culture that is still dominant?'

How do you feel about hip hop being part of a larger urban culture?

JD – I struggle with the sense of closure that some people have for hip hop, both culturally and formally. These four pillars – graffiti art, the dance, emceeing and turntablism – are a nice structural beginning, but I think we have now really got to address the other elements, too. Beatboxing. Parkour – I think parkour is hip hop! For me hip hop is about the socio-economic context in which you make something from nothing. Parkour fits in there completely.

SK – For me it is a question of heritage and history – again jazz is a great analogy here. People throw up a lot of quite nebulous improvised free music and say, 'oh it's jazz music, it defies categories', thereby negating the very specific history jazz had at its inception; growing up in Congo Square in New Orleans out of an African-American experience in certain states.

To not understand hip hop's history, its relationship to the Jamaican immigrant community in New York in the seventies; to not understand what DJ Kool Herc did in the South Bronx, or how Afrika Bambaataa developed the five elements (including knowledge of self as well), is to misrepresent what hip hop was. That is not to limit what it could be in the future, but I think you really have to understand its past and its significance. I hear all the time that emcees who are 'new skool' don't know how to freestyle, that they've never checked out the rhyme styles of Daz Dillinger or U-Roy; that they don't even know the Jamaican sound system culture that birthed hip hop. They don't understand where Busta Rhymes was coming out of, let alone what other emcees could be now and in the future.

Indeed, rather than an aesthetic of distanced, disengaged, formalist judgment, rappers urge an aesthetic of deeply embodied participatory involvement, with content as well as form. They want to be appreciated primarily through energetic and impassioned dance, not through immobile contemplation and dispassionate study.[11]

GC – Talking about the institutionalisation of hip hop: Jonzi, the new piece that you are premiering this week deals with institutionalisation too, doesn't it, on a more personal level. Can you introduce *The Letter*?

JD – Sure. At the end of last year, I received a letter. Which I thought was me being bad with tax, because it was from Her Majesty's – I'm sure it said Secret Service. It didn't, it was Her Majesty's Service or something, and when I opened it, it was an invitation to Buckingham Palace to accept an MBE for 'services to dance'.

On the one hand I was really proud and honoured, and then quite quickly I realised that MBE stands for 'Member of the British Empire'. For so long I'd been cussing empire, cussing the Queen, cussing the government and all of a sudden I get this invitation: (seductively) 'Hey Jonzi, come! Join us!'

That aspect of it was what made it very easy to turn down. There were two voices in me, one said, 'You've been given an award, Jonzi! They've acknowledged your success, come on Jonz, isn't that what you've been complaining about, being voiceless and nobody hearing.'

And the other voice was like, 'Yeaahhhh – BUT'. I think it leads into this same area of commercialisation. I'm quite happy being marginal as an artist, and I think marginal doesn't necessarily mean quiet. I actually think it's the opposite.

So the new piece is about responses to this letter.

GC – And the two of you also have a new collaboration, which you initiated, Soweto.

SK – Yeah, it's based on an album I've just finished working on and it follows the story of an emcee called Mike Smith, who is played by each of the seven deadly sins in turn; it is called *The Legend of Mike Smith.* A lot of my previous albums have had a lot of narrative in them but this is the first time I'm trying to actually convey the story on stage. With the choreographic and directorial skills of Jonzi, two performers, two dancers, as well as my band, we're going to translate this epic story to the stage.

GC – Is choreopoetry a good description of what you are doing?

JD – I think it is a description of what I do. Another one is 'lyrically motivated movement'. I was bandying around a few ideas in the early nineties trying to establish what this new thing was that I was doing, and I kind of settled on hip hop theatre because it gave the clearest image. 'Lyrically motivated movement' sounded a bit too much like a scientific experiment. 'Choreopoetry' – I quite like the feeling of that.

GC – When I first prepared this talk I gave it the title 'The Urban Body', but then it felt like that was too limited. And when I saw the show, I changed it to 'The Poetic Body'. It reminded me of one of my favourite philosophical quotes ever, by Foucault, in which he makes a link between poetry, dance and drunkenness as being three related 'art forms' in the Dionysian style: 'Noisy ear, unstable repetitions, passionate violence and desires ... of intoxication and dance, of organic gesticulation: the flash of poetry and of abolished time, repeated.'

JD – Well, let's see. 'Noisy ear' – I think you have to turn up the music a bit more; 'Unstable repetitions' – um-ch, um-ch-ch-um-ch – That's what makes me dance!; 'Passionate violence and desires' – Hey, we all love that, don't we; 'Intoxication and dance' – I don't know if intoxication is the right word, but I would definitely say that once you get into the cipher, you know that you've just got to keep going and you connect to something uncontrollable that happens there; 'Organic gesticulation' – (*giggling*) Yeah. There are a few people that understand what I'm getting at now; 'The flash of poetry and of abolished time repeated' – Soweto, maybe you've got an angle on that?

SK – I think it neglects the kind of restraint and control that you need to pull off a lot of hip hop disciplines successfully – you're not abolishing time at all, actually, you are very conscious of the metre and the constraints of time when you're dancing or emceeing, certainly when you're deejaying. But I do like the allusion to being intoxicated – being possessed, if you like, by something else.

GC – My experience – and this is also the reason I go to see dance in the first place – is that it energises me. It happened in your show last week; I had been travelling all day, I was very tired, but while I was in the show, my energy levels went up.

I think it is the reason why people originally danced, but a lot of theatrical dance now lacks that aspect of it. You activate it really consciously.

JD – I always make a point of ending my shows with improvisation, I think that it is the initial key thing in hip hop from which we start to want to organise the movement into space and time and theatrical form. There are no boundaries. The only boundary, as Soweto mentioned, is the beat. As long as you're on beat, you can do what you like.

GC – Having said that, do you feel like closing this talk with some freestyling? (*Jonzi D starts giving a beat on the sofa.*)

SK – *Ahhh it feels like this talk is almost over*

What's this guy doing? He's just beating on the sofa
It's all great – 'cause I'm too dope
I feel like I'm high on hip hop
And fructose.
Ay-oh that's the way we break the rules
Jonzi D, Soweto – and Guy Cool
Yo, it's like pre-school.
What can I say
I freestyle to what he drools and he moves –

JD – *Thank you very – much*
'Cause I'm on the mic
Speaking double – Dutch.
Kinda like – Malcolm McLaren
But right now my style feels barren
Because I guess you showed some old work
I'm wondering I don't come across like an old jerk
Forty-three – you caught me, G.
Luckily for that I feel really lively still,
'Cause I'm a geezer that doesn't use
Erm – stuff that some would say abuse
And if you see the show I'm doing at the weekend,
After that you will be freakin'
– out
Without a doubt
You see me
J-O-N-Z-I-D
Refuse an MBE
What did he do that for?
I deserve to get a slap in the jaw
Once more!
So any-way
I'm not gonna be no fool
'Cause I heard
Next to me, this guy, Guy Cools
Is gonna do a rhyme
It's kinda cool
I wanna really know
What'ya gonna do!

GC – *Oh God, oh god, oh god*

I first have to find a rhythm
Because it's my first, first, first
First time,
I've been challenged to do this
Thank you, thank you guys

JD – *You hear the flow*
I really really hope
That was caught on vide-o!
YouTube! That is going ONLINE dude!

Notes

1 Michel Foucault, *Sept propos sur le septième ange* (Monpellier: Fata Morgana, 1986), p. 52, translation by Guy Cools.

2 Big Intensive: An intensive annual workshop organised by Sadler's Wells between 2006 and 2010, aimed at choreographers looking to develop their work for large-scale venues.

3 Richard Shusterman, 'The Fine Art of Rap', in *Performing Live* (Ithaca: Cornell University Press, 2000), p. 63.

4 The short film version of *Aeroplane Man* is available to watch on Jonzi D's myspace page.

5 Jenny Rossier, 'Characterisation in Jonzi D's *Aeroplane Man*', in: *Hotfoot Magazine* 5, ADAD (Association of Dance of the African Diaspora) website.

6 *Wild Style*, released in 1983, the film is regarded as the first hip hop movie, featuring graffiti, breakdancing, deejaying and emceeing. It was shot entirely on location in the South Bronx and takes a semi-documentary approach, with several hip hop pioneers appearing as themselves.

7 Shusterman, *The Fine Art of Rap*, p. 61.

8 Richard Shusterman, *Pragmatist Aesthetics: Living Beauty, Rethinking Art* (Lanham: Rowman & Littlefield, 2000 c1992), p. 208.

9 David Abram, *The Spell of the Sensuous: Perception and Language in a More-Than-Human World* (New York: Vintage Books, 1997).

10 Shusterman, *The Fine Art of Rap*, p. 66.

11 Shusterman, *Pragmatist Aesthetics*, p. 214.

The Subversive Body
A Conversation with Sue Buckmaster

The one thing that seems clear is that there is an uncanny force inherent in the very poverty and transformability of the puppet, in how readily it offers itself to us, offers itself for a dangerous relation to the world.[1]

Guy Cools – Sue and I met for the first time during the first 'Big Intensive', a kind of research lab for choreographers, initiated by Sadler's Wells in 2006. I was fascinated at the time that Sue is a puppeteer. And she at this point already had the desire to work with choreographers, which eventually she did.

This is one of the reasons why she is here. Personally I am very interested in how a number of high-profile contemporary choreographers are increasingly working with puppets or the manipulation of objects. My own experience has been mainly with Sidi Larbi Cherkaoui, who has been using puppets and objects in, among others, his collaborations with Antony Gormley, *zero degrees*, *Sutra* and *Babel*, where the choreography of the sets is as important as the choreography of the people.

Finally, in classical ballet there is also a long tradition of puppets coming alive and ballet dancers enacting puppets – think of *The Nutcracker*, *Coppélia*, or *Petrushka*. Even more recently, in Akram Khan and Sylvie Guillem's piece *Sacred Monsters*, there is a scene where the human body becomes a puppet.

These are the topics that we will be circling around in this conversation: What is the fascination of the puppet as a body? How does the object come alive through the puppeteer's manipulations? But before we go into this more philosophical discourse, maybe we can start with your history – your very particular history as a fifth-generation theatre practitioner.

Sue Buckmaster – My great-grandfather was an inventor and a unicyclist, who designed a revolving circular table so he could unicycle and juggle on it. My grandfather on my mother's side and his troupe, my aunties and uncles, were a musical act, *The Musical Elliotts*; they performed with musical instruments and with anything they could make into musical instruments. They would play chairs, horns, bells, and often they would pretend to be marionettes, or have a *Punch and Judy* show in the middle of the performance. They were very playful and inventive, and it was always about the play of the object, as well as the musicianship. It's a rich history – and a rather wacky one.

My grandfather was the musician and my grandmother the businesswoman, the business brain who formed the team – kept re-forming the team, actually. When a lot of the men went to war, she created a troupe of women, The Candies, who went around in crinolines, playing saxophone. She was a resourceful woman.

GC – And your parents?

SB – My parents founded the Buckmaster Puppets in the fifties: 'Modern puppetry in a modern manner', their promotion leaflet stated.

GC – How was it, growing up in a family with that kind of profession?

SB – It felt normal to me, completely normal to be surrounded by marionettes hanging around, and going off every weekend to some working men's club or holiday centre, or some burlesque show, watching a woman being sawn in half – and then going to school during the week and watching Benny Hill on TV. But I suppose I became more and more aware that other children weren't getting access to these specific kinds of comedy or speciality acts. It was a real British working-class, seaside influence, in terms of culture.

My father was a puppeteer and used to make his puppets at home, so I got involved in moulding plasticine with him. The intimacy with my father had very much to do with making.

GC – So your first entrance into the art form of puppeteering was through making puppets?

SB – Yes. And watching him, really. I used to sit in the audience and give him notes about how to do it better, and occasionally he would let me do a show. I got my Equity Card[2] through working with him. As I became more interested in the visual arts, my making probably got better than his and I started making puppets for him.

GC – Are they all still there, your father's marionettes?

SB – They're all in a shed. He is retired now, but if you want to know about trick marionettes, for example the striptease marionette – he has one of those, and one that comes apart, where all the limbs seem to fall off. Amazing constructions, but they are for entertainment purposes. There is nothing analytical about what he did. He was an entertainer.

GC – There is nothing wrong with that.

SB – No! That is also where my interest was born.

The triadic nature of the puppet art form is what makes it unique – the presence of the relationship between a puppet and its operator, and that puppet to its audience, which makes the experience different from the actor's performance or the observation of a piece of sculpture.[3]

GC – One of the books that Sue proposed as a background text to frame the conversation is Kenneth Gross's *Puppet: An Essay on Uncanny Life*. I have also been reading Sue's own MA thesis, in which she links psychoanalytical theory and puppetry. One of the striking things you say in the first pages of your thesis is about the triangle – the triadic relationship between the puppet, the puppeteer, and the audience. Why is this so important, and so unique compared to dance and other forms of theatre?

SB – It is inevitable in puppeteering that this 'other' force is involved. What I have always loved about the visual arts is that in an art gallery – or wherever a piece of art is placed – I have my own time to respond to the object. I like the fact that you can wander past it and it be very momentary, or that you can spend three hours with it. I often crave to be in a visual arts world, because that is exactly what live theatre, or live performance, doesn't allow for. Even though we as theatre performers only have a limited time frame, I always try to give as much freedom to the viewer as possible. I suppose I want to put visual art on stage.

In the visual arts the maker is not present, so it is a one-way process. Of course you can read the placard if you want (I often don't), but it is still different from the performing arts, where you have to engage directly with the actor or dancer. You are projecting whatever you want to project, but there is this other person, who is saying, 'I will help you. I will make sense of these projections; I will guide them.'

The intriguing thing about puppeteering is that there is this thing that you engage with and project onto, but it is moved, manipulated, operated, animated – there are so many words for it – by a third person. There is always this presence of the other person, whether they are very visible doing it, or are invisible. The different psychological meanings to this triadic relationship are endless, I never get bored.

GC – Can you give an example?

SB – If you are watching a child manipulating a toy, you absolutely don't assess their technique. All you are engaging with is how the child plays with the object or puppet. It is authentic, and the joy is in the authenticity.

With actors, you can see that their main concern is for what the object thinks or feels, and how it uses its brain power. Even when the object doesn't have a head, they will give it one, and they will give it thoughts and meaning, and that is what is exciting. Can they transfer all that psychological energy through the puppet, or does the puppet or object tell us something about *their* psyche? It may be a part of themselves which they are animating, or it is all of them, which makes them disappear completely. I find that a fascinating number of choices.

Watching dancers with puppets or objects is like looking at an outside but seeing an inside: There is something about the way someone handles an object that tells me about their inner self, and whenever I see dancers with objects or puppets, I immediately understand the muscular structure of the object. I understand its motivation for movement much more. It doesn't necessarily need to have a head, but I absolutely understand its centre of gravity.

A visual artist moves the object for what it is – they listen inherently to the object. You become more interested in what the object is made of; maybe it is a soft object, and it might meet something that is hard, which might devour it. So with the visual artist, it is about the substance and material of the object. Now ideally, the perfect puppeteer knows all of that. They have a visual artist's eye, a movement eye, a psychological eye.

GC – Is there also something about the act of manipulation itself that is interesting to show on stage? If I look at a lot of contemporary dance vocabulary, I often see bodies being manipulated by other bodies, as if they were puppets.

SB – There are many options for how you observe that transference of the motor force to the object, even if the object is another body. The interesting thing is the duality: the transference between the object and the audience, and the transference between the manipulator and the object. Both those spaces – I can only describe them as spaces – help me to listen to my intuition. There is a special awareness because it happens in two directions. You get to observe it more carefully.

And when one of these spaces is an object – one of them is innocent. The object is doing nothing. I think the audience works extra hard because they have to believe. And at the same time the person manipulating the object asks you to disbelieve that this is just an object. Something incredibly beautiful happens in this agreement to disbelieve. Something invisible becomes visible. The space becomes very alive, and the power struggle becomes the subject matter, I think.

They conjured up our feelings about independence and dependence, attachment and separateness. Issues such as control, power games, autonomy, life and death. These are the themes that puppet theatre creators return to again and again.[4]

GC – In one of your most recent pieces, *Mojo*, there is only one puppet, which is manipulated by a large group of puppeteers. Why did you make that choice?

SB – My work has always been very personally driven. Early on it was often about the relationship of the puppeteer or the mover of the object as being like a child playing with a toy. Or a mother playing with her child – because when children play with toys, it is often an imitation of how they experience their parents interacting and playing with them. I think *Mojo* is maybe the completion of this whole journey for me. The theme that I wanted to explore was how we handle an object if the object is a child. So the puppet in the piece is a child, from baby through to fourteen. I wanted to look at how a dancer, an actor, a puppeteer and a musician would manipulate this object.

When a child is very young, it is all about supporting them, handling them, helping them walk. There was a connection there to the musician playing the xylophone. We used the idea of attaching the sticks which the musician played a xylophone on to the feet of the child puppet. Their first tentative steps were played out musically and physically. This and other artistic abstractions when playing with an object became metaphors for various stages in child development.

It has always been popular to give puppets the power to be subversive, to act out what we normally feel should be repressed behavior. ... Perhaps their most absolute subversive act is, in fact, the puppet's ability to make us confront our own acknowledgment of death.[5]

GC – You mentioned earlier that the object is always innocent. But often puppets are used to allow things to happen to them that we would never do with a real body. There is a subversive element about puppetry, whether it is *Spitting Image* or *Punch and Judy*. How relevant is that to your own work?

SB – Very important. The fact that the object can hold, or declare, something about the people near it is what interests me. We are asking of the audience to project parts of themselves, which are then reflected back by the puppet.

In psychoanalytic theory and the texts of Melanie Klein there is this idea that when we are very young, as babies, we don't understand that we are all separate. The baby in the womb is one with the mother and when it comes out, it understands all objects as being the same as it. A lot of beautiful things have been written by psychoanalysts about the moment of separation, when the baby recognises the object as outside of itself.

From that moment of separation onwards, we have to find different ways of internalising the object, and one of them is to project outwards. As we grow up, we separate things out and we put many of our repressed feelings onto external things – buying the flash car to make ourselves feel better about getting old, for example. We place different parts of ourselves into different objects, and puppetry exploits that. An object can become a repressed feeling. Puppets are wonderfully safe to do that with because they always repair themselves. Particularly because I do a lot of family work, it is always necessary to show the reparation.

The relationship with the puppet can also be very humble. I often think that the puppet comes off looking better – it knows it is dependent and reliant on this other force, and it succumbs to that, beautifully and honestly, whereas the puppeteer can actually come across as quite controlling and mean. In a way, the human looks less human, and the puppet more so.

GC – An example for this that I can think of is in *zero degrees* by Akram Khan and Sidi Larbi Cherkaoui: towards the end of the piece the story becomes about a dead body, who is treated badly. The only way we could present this happening on stage was for Larbi to kick the dummy that Antony Gormley had made using Akram's real body as a model, and Akram acting out the impact which the dummy received. The funny thing was that for an adult audience it was still a shocking scene, but children were always hysterically laughing – they responded to a kind of subversive humour in it. Your own work also contains subversive humour and images, and maybe we can look at some of them.

SB – This image for example is from the piece *The Thought That Counts*, where we manipulated variously sized, physical thought bubbles, so that if you were holding the bubble, it was your thought. One of its themes was how to tackle bullying, for under-six. The thoughts in the bubbles were quite strong, sometimes even brutal, but the object was able to abstract the bullying. Although the characters were thinking about what they could do to the girl they didn't like, it was in their imagination and they were not actually doing it. Children do actually have these feelings, so it was important for us to explore what to do about feelings of wanting to throw someone around who is irritating you in the playground.

In the puppet, a hand transmutes itself ... into a body.[6]

GC – In the tradition of puppeteering the hands of the puppeteer are often seen as the essence of the art form. You have told me that for you the starting point is never the hand, but always the object.

SB – I think it goes back to when I first started directing. I was given an actor and I just didn't know what to do with him. I had no idea. And then someone went off to get lunch and came back holding an orange. Suddenly I was watching the way the person was handling the orange, and I knew.

The object was telling me something about the actor. Out of that developed my method of working – not with a script or an idea. My method is to give a person an object. The process now is about the choice of object, and the choice of person.

GC – Do you also follow this process when you are working in dance, or with dancers?

SB – When we started working on *Mischief*, which is a dance piece, we wanted to find an object that would really respond to dancers' hands. Sophia Clist,[7] who I was working with at the time, said, 'I want to work with lines', so I thought about how to create an *object* of a line, rather than a flat marking, and we came up with these lines of foam.

Then we introduced a number of dancers to it, and I worked with the choreographer Arthur Pita to create the piece. Different people moved the line so differently. Maho (Ihara) was so centred and graceful in her movement that she was the only one I could give the biggest, longest line to. Performing with such centeredness with such a huge thing (which for many weeks did look clumsy in her hands, but I knew she would get there), she could show how to take charge of an object without grabbing it. It is not about grabbing and moving and manipulating, it is an art of listening to the object. She was able to listen to the very long, heavy line.

James Painting,[8] the hip hop artist, would bend the foam and then respond by bending his body, which again would make the foam bend. It was a wonderful understanding of muscular structure. There was a real relationship that each of them had with the same object. We then started to make very subtle changes to the objects, where Sophia would put some wire up the middle of one of the foam lines to give it a little more resistance, or, for somebody else who was very fast and who was moving it around very quickly, we made sure it was the softest, bendiest piece of foam. The lines danced.

GC – Was it your first collaboration with a choreographer?

SB – I had worked with Anna Williams before, a little bit on the thought bubbles, but with *Mischief* the choreographer was involved from the very beginning.

GC – What were the things you discovered in this collaboration with Arthur Pita?

SB – We had to learn how to count, that was one of the most difficult things. Puppeteers do not count, they respond to impulse. We train – if we are lucky enough to get any training – to study movement through watching it. So one of the exercises I had to do in training was to lift a cloth, and drop it, and watch its movements. To see every tiny movement it makes, and then to try and recreate that movement. Which of course is impossible. You learn that an object always moves differently. You train your eye to see it so that if you are operating an object, or if many of you are operating an object, you are always looking for that same little movement of the cloth, which is the impulse for the next movement.

In this project, we puppeteers learned to count, and the dancers learned to look for the impulse in the object: Regardless of the counts, if your object is behaving differently, you have to go with that. The object is innocent.

The life of the puppets does not just survive destruction; it feeds on it. ... The puppet belongs to a family of things partial, fragmented, and broken, a family of relics, remnants, and skeletons, a world of small pieces gathered to make up an image of a larger world, parts enacting the whole, transforming our sense of the whole. The poetry of the puppets is the poetry of inadequacy.[9]

GC – (*He shows a clip of the song* I don't want to get serious[10] *from the piece.*)

To change the topic a little, and as you said that it was OK to go there. Disability, or personal physical issues, have informed you as an artist and influenced the way you approach objects. You said that your relationship with objects has become more intense because of it.

SB – Yes. At the age of thirty I lost the use of my body and I was in and out of a wheelchair for almost ten years. Most of my early work was created from a place of immobility, and it made me want to project all my energy outwards, through an object or a person. I felt that if we got it right, I would have some reparation. Objects began to work for me. I wanted to find objects that could be liberated. I then wanted to find other objects that would kill them off, annihilate them, and for them to be re-born and become robust again. But it was from a point of stillness that I learnt how to direct movement. By the time I got to do *Mischief*, my own body had come back to me, and that gift – when you lose something and then you are given it back – is very profound.

On stage, I like seeing something come to life, be killed, come back to life. With this work particularly

I wanted the puppetry to be very momentary, so that you wouldn't get too attached to any one figure. We really had to work on the constant transformation of the object, so that the abstraction in the object remained more important than its psyche: one object becomes another object, which maybe needs to disappear or die to allow room for the next object, or it changes or transforms within itself. Death becomes the obsession of the puppet artist. If you imbue something with life, it means you can remove its life.

This link with the dead, with the realm of the uncanny, the threshold realm of things unknown or repressed yet half-revealed, can be felt in the most secular of puppets, in the impression of their dead life, the sense of will and power in them despite their being objects to be manipulated by others.[11]

GC – I like how you express this as an optimistic thing: Death is there to allow the resurrection.

SB – I think for me *Millworks* is maybe the best example of this. I was asked by the Greenwich and Docklands Festival to make a piece in response to a mill – the Three Mills Island in Bow, East London – and it really allowed me to explore the cycle of life and death through the symbolism of the milling process. We started with the wheat, and I made a wheat figure, who was then sacrificed to make grain. The grain went into some sacks and I made sack men, who were competitive and hungry for grain; quite *Punch-and-Judy*-esque anarchic hungry sacks. They were then crushed to make flour, which was given to the children to make dough. We put the dough in the oven and made bread, and out of the bread we made the bread man, who had a likeness to the original wheat figure. And then the millers came and ate it.

I really enjoyed that at the end there was just a little bit of flour left, a very ethereal image. And I enjoyed making a puppet out of bread; it had to be made especially for each show.

GC – *Millworks* is also a good introduction to the other strand of your work: the site-specific, where space itself becomes an object to work with. Has this been important for you right from the beginning?

SB – In the beginning I didn't have much space to work in, so I concentrated more on materials. What happens if this kind of material meets that kind of material? Working with visual artists led me to installation work, which is all about listening to the space.

Hospitalworks, for example, was about the spaces, materials and objects you can find in a hospital. We had been given an empty ward in the Mayday University Hospital in London, and for a long time we struggled creatively with the fact that there were no patients there. We thought about getting large numbers of actors to play patients, or using the audience, until we realised that the problem was the answer: There are no patients. The objects themselves became the patients. We had a breathing bed that you had to listen to with the stethoscope, and as the children listened, it actually did breathe, which was lovely. In one performance it went wrong and it died, and we had to repair the audience! We resuscitated the bed, and in the next version of the show we actually put the death and resuscitation in because it had become a very dramatic and profound moment in this experience.

One room had cracks, which Sophia (Clist), the installation artist, had put in the walls, and the children had to literally put plasters over the cracks. Another was in UV light, so you saw the X-ray version of the room. We looked at the space as if it was the patient.

Space is a beautiful object to be given. And I suppose now, where I have been given many things to animate, with many different people, I have got to the point where I want to animate the impossible: a brick wall, a door, light, a cloud.

Paradise, our most recent site-specific production, had a nice big budget, which allowed me to explore some of these big concepts. Which in a way you can do in a poor theatre as well – the big concepts are the small concepts, too.

GC – This was produced for the Ruhrtriennale 2010, and

you worked with another choreographer, Luca Silvestrini. Was it different to working with Arthur?

SB – It was different in that it wasn't a dance commission, but a collaboration between a visual artist, a choreographer, a composer and myself, in response to a building in the Zollverein complex in Essen. Its theme was religion, and pilgrim's travels. Because I had enjoyed working with Arthur and was beginning to enjoy the idea of the body in space, I wanted to work with another choreographer. I chose Luca because I thought he could respond to the sometimes harsh reality of this concrete, industrial building. I needed someone who wasn't precious, with dancers who weren't precious – they ended up climbing, on aerials, throwing themselves against concrete walls and doors. It was hard work.

The piece was a journey through a number of rooms, and it was a matter of which artist spoke to a specific room in the wisest way. Luca would try moving in that room, I would try an object in there, and Jeremy (Herbert)[12] would try an installation. And I think we all found our strength in different rooms. For example Luca really came into his own on the steps, whereas steps to me were scary. In another room he preferred choreography and I a puppet which I had placed there, but it all got cut because actually just falling gravel in front of a huge projection, provided by Jeremy, was enough. Then we had a room of cloud which was beautiful, and we had all planned something for it but cut it all, because the cloud was powerful enough on its own.

GC – We have a fragment of *Paradise* to show. (*He shows a short video clip of the piece.*[13])

You haven't presented site-specific work here in the UK for a number of years, but are now planning a new project for 2013. Can you tell us a little bit about that?

SB – Yes, *Hospitalworks* was the last work we did here, in 2005. All the others have been in Europe, because budgets are a bit friendlier there. But we are going to do one on a smaller budget in this country. The kind of building I wanted to work in this time was a bureaucratic building – a bank – to make a piece about economics. It will be called *Bank On It*, allowing children to play in a world of economics to see what they can make of it, given that we just can't. For me it is a little bit like when you go to a funeral and there are children there – they help remind you of another way of thinking about it.

I am interested to see what it will be like to do a piece for children and adults to experience together which is about such a hot adult topic. The children will just play with whatever metaphors I come up with for economics, and the adults will hopefully be more politically aware of the subject and the difficulties surrounding it. They will be observing the children play and having their own process. I think it is a very rich time to ask adults and children to share an arena like that.

In terms of objects I am looking at the big object of the bank and the small detail of the coin as my starting points.

GC – You are also working with rubbish. But that is for another piece.

SB – Yes, our next performance piece is in response to 'value'. None of us have liked how art is now being valued, or not valued, or being asked to value itself, so I think many artists are looking at rubbish, and things that feel full of poverty but in fact are full of resourcefulness. For the piece *Rubbish* we are animating a pile of bin bags to explore how to re-see promise in things that don't on the surface look so promising – and also how a surface can look promising but may not in fact deliver. So yes, it feels important right now to make a work about rubbish, and one about economics. It responds to a certain current climate.

Whereas when we created *Mischief* there was maybe more risk-taking involved in terms of big venues putting on non-narrative work for families and building up an audience, right now venues have to be more cautious. It requires a different kind of work.

I feel lucky enough that I have gone through many trends – puppetry has been in, and out of fashion, and money has been on different levels of availability – and the work always reflects that. It reflects what is relevant to us as a society, but also to me personally: being a mother, an artist, a disabled artist, my history, the history of the company. We haven't touched on this, but Theatre-Rites was set up by myself and Penny Bernand,[14] who then died of cancer, so for me it is very important and very meaningful that Theatre-Rites has survived, and has become a legacy for another artist.

We always hope that out of all these personal and cultural and political influences we can make something universal that goes beyond all of it. A residue that just means something, regardless.

GC – I think that is a really nice note to end on.

Notes

1 Kenneth Gross, *Puppet: An Essay on Uncanny Life* (Chicago: University of Chicago Press, 2011), p. 107.
2 In the UK, an Equity Card is proof of membership of the British actors guild also called Equity.
3 Sue Buckmaster, *A Psychoanalytical Study of the Power of the Puppet*, unpublished MA Thesis (Colchester: University of Essex, 1997), p. 4.
4 Ibid., p. 12.
5 Ibid., p. 27.
6 Gross, *Puppet*, p. 52.
7 Sophia Clist is a sculptor who works primarily in the context of performing arts and public installation, and whose work is based around audience interaction. She was Associate Artist at Theatre-Rites from 1998-2008.
8 James Painting died in 2014 at the too young age of 32.
9 Gross, *Puppet*, p. 95.
10 *Mischief song*, composed by Charlie Winston.
11 Gross, *Puppet*, p. 23.
12 Jeremy Herbert is an installation designer and multimedia artist who specialises in theatre work.
13 Clips of many of these shows are available on the Theatre-Rites website: www.theatre-rites.co.uk or on their YouTube Channel.
14 Penny Bernand (1946-2001): Co-founder of Theatre-Rites, she was a theatre-maker who revolutionised children's theatre, harnessing the power of ritual and taking performance out of the theatre and into found spaces.

The Rhythmic Body
A Conversation with Hofesh Shechter

Music is the reason I do dance. That's it. I love the feeling when music is played in a theatre. It just gives me a thrill ... It can create an atmosphere, it can create rules, it can create thoughts, it can take you somewhere in a split second.[1]

Guy Cools – I remember very well the moment that we first met, which was in 2004, in London. I sat on the selection committee of The Place Prize for dance and you had to pitch your piece, which was to become *Cult*. My memory is that you managed to pitch the whole piece by only talking about the music score, and saying nothing at all about the choreography.

You are unique in that you combine the creative roles and talents of composer and choreographer, so today I would like to talk about music, with a specific focus on rhythm and its importance in your work.

The other thing we always do in these talks is to use some background reading to frame the topic. One of the books I will quote from is *Art as Experience*[2] by the American pragmatist philosopher John Dewey, in which he talks about the essential role of rhythm in art, and the second one is an amazing book called *The Conversations*.[3] It is a conversation between Michael Ondaatje, the Canadian writer and novelist who wrote *The English Patient*, and Walter Murch, who is the film and sound editor on many major films, including the Coppola films *The Godfather* and *Apocalypse Now*.

Murch discusses two approaches for how the creative mind works. He says that there is the 'Hitchcock approach', which is about always being very much in control and devising everything in advance, and then there is the 'Coppola approach', which is more about trial and error and letting chance happen within the process. Where would you situate yourself on this scale?

Hofesh Shechter – I think I am a sort of 'Hitchcoppola'. When I start to work on a piece I am a very Hitchcock-like. When I create, or before I create, I worry a lot about the void and the emptiness – the feeling of walking into a studio with dancers and not having anything solid to go on. Dance is like that anyway: even when you have built something solid, it doesn't survive the test of time; it's there and it's gone. Because it is so difficult to grasp, I have this panic of trying to be prepared. When I'm coming into the studio I try to prepare myself as much as possible with imagery, ideas, the atmosphere that I hope the work will have.

You brought up the example of The Place Prize 2004. I didn't really have a choice; I had to present the pitch for a piece without having a piece. You guys imagined it in your heads when I described it – it wasn't real. The music defined the atmosphere and the 'world' that the piece was going to have.

But you can plan all you want, when you go into the studio is when things start to go wrong. You discover that many of your ideas don't work, so all the preparation is only ever an inspiration that starts a chain of events. Which, if you are a believer, you think is fine. And if you are not a believer, you have to practice until you believe that it is fine. Because otherwise you lose hope and then it really goes wrong.

What I am trying to say is that there is a sense of planning and a sense of connecting to something that is real, and something that is premeditated, and then there is the trust that once you are in the studio and things start to go out of control, that is what is supposed to happen. It is a situation where you lose control and try and re-gain control, and lose control and re-gain it. So, Hitchcoppola.

GC – Is it also a question of scale? The larger the group of people you collaborate with, the more you have to let go and let things happen in the moment of interaction?

HS – You can argue that the more people you have in the room, the more control you need to have. I actually feel that I am more able to let go and share responsibility of creation with fewer dancers in the room. If I work one on one, I feel that I can give more responsibility to the dancer because we are in constant conversation; there is a chemistry and the connection is very immediate – I have my hand on the pulse and I know where it is going. If you have sixteen dancers in the room, unless you are looking for some sort of chaos, you have to have a more constructed idea.

But it is something I play with – obviously I have control issues (laughs) and find it more difficult to let go if I have sixteen people in the room because it really could go anywhere. I suspect it has something to do with generosity: on the one hand, when you come to the studio with a lot of information it is very generous, and on the other hand, if you try to stick to that information and to that energy and not let anything else happen, it's not so generous because other people don't find themselves or their place in it. I am working on generosity now and we will see how that goes.

The ear and the eye complement one another. The eye gives the scene in which things go on and on which changes are projected – leaving it still a scene even amid tumult and turmoil. The ear, taking for granted the background furnished by cooperative action of vision and touch, brings home to us changes as changes. For sounds are always effects; effects of the clash, the impact and resistance, of the forces of nature.[4]

GC – You have a double role of composing both the music and the choreography. How do these parallel tracks develop?

HS – It is a messy business, not linear in any way. It never actually happens that I make the score and then just do the choreography to it. There are little explosions of creating music, little explosions of choreography – the two inspire one another.

In the preparation period, I will have an energy or an idea in my head and I will try to make music to serve that idea or to portray this energy. But often I start making sounds and it turns out very differently, so again it is about letting things happen and be awake when something amazing happens, even if it is not exactly what you hoped for.

Often when I work on some music I will then have an image of movement and start dancing in my room and – this is where the iPhone comes in handy – record myself. It turns into an eclectic, messy collection of information and I try to preserve this chaos for as long as possible. The more information I collect, the richer the piece can be and the more of a journey I, the dancers and the audience will have.

Then comes the other element, which is the panic of the deadline and what I call the 'point of no return'. If at a certain point you don't start making decisions, the piece is not going to be ready. Simple. You never really know when it will be, but again it is a matter of trust and I kind of trust myself there. There is always a morning in creation when I wake up and say, that's it, we have to start to put it in order, to use this eclectic information and make something coherent out of it, or not coherent – whatever the structure is – but we have to start to form something that has a rhythm to it.

GC – What kind of information do you feed your dancers in these early days of generating material?

HS – In the very early days as little as possible. I try to stay very secretive, or at least to appear so, mainly because I don't know exactly what I am doing. I will have a sense of what is happening, but if someone asked me to talk about a piece before I did it – it is like me talking about my daughter before I get to know her, before her growing up. Once a piece is done you can talk about it forever, it is right there. When I go into the studio with the dancers it is a matter of chemistry, of energy. I have a feeling for a piece, and I create movement from that place. I try not to analyse it too much, and therefore not to speak about it too much. There is always information, but it might not necessarily be information that you can talk about.

Sometimes I ask the dancers to improvise in the atmosphere of whatever we are working on, and there always arrives a point when they go, 'Sorry, we don't know what's going on.' That is also a very important moment, because this is where I actually have to start to define in words – which are a more focused form of energy – what we are doing.

GC – You mentioned earlier that you do visualise ideas for yourself. Would you also pass these images on to the dancers? Can you give an example?

HS – When we worked on the very early stages of *Political Mother*, we had a month of research in Brighton. I knew that I wanted to do something about performers – people who exist solely to satisfy an audience. There was something about this idea of servitude that intrigued me. We were working with two words, one was 'tap dancing', and the other was 'gypsies' or 'travellers'. We were trying to capture that sadness of the performer, trying to make an audience laugh, trying to lift spirits and get everybody on their feet and happy.

We make so much movement material that doesn't make it into the piece, but every experiment teaches you something. I pick up the things that I feel are maybe more mysterious and weird.

GC – We have a fragment of this section of the piece, shall we have a look? (*He shows a video clip of* Political Mother.)

HS – I may have ruined it for you now. You talk about what something means, and it kind of doesn't mean anything anymore. Explaining too much takes away your ability to think what you want, the audience's ability to imagine, to fly.

Cooks are always trying to find unusual substances that, if you put them together, seem to excite the taste buds in new ways, because of the talent of that one contradictory taste to precipitate the elements of another ... It happens in the chemistry between sound and picture as well. A certain sound colour will make you see colours in the picture in much more vibrant ways.[5]

GC – But then again – if you go to a good restaurant, it is of course about the experience of the food, but sometimes you also want to know how the chef made it. This talk, for instance, gives the audience a different experience to just watching the show; it is about providing an insight into your process.

Can you comment a little bit on what we just saw: how you brought together the aural and the visual? Is it typical for your work or does it deviate from your usual process?

HS – Oh yes, it is absolutely typical, typically Shechteresque. I love fast editing. The parts themselves carry emotions, but for me the cuts are more interesting. A cut or stop is almost like catching someone in the middle of a photo, or a sentence, and telling them, 'That word, that you said just now – keep it', so people are left with an emotion that is hanging there, and then you smash another emotion into it, which can flip it around or develop it further. I love playing with timing and emotion in that way.

In dance it is often very difficult because dance is so much in the here and now. Everything happens in one space and time, like in very old-fashioned films where the hero walks along, gets into a car, drives, gets on the plane, sits on the plane. In films today he leaves his house and next thing he is in New York. You pump in more emotions by editing like that. I find it exciting.

GC – Film is a source of inspiration for you. Can you give some examples?

HS – I didn't see any dance when I was a kid. When I was seven or eight years old, if a ballet was shown on TV, I would have certainly tried to find another channel. I grew up on TV and film and they still excite me. Films are like dreams for me; amazing things where the visual and the aural come together in an engulfing way.

When I did get into dance the attraction was different, it was much more connected to my limitations – I was very shy and I felt that it was a huge challenge to feel comfortable with myself and in my body. And I think it was a social thing as well, being with other people.

I did discover eventually that dance is a very unique art form with a mysterious power. But it is very important for me to feel that I am interested in it – when I make a dance piece, the best test is when I imagine myself sitting in the audience. Do I want to sit there and go through it, or is it simply a nightmare? The answer could be, 'It is a nightmare, but I want to feel that nightmare', or it could be, 'I'm just not interested.' I think this is somehow connected to my love of film.

Film also influences how I connect the music and the visual – in *Political Mother* it is certainly the music that carries the story. Stanley Kubrick is a big influence.

Seeing his films shocked me because he doesn't really care about right or wrong, good or bad. Only interesting. I remember seeing the beginning of *2001: A Space Odyssey* – I had heard a lot about the film but didn't see it until I was in my twenties – and I remember it starting with this nothing on screen, only very old-fashioned, operatic music and I thought, 'the title sequence is about to come', but it didn't. Then you realise that you are just staring into empty space with this music building an atmosphere for you for two minutes. I rewound and measured it, 'Really, two minutes of black out at the beginning of a film?' It is genius. It is like wine tasting: you eat a cracker before the next wine, so your palate is clean. And he clears our mind and re-sets the atmosphere, and here we go.

Rhythm and its entrainment of movement (and often emotion), its power to 'move' people, in both senses of the word, may well have had a crucial cultural and economic function in human evolution, bringing people together, producing a sense of collectivity and community.[6]

GC – You just mentioned that one of your original reasons to go into dance was also this sense of community. It seems that rhythm, also in the folk dance tradition, is such an element that brings people together. You also refer to that in *Political Mother.*

HS – Yes, I do make a comment on folk dance in *Political Mother.* It is certainly something that I learned a lot from. Folk dancing was how I got into dance and there was an element of the tribal thing that you speak about. Being quite a lost particle until the age of eleven, it gave me a sense of belonging for the first time in my life. I suddenly belonged to this very awkward group of people who were part of a youth dance company and it gave me a lot, but with time I also got a bit judgmental about the institution of folk dance. It is a very nationalistic tool. Nobody really wants you to be happy – or they want you to be happy, but for a purpose. It is like the American songwriters who composed folk songs during the war to make people want to sign up. The songs are beautiful, but they had a purpose. With *Political Mother,*

I wanted to show this aspect of folk dance as well.

In a sense, I now have a company that is my tribe. I love it and it feels like we are re-creating a society in the way we want it to be. Something about dance, too – the fact that it is so obviously multicultural and multinational. It breaks barriers. At some point tribalism has become contaminated. And we are trying to revive it through dance.

GC – You already mentioned earlier that you are a ruthless cutter and editor. I remember hearing you say that you use less than twenty percent of the material.

HS – Yes, for sure.

GC – How does it feel to let go of all that material?

HS – Good! It feels good. It is like going to the toilet when you really, really need to.

You have to get rid of what is not useful, because if it is not useful, it is poisonous. With *Political Mother* I was struggling with one bit for a long time and one day – it was a week before the show – I came to the studio and realised that it just didn't work in the piece. It was a great section in itself, but it had no place in the piece. I said, 'Sorry guys, it's going.' We all got a bit depressed because we had worked hard on it and everybody gave their hearts to it, but it did feel good to let it go. That is the test of a good cut – if you feel a sense of relief.

It is like a break-up, maybe. You ask questions until you do it, and when you do it, you either feel great, confused but great, or you feel like something really bad just happened. The same thing happens when you throw out movement material. I think it is healthy.

GC – Which again resembles the attitude of a film-maker. Walter Murch mentions in the book that in film often only one fiftieth of the material gets used – in extreme cases, like *Apocalypse Now*, only one percent.

In film, the 'director's cut' has become popular, as it gives the director the chance to restore material that was cut under pressure from the producers or the studios.

You have also made a couple of pieces where there is an original version and then a 'choreographer's cut', although for different reasons.

HS – Yes, people ask me, 'Why, did producers tell you what to do in the first version?' No, they didn't. They just came with more money for the second version. And they said, 'Listen, we want to do something exciting and fun.' It is not that much more money, it sounds better than it is and of course everybody ends up losing money in the end, which is the beauty of art. Sorry – spending money, not losing money.

The first time that Sadler's Wells came with that kind of statement, I said, 'Great – let's do a version with an orchestra!' And it worked out.

GC – Is it just a matter of scale?

HS – In these cases it was a matter of scale. You can imagine how difficult it is to stage a show like that – you need a special occasion as it is untourable, but as a special event it is great. It is about enjoying and exaggerating everything, the size of the orchestra and the size of the cast. I wouldn't do it with pieces that don't lend themselves to it, but *Political Mother* for example explicitly deals with mass, and to have a real mass on stage makes it doubly powerful and overwhelming.

GC – You said to me beforehand that you like to re-mount your work because there is less anxiety about the unknown. Is it also about that?

HS – When staging work with other companies, creating a work from scratch is very difficult because of the time it takes me to get to know them, plus the usual anxiety of creating something out of nothing. I don't know who said it but it is so true: 'Each time I make a piece, something dies inside me.' I am one step closer to death. And doing it with a company you don't know takes you two steps closer. Something is probably wrong with me because it is supposed to revitalise you, which it sometimes does afterwards. But it is so painful.

So I now think that it is better to re-work existing works for other companies. The piece is there and you can sound like a wise man when you talk about it rather than being a fool who is searching for his arms and legs. It is also better for the dancers because they can take it further. With new work, they often don't go far.

GC – The choreographer's cut also allowed for a different relationship with the audience, because you had the audience standing, like at a rock concert.

HS – We had been touring for two or three years when we did the first choreographer's cut, and so many people came to me and said, 'I wish I wasn't constrained to a chair – I want to stand, I want to rock out, I want to move.' So part of it was finding a different kind of venue. One of the first ones we looked at was the Roundhouse[7] and standing up really made sense in that space. It gave so much freedom to the audience and it made them much more shouty and loud. People feel freer to express themselves and to feel the show through their body.

It was great to see people experiencing dance, not analysing dance. It kicked people out of the mindset of 'Let's try to understand what that piece is about.' I am probably guilty of it, too, but a lot of people see a dance show and just before it finishes, or as it finishes, they try to find that one sentence for the discussion afterwards in the bar, where you define what you have just seen. In one sentence! I wish people would see dance like they go to see music concerts. Concerts do have a visual element, but nobody comes out and tries to say, it was about this or that. It is an emotional experience. If you have thoughts then let them be, they will pass, don't worry.

GC – Shall we look at another fragment? We haven't defined what it is about, so we will just let everyone enjoy. (*He shows a clip of* Political Mother.)

Not to explain this fragment – but you chose it because there is a very particular relationship between the music and the choreography here; you said it has 'different rhythms'. Can you explain that?

HS – When we worked on this part in the studio we tried many different things. In the end, and to the dislike of the dancers, I fell in love with the idea that the music is completely separate from the choreography – the music is very sweet and almost Hollywood-ish filmic, and the dance is very rhythmical, busy and complex. It gives you a sense of distance.

I enjoyed playing with the idea that you have a bird's-eye view of these puppet-like miserable characters, and when the music disappears you suddenly feel like your head is being pushed into the water. You're back in it. The music makes it sweet-sad, and when you're in it, it is hard-sad.

It was emotionally more effective for the music *not* to describe the situation. And choreographically, the monotone of the music meant that the colours, rhythms and textures of the dance were more watchable and more engaging.

GC – *In your rooms*, which was the piece that introduced you to a larger audience, you were allowed to re-work it three times on three different scales. It started at The Place, then moved to the Southbank Centre and eventually you made a third version for here, at Sadler's Wells. Why was that process so important?

HS – It was an amazing opportunity to be able to re-work the piece, especially as it was my first long work. The process is always messy, but at least when you are making a short piece you can make a bite of music and bring it into the studio and here you go – a third of the piece is done. When you come to a bigger piece, suddenly you are swimming in a much larger ocean and every change in the current moment changes everything else – everything is moving underneath your feet all the time.

So the challenge of connecting the music and choreography was very difficult and I felt that I was giving myself the chance for it not to be perfect the first time, because I knew I would have more goes. Each time I came back to the studio I felt smarter. I had had the chance to see it on stage and to get a sense of the problems in the rhythm, what was missing, where it was too much or too long. Each time I felt like I was able to make the right decisions more quickly. It was an invaluable opportunity and I think that choreographers are not often enough given the chance to re-work. It is expensive.

GC – Is it re-working, or is it about having pauses in the creation process that help you to get some distance and then go back into it?

HS – I think it is both. When I work with my producer on the schedules for creating a new work, we always include breaks in the middle of touring. We tour old work in the middle of creating new work. It just means that I am not constantly dealing with it, because at a certain point you start going in a loop, and things have to settle.

I am a big believer in pauses, also as a dancer. When I was at school, every time I had two weeks or a month off, I came back and felt like a better dancer. And I always got feedback from people, like, 'Wow, did you do a summer course or something?' Progress can happen just by letting go.

In rhythmic ordering, every close and pause, like the rest in music, connects as well as delimits and individualizes.[8]

GC – It is probably also a rhythmical thing. One of the people who had a huge influence on the development of dance in Belgium was the percussionist and rhythm teacher Fernand Schirren, who worked with Maurice Béjart and taught at PARTS. Anne Teresa De Keersmaeker often refers to his teaching. His theory was that consciousness happens in the non-beats.

As a dancer you decided to study percussion. Why was that, and how has it influenced your work?

HS – Well, I went into folk dancing, I started to get to know people from the academy, went into the academy, went into the junior company of Batsheva, went into Batsheva, and then there was a moment when I asked myself, did I choose this? Did I actually choose to be a dancer? I don't know what I am. Maybe I am a musician after all.

I felt a little bit like I had been injected into the world of dance and in the process music had died inside me, even though there was a great love there. So I decided to study percussion and to see what would happen. There were a few years when I was searching and hadn't found the answer yet. I went into percussion very obsessively, practicing non-stop for about three years.

Of course, being a professional dancer, when I needed cash again I had to dance. And then came a point when I felt that I really wanted to create my own stuff, and a big part of the attraction of that was that I would create the music as well. I was much more thrilled about the idea of people sitting in a theatre listening to my music than about them watching the dance.

I saved for a long time to buy a computer so that I could record and edit multi-track. Everybody told me, 'It is not the computer that will make you start creating – just start', but I said, 'No no no, I need the computer.' And you know what? I needed the computer. Once I had bought it I could do it. Of course it was in my head, but I did need this device to be able to start creating.

Knowing percussion really felt like going back to not just the basics of music, but the basics of time, and the basics of art. You go through weird things when you practice rhythms. For example, you start to work on a very complicated pattern and after about five or ten minutes... Some of you must know the feeling, like when you play the piano and you come back to an old piece which your fingers remember but your brain doesn't. So when you practice complicated rhythms you suddenly start to think about other things, and you realise, 'Oh my god, if I am not flying this plane, who is?' You start to understand that rhythm is absolutely connected to your body. It helped me with my dance work, too.

GC – You recently worked on a piece with Antony Gormley, where he was in charge of the space and you felt that you could add a time element to it.

HS – Yes, we collaborated on *Survivor*, at the Barbican. We were dreaming together – what a privilege. At a certain point I realised that Antony doesn't really have a sense of time or timing. It doesn't function like that for him; there is just an incredible sense of space and it doesn't matter if it exists for a second or ten years.

I wondered if it was my responsibility then to be the time master or the storyteller. But I decided not to push it and just to go with how it was; to allow it to be quite loose and experimental. I knew that I could force the piece, but then I don't need Antony to do my own thing. I discovered completely new things. Depending on the day, I felt in awe and in love with it, or hated it. It was more than anything a work to be watched in a state of nothingness; a state of experiencing and not trying to figure out anything. Much more difficult than dance, even, because it was undefined.

GC – Richard Shusterman[9] is one of the major contemporary American philosophers who is really working to put the body back into philosophy. He believes that if knowledge is your goal, the first stage you have to go through is self-exposure. You have to put yourself into unknown, uncomfortable situations. Is that something you recognise?

HS – When I make work, I almost always have regular nightmares that take place in different places and different situations but the idea is always the same (this might be disturbing for you, I am sorry): I am naked and running through the streets, trying to find a place to hide. Even worse, I am trying to find a toilet. And when I find it, it is always in a public place, with people watching. The most intimate, and in our culture the most embarrassing, situation you can be caught in.

When I wake up I know that it is about that feeling you have when you really throw yourself out there. It is a very fragile place and I try to encourage myself not to be afraid and not to worry about it, because nobody can hurt me. It is a psychological place.

GC – We have a fragment of *In your rooms* to show. (*He shows a video clip of the show.*)

Both in the studio and to motivate dancers, you often work with vocalisations. Why is that?

HS – Not intentionally. I make sounds and noises when I make the movement material, and I think it gives a sense of the energy and the timing – it is very rhythmical, so we almost sing it. The dancers kind of learn it and start doing it this way themselves. If I ever did a dance piece without music you would hear them, they all sing.

GC – Would you be interested in using the voice more? *Political Mother* has an actor in it.

HS – If it worked, yes. But I am wary of using voice. At the moment I don't know how to make it belong to the piece, it has never felt necessary. There is a moment in *Political Mother, The Choreographer's Cut* where the dancers are singing – more like wolves. They all stand in a line. But nobody can hear them, because the music is so loud.

GC – You also mentioned that eventually there will be a desire to make a film.

HS – A great desire, I am very attracted to this art form. I don't know exactly how making films works, and really I am so busy at the moment that I can't go there. But there are talks with various partners who are interested. I guess you either just clear half a year in your diary, or you don't. And I haven't yet. But I will, and now that I have said it in front of an audience, it will be so embarrassing if it doesn't happen.

GC – But for the moment there is another rhythm that is taking over.

HS – Yes! It kind of wakes up every two hours. What is wrong with her?!

I am very excited because my life had started to become kind of boring – or if not boring then quite repetitive in its chaotic nature. And probably quite self-obsessed. It is always about the work, and about me, so it is great to be kicked into a different situation. But don't ask me too much, at the moment I am just in love. I feel like

I am fifteen again, she is so... It breaks my heart. And I am curious how being in love affects you when you make new work.

Notes

1 Hofesh Shechter, *Political Mother: A Resource Pack for Teachers and Students* (London: Hofesh Shechter Company), p. 9.
2 John Dewey, *Art as Experience* (New York: Perigee Paperback, 2005 c1934).
3 Michael Ondaatje, *The Conversations: Walter Murch and the Art of Editing Film* (Toronto: Vintage Canada, 2002).
4 Dewey, *Art as Experience*, p. 245.
5 Walter Murch in Ondaatje, *Conversation*, pp. 246–47.
6 Oliver Sacks, *Musicophilia: Tales of Music and the Brain* (New York: Vintage Books, 2008), p. 268.
7 The Roundhouse in Camden is a former Victorian steam engine repair shed. Perfectly circular, it has been a cult performance and music venue since 1964, housing performances by Jimi Hendrix, Pink Floyd, Peter Brook, the Royal Shakespeare Company and many others.
8 Dewey, *Art as Experience*, p. 179.
9 Richard Shusterman is an American pragmatist philosopher who created the philosophical discipline of somaesthetics. His book *Body Consciousness: A Philosophy of Mindfulness and Somaesthetics* (New York: Cambridge University Press, 2008) aims to put experience and the body back into a central position within the philosophical discourse.

The Luminous Body
A Conversation with Russell Maliphant & Michael Hulls

For sound is not the object but the medium of our perception. It is what we hear in. Similarly, we do not see light but see *in* it.[1]

Guy Cools – Russell and Michael and I go back to 1997 or 1998, when you came to Ghent and presented *Shift* and some other early works.

Each time I choose a theme to frame the talk and as Russell and Michael's collaboration is so much about the relationship between body and light, this is the obvious theme that we will explore today.

You just had a premiere in Eastleigh, a new collaboration, and this is a result of almost twenty years of working together, maybe twenty productions also...

Michael Hulls – ... actually more than forty productions, I think, roughly.

GC – It is quite unique that two artists have such a long ongoing collaboration. Can you go back to the beginning, to how it all started?

MH – I didn't train to be a lighting designer. I trained in theatre and dance at Dartington College of Arts. The dance training was mostly contact improvisation, with Steve Paxton. It had always been my long-term goal to be a theatre designer and design sets and costumes, and I went a very long way round to get there. When I started doing it I decided that the thing I had always wanted to do wasn't the right thing, and I wasn't sure what to do. One day I bumped into the dancer, improviser, choreographer Laurie Booth, who'd also been at Dartington a little bit before me, so he had also been trained by Steve Paxton. Laurie knew that I'd had the same improvisational dance training as him and he knew that I was a sort of visually based life form, so he asked me if I would consider coming to work with him and make lighting for him. Which was something that I'd never thought about. So I said, 'Yes, let's give it a go', and I became a lighting designer by accident.

I started off by improvising lighting with Laurie Booth performing a solo. I enjoyed doing it, as it was aesthetically and visually interesting, and improvising was fun. Laurie then asked me to make a new piece with him, which was going to be not just a solo but involve a couple of other dancers, too. I went along to one of the first rehearsals for this piece, *Spatial Decay*, and there were three other dancers that Laurie was going to work with. One of them happened to be Russell. This was how we met, working on an improvisational piece by Laurie Booth.

GC – And Russell, what was your journey from the Royal Ballet to working with Laurie?

Russell Maliphant – Well, from the Royal Ballet I went to DV8 Physical Theatre, by way of a company called Dance Exchange. That was quite a big jump already. And then I saw Laurie perform a solo at the ICA, and I really loved what he was doing. I spoke to him after the show and he said that he was leading a workshop at Dartington and invited me to come and do some improvisation. I did, and he said, 'Why don't you join me for this project that I'm working on' – which was the one Michael was talking about. I'd never done improvisation really; we did some on the making of DV8's piece *Dead Dreams of Monochrome Men*, but I hadn't learned any improvisational techniques. On this project we did six weeks of tasks and learning about it, and then started performing. That's when Michael and I really had a chance to interact on stage through being in a place, bringing up lights, moving away.

GC – Already at that point, you told me, you started talking about wanting to collaborate on this thing about dance and light.

MH – Yes, over the next year or so we did. The piece was a quartet for the premiere, with Laurie, Russell, Gill Clarke and Scott Clark, and then Gill and Scott went back to Siobhan Davies Dance Company so it became a duet, which actually for me was more satisfying. Over the next eighteen months to two years we toured it – not intensively, maybe once a month. I was enjoying, as Russell said, meeting him on stage, with me improvising lighting and him improvising movement. One of the things that I was interested in was that Russell seemed very sensitive to the light on stage and would dance in a different way if he was in the centre of a light to how he would dance if he was on the very edge of a light.

Over time, touring and hanging around in airports and hotels and things like that, we started to talk and hatch the idea that what we both liked to do was to work together, with dance and light. We wanted to use improvisation as a tool to discover and create material, but then to put it into a structure and composition, so that the performances themselves wouldn't be improvised.

In terms of lighting for dance, I guess, it really started with Jean Rosenthal and her works with George Balanchine and Martha Graham that gave birth to lighting for dance in the era of Modernism. That was then developed and taken forward by Jennifer Tipton and that's the start of the recognition of lighting design in itself.[2]

GC – There were very few role models at that time for lighting designers working specifically in dance. One of them was Jennifer Tipton, with whom you worked later and also did workshops with.

MH – The year before I started to work with Laurie, he had been to the United States and worked on a project with Dana Reitz, with lighting by Jennifer Tipton. Laurie had started to talk to me about Jennifer and the way that she approached light. It seemed interesting to me and a kind of parallel to what I was trying to do with Laurie, and then with Laurie and Russell. Very kindly, Julia Carruthers, who then was Arts Officer at the Arts Council, asked me what I would like to do if she could get me a training bursary, because I'd had no training in lighting. So I said that I would like to go to New York and work with Jennifer Tipton. I knew that she was going to do a two-week workshop for choreographers and lighting designers the following year and thankfully the Arts Council gave me the money.

Jennifer and Dana were making a new piece and they were working on the piece themselves in the mornings, and I guess that they were funding the time to do that by running this workshop for eight choreographers and eight lighting designers in the afternoons. I actually spent my mornings working for Jennifer, rigging and focusing lights. They would then repeat the workshop in London the following year as part of the Dance Umbrella programme in 1993.

GC – And then you and Russell went into the studio to create your first solo collaboration, which I think was *Shift*?

RM – Actually, the way this first solo happened was that I'd suffered an injury and wasn't able to work for nine months or almost a year, and then when I was free, Michael wasn't available. So I made my first solo with someone else, Margie Medlin, a lighting designer from Australia who was working here. After a while she went back to Australia and as I was touring the piece, Michael came out on the road. We started to play with the piece and remake it along the way. It was a kind of workshop piece for us, trying things out this way and that way. Then we made *Shift*.

Limitations are good in lots of ways.[3]

GC – In that period when you started, you had to make work in really limited conditions – but somehow these limitations also stimulated creativity.

RM – Well, we were limited financially, that's for sure. But there was support. We were given some weeks at Middlesex University by Professor Christopher Bannerman to work in a room with light.

MH – Over the summer holidays.

RM – That was fantastic. I can't remember how many weeks we had there. It was a glass room that we had to black out every day, because the black would fall off the windows, but it worked and it gave us the opportunity to try things with a set rig. We would just sit with one particular lighting state and work with that all day, or try a run of movement in the light, or play with different levels of light and stop it at a certain level. Looking at things – you don't often have the opportunity to do this, because usually you have a piece and you need to get it lit and you only have a few hours to do it in.

MH – There were limitations in the space: not much equipment, no money, just Russell and myself. Later another dancer came in to work with us.

Just to go back, when Jennifer Tipton came to London the following year, Russell did her workshop, so we both had that experience of working with her.

RM – That was very interesting, as she was so fantastically experienced. She would invite all the choreographers to try a lighting state and then look at movement in it, and she would always get them to test which way was better. She didn't *tell* us, she said, 'I don't know – you look at it. Which state gives you more of the result that you want?' She wouldn't work with her past, but instead encourage us to see everything afresh, look at it in many different ways, and then make a decision.

GC – Shall we have a look at a fragment of this second work, *Shift*?

MH – Yes. The piece was co-commissioned by a dance festival in Nottingham, and it was going to happen in a gallery. So one of the things that we knew when we went into the studio to make something was that ultimately it would be performed in a white-walled gallery space. There were very limited possibilities for overhead lighting. I thought, well, ok, it's in a white space and we better have lights on the floor to give us a bit of flexibility.

RM – We had one week to make the work. That would scare me phenomenally now. At that time, because I was doing improvisation, I thought, great, we have a whole week to play around! We could go and do it in a day.

I had been in the studio thinking about ideas and when we got there Michael had a plan for what he wanted to try. You'll see on the video that there weren't a lot of movement possibilities in the final plan we settled on, so most of my ideas went out of the window.

(*Guy Cools shows a clip of* Shift.)

GC – You are dancing with your shadow. And as you said, the lights create a lot of limitations here.

RM – Yes. You have a light at the front of the stage, ten metres in front of the cyc,[4] and the closer you are to it the bigger your shadow is. The range is about a metre and a half across, so if you are right at the back you have almost this much space, but as you get closer to the light and are able to keep your shadow well placed in the frame, the space to move in gets smaller and smaller. The movement had to be very much in the body and not much through the space.

We also knew that we wanted to unveil this idea, so that there would be one shadow, two shadows, three shadows at different intersection points of the lights. Because of this idea, the piece kind of suggested itself quite quickly.

GC – It became extremely interactive right from the beginning, which was also your aim of working together. And it is interesting that in a lot of your lighting designs the light forms a grid on the floor. Did you always want to include this notion of the interaction between light and body, and light as a landscape?

MH – Both those things. Light is a landscape, but more importantly in collaborating with Russell, it is something that is indivisible from the movement and from the piece as a whole. If you take the lighting on its own it doesn't make sense, and if you take the dance there is no other way of lighting it – it has to be like this.

For two days we worked with taped out beams of light on the floor to establish the principle of dancing between various quite small intersections. Maybe half the size of this table top. As Russell said, the movement had to be in the body because the angles were so tight.

We wanted it to be indivisible, and the only way of doing that was to start with the lighting on day one of rehearsing.

GC – And you continue to do that to this day?

MH – Yes, though not always with lights. It is something that we would always like to be able to do, but sometimes it is not possible.

RM – We made a piece recently with BalletBoyz that was probably the shortest time that we have ever worked practically with lighting. I think we had a day or two days...

MH – ... twelve hours, just before the premiere.

RM – It was the least amount of time of any project we've undertaken, but Michael was in the studio a lot and we were discussing ideas and because we've worked together so much before, we knew when things were shaping up in a certain way and we could say, 'Let's do that, let's define it.'

MH – We do a lot with tape on the floor. We tape out compositions of spacing and this helps dancers to be in the right place spatially. It's a bit trickier when it's not a mark on the floor but a light. Some people are more skilled at finding the light than others.

The strange thing is that this is kind of the norm, not getting any lights on until a day or two before the premiere.

GC – You continued to make a whole series of solos and there is a second solo that we will show a fragment of. I think that this piece is especially interesting because the lighting is so dark. There is something about darkness that is as triggering as *Shift*, which was created for a white space. This almost feels like the opposite. Can you comment on that?

RM – It's always about what is highlighted, and what is taken away. Both are part of it.

We did a project recently, *The Rodin Project.* Rodin had a lot of sculptures present in his studio and home for inspiration, and he used to cover parts of them in which he was less interested in order to make the beautiful parts resonate even more. I think sometimes it's a bit like that with light. Working in the studio where light is all around, it is very different to looking at movement in a specific light.

In this next piece there is a lot of backlight, so what is highlighted are the arms, shoulders and head. If you make something that is very intricate for the feet, it doesn't work. Strangely, on the project that we just made now, I made five minutes of work that was great in the studio but when we looked at it in the light it was nothing.

You can't have lighting without darkness, and the quality of the darkness is really important.[5]

GC – Michael, what is your fascination as a lighting designer with darkness?

MH – Well, you can't have one without the other. We talk about having good lighting, but the other side of the coin is having good darkness. One of the important things for me is the ability to maintain a really high quality of blackness, which is sometimes really difficult to do.

It's exaggerated on film because the camera is not as sensitive to light as the human eye, and sometimes you have to make your lighting a little less bright than perhaps you'd ideally like, because that's the only way that people can preserve the quality of darkness in a space. You have to find the right balance.

With Russell's work, it seems to me that the movement is coming from inside the body rather than from having an idea of creating a pattern with dancers in space. There is an intensity to it. It needs a particular focus that will complement this experience, so it's very clear that you are tightly focused on something.

GC – Shall we have a look at the piece? (*He shows a clip of* One – Part Two.)

Darkness also completely influences your sensory awareness. Is that why you like to play with it?

MH – Yes, it would never be my intention to try and frustrate people, but obviously I like the work of Caravaggio,

I like sculpture, and for me being able to light something with one light source makes it sculptural because of the contrast between light and dark. Given that, given what I said earlier about the quality of darkness, working with a low level of light is sometimes a way of achieving both of those things. I also think that when you're not quite sure what you are seeing, there is an ambiguity that opens up your mind. We have a heightened sensory awareness of things in that ambiguous low light state, which relates to thousands of years of not having electrical light, or much light at all.

In the theatre of course we don't want to create a 'flight or fight' response in people, but that heightened sensory awareness, where all your senses have to sit up and take a little bit more notice because you're not quite sure what you are seeing, is a useful state.

GC – Russell, when you are moving in a semi-obscure environment, how does that affect you and influence the development of the movement?

RM – This piece is really three times of coming into the same light, and three different ways of working with entering into the light. There is an interaction between the speed of movement and the intensity of the light. The light remains constant in all three instances, and I play with different speeds and levels in the space, but also the reflection of the light from the arm on the face. You see it at the beginning when the arm moves into the light and then back, and then gets a bounce off the face.

You play with the light – is it compressing you, are you being drawn up by the light? What kind of viscosity are you moving in?

I've often called the lighting for the stage the 'music for the eye', because it has the same way of making an atmosphere, making a landscape, changing fluidly from one place to another without seeming effort. And I feel that the same rules apply as in music: variation, structure and form, and statement of theme, and development of theme. And I also feel the rhythm of a production is made by the lighting.[6]

GC – I'm quoting Jennifer Tipton, where she calls light the music of the eye, because it follows the same rules. Can you recognise yourself in that? Is the light like music?

MH – Yes. It operates in the same way in that it is a composition, and it has a variation of rhythm and structure, and different notes and different qualities. It is also the way that the space breathes, expands and contracts. Sometimes it does that without anyone being aware until afterwards, when you realise that it has happened.

RM – It also has energy. In the piece that we just looked at the light has a very low energy – the lamps are slowly coming on, they stay at a low level, but it is a very constant, slow rhythm. The dance is the percussive element on top of that.

We worked on a piece recently that has a very different use of energy. We were looking at something that felt like a very nice state, but it wasn't energetic enough. Just like music rises and falls and gives energy, we looked for ways for the light to give us more energy.

MH – Sometimes you don't necessarily want the music and the light and the dance all doing the same thing. If you are in counterpoint, you create a different kind of energy and tension.

On a very fundamental level, there is no time or space without energy. And that is something that lighting creates. In this work we have a black space, so until we have some light, there is no space.

GC – After these original collaborations, which resulted in a number of solo works, you got other people involved and collaborated with Sylvie Guillem and the BalletBoyz, and others. How did that step arrive?

MH – Actually, there were some group pieces before that, it wasn't just solos.

RM – I knew the BalletBoyz Michael Nunn and William Trevitt from the Royal Ballet. When they were leaving they asked if they could perform a duet that I had made, titled *Critical Mass*. The following year they asked if I would make a piece on them, which became *Torsion*. We were performing on a bill at The Place together where Michael and Billy danced *Torsion*; Dana Fouras performed a piece called *Two*, and then Dana and I danced another piece, titled *Sheer*.

Sylvie Guillem, who knew Michael and Billy well, came to see this show and enjoyed it, and when I met her in the dressing room afterwards she asked if I would make something for her, Michael and Billy. This would become *Broken Fall*. It was performed at the Royal Opera House, but it wouldn't have happened without her.

The thing that is really important is light that moves, rather than having a series of lights alone a line.[7]

GC – In your recent work you have begun to work a lot with projection and animation. Can you explain what interests you about that?

MH – The interest is to be able to move the light. To use a projector as a light source and then to work with video software or an animator to make it move.

It is something that we've always been interested in and tried to do, even just working with fixed generic lighting. Earlier we said how we wanted to create an ebb and flow of light in the space, and using a projector with software or animation is another way of achieving that.

RM – There are also some practical reasons for that. For *Afterlight*, when Sadler's Wells asked if I would be interested in doing something for the Diaghilev season, I remembered the paintings by Nijinsky that I had seen. We knew that with a certain level of light you could get this tracing effect of movement through space, and I thought that we could utilise this tracing reminiscent of Nijinsky's paintings. We'd also done *Transmission*, where we had used a very small box of light, no bigger than a cigarette packet, and when you put your hand through it quite fast you got this flash. I wanted to do something that had this kind of flash all over the stage.

Michael said that we would need hundreds of pin spots and that we would never get that set up in a full evening programme – but we could get the same effect by using a projector, and a projected pool of light, with lots of shafts of light and dark. I was interested in textures in the space, and animation and projection was a way of achieving this.

GC – When I came two weeks ago to see rehearsals of your most recent piece, I also got the sense that when the light moved, it allowed the body to remain very still.

RM – Exactly, it allows you to play with juxtapositions and energy.

Afterlight was the first animation piece that we made and it became something that I wanted to do more and more of.

GC – The projection very much has the quality of a kind of weather constellation. Is that something that you thought about?

MH – It was consciously intended.

RM – It's more about textures, about light and shade, cloudy kinds of pictures.

MH – It's about texture, depth, and movement – exploring them in a way that would be very difficult with generic lighting or even moving lights. One of the first things that I said to Jan Urbanowski, the animator, as a reference was to think about how a tropical storm or cyclone appears on a weather satellite image: this swirl of cloud that has trailing end bits coming off it, and a dark hole at the centre of it. It has light, dark, and mid-tones in it, and it has a lot of movement.

GC – You mentioned that *Afterlight* was created as a solo for a mixed bill, the Diaghilev evening at Sadler's Wells, and that you then decided to develop it into a full-length piece.

RM – That's not how it worked, actually. We started by making trio material and solo material, but when we tried it for the first time with the projector, having the projector with three people was weaker than having the projector with one person. So we developed the solo part first for the mixed evening and then went back to the trio parts afterwards.

It's harder to make it work with people stretched across the stage, because the projector only has a limited frame. And we could only afford one projector – not four, or nine – so it was better to have one person at the centre of it.

GC – Is it about the relationship between body and space, in that every body is a centre of attention, and the light kind of creates a landscape or a frame around these bodies?

MH – The strongest relationship is between one dancer and the lighting, because once you have two dancers, the strongest relationship needs to be between them. It can still be a collaboration with light, but it needs to be a less powerful one. The more people you have on stage, the more you multiply those relationships.

GC – You have chosen a fragment of *Afterlight* to show, would you like to introduce it?

RM – Actually there are two fragments in this – it is part three and four of a four-section solo. The dancer is Daniel Proietto. (*Guy Cools shows the final seven minutes of a recording of* Afterlight.)

GC – One of the original sources for *Afterlight* were Nijinsky's drawings, and for *The Rodin Project* you also worked with Rodin as a source. Not only with his sculptures but also some drawings and watercolours.

RM – Yes, the Nijinsky piece was the first one where we really had a theme as our inspiration, and chose to follow that. We had lots and lots of books open in the studio throughout the process and used photographs and drawings for reference, and I think they were good for all of us – from costume to lighting, to movement, to interpretation. As we enjoyed that process so much, we wanted to follow it again in *The Rodin Project.*

GC – In *The Rodin Project*, it is the sculptural quality of the body that almost transforms it into a kind of set design.

RM – Yes, for parts of this piece we had very little costume. In the fragment which we are about to show, which is from a film adaptation of the piece called *Erebus*, we did still want some kind of costume. Sometimes it is about giving some flow to the movement, and I think you probably see that in this. But there is a lot more body than costume.

GC – You were also consciously looking for a different type of body for the dancers.

RM – The weight of muscularity of Rodin's figures, particularly the weight and physicality of the men, seemed very important. That brought me to the dancers that I chose for that project, Dickson Mbi, Tommy Frantzen, and Thomasin Gülgeç, who you are going to see here. There are also three women in the project who aren't present in this clip.

GC – You said it was a clip of the film version.

RM – Yes, *The Rodin Project.* was a seventy-minute piece and from that we made a fifteen-minute film adaptation called *Erebus*. (*Guy Cools shows a short clip from the film.*)

GC – When I came to see rehearsals for your new piece, I observed a long, very detailed conversation about costumes, how they would be draped around the body. Also in this clip it all looks very casual, but it is actually very constructed. It looks like skin. Clothing is the interface between light and the body and it is something you very consciously work with.

RM – Yes, very much. And we had time to look at costume in the piece, to get the red colour in the beginning for example. We also realised that it worked much better in the light when he had a hat on, because he had very dark hair and it just looked like a dark shadow. The grey pants meant that they could kind of disappear in the darker parts, but they also gave enough sheen on the material that allows you to fill in that part in the picture.

GC – The relationship between skin and clothes, is that something you researched as well?

RM – Skin. You can't beat skin in the light really.

But sometimes there are parts of the body that you want to drain away a little bit, so you don't put them in white tights or white shoes but something a little bit more muted.

MH – It is always a long conversation that starts with the question of how much or how little skin, and then when you get somewhere with that, it is about how light or dark the costumes should be to be able to make visible what you want to be visible, and to hide what you don't want to be so prominent. You have to keep trying things out to find a balance between all these things.

GC – Keep trying things out. That is a great statement to finish this talk with.

Notes

1 Tim Ingold, *Being Alive: Essays on Movement, Knowledge and Description* (Abingdon: Routledge, 2011), p. 138.
2 Michael Hulls, from a personal e-mail, 29 June 2016.
3 Michael Hulls in theartsdesk Q&A, 21 January 2012, www.theartsdesk.com/dance/theartsdesk-qa-lighting-designer-michael-hulls.
4 'cyc' is an abbreviation of Cyclorama, typically a full stage width and full height white cloth hanging and stretched across the rear of the stage that is illuminated with white and coloured lighting to create a luminescent, and often 'sky-like', background.
5 Michael Hulls in theartsdesk Q&A, 21 January 2012.
6 Jennifer Tipton in Hamilton Dramaturgy, 7 December 2011, https:/hamiltondramaturgy.wordpress.com/2011/12/07/theatrenow-interview-with-jennifer-tipton/
7 Michael Hulls in theartsdesk Q&A, 21 January 2012.

The Meteorological Body
A Conversation with Ruth Little

Dramaturgy isn't a career: it's a way of knowing common to all of us, rooted in embodied experience, dialogue and interaction, and developed in sensitivity at every level of scale to the fundamental relationship between movement and meaning.[1]

Guy Cools – Having gone into the fourth season of these talks now, I've kind of exhausted my circle of British friends, so I've shifted my focus a little bit...

Ruth Little – ... to your enemies!

GC – No, no! I've started to invite people I would like to get to know better, using the talks and the preparation for the talks to have that possibility.

Ruth and I have a lot of affinities – we have the same profession, we are dramaturgs, we have both worked with Akram Khan at different stages in his career, and during the preparations for this talk we've also discovered that we share a passion for and an interest in contemporary eco art practices. So these will be the three topics that we want to cover. But as it is a real conversation, we will find our way through it.

We will illustrate the talk with some video material that Ruth selected and that she will introduce, and I will also bring in some quotes, depending on where the conversation goes. Ruth said she would like to start the talk with a quote that she selected herself. Could you tell us where it comes from and why you chose this quote?

The life of the body, birth, death and illness, has vanished from the private sphere into professional seclusion; the production of the conditions of life has vanished also, with energy and materials that come from what is no better known than nowhere. Together, these disappearances mean that both the exterior and the interior of the body – the interior of metabolism, the exterior of sustenance – have been lost. The body is no longer experienced as a natural system integrated with natural systems.[2]

RL – It comes from the writer, art critic, and traveller Rebecca Solnit. It was written over twenty years ago and I think I came across it when I was working with a dance company in Montreal – someone sent it to me. It is from a catalogue essay that she wrote for the artist Ann Hamilton in the nineties. It struck me like a blow, actually, because I think it coincided with something that was already developing in me, in my theatre practice. I had been working in theatre for about sixteen or seventeen years as a script reader and then as a literary manager, so I'd been on both sides of the organisational fence. But I had begun to feel frustrated by the ways in which the making of plays and the articulation of the meaning of plays as live performance art were being communicated, particularly to young playwrights.

Something wasn't right as far as I was concerned, and that lack of rightness was tied up with Aristotelian approaches to dramaturgy and what I would now describe as a linear understanding of how a play is made and therefore how it influences or has an impact on its audience. I started a journey that has taken me on an unbelievably circuitous and roundabout path, and I would encourage you all to go on it. It is absolutely fantastic. All you have to do is read a biology textbook. Or a physics textbook, it doesn't really matter which of the sciences you enter into in order to bring some of the knowledge of contemporary science into the ways we think about and understand the structures, particularly the dynamic structures, of the world. Once you start that process, it kicks open a series of completely unpredictable doors. If you are as lucky as I think I've been, you end up without a career – which is a fantastic place to be, I think, in a world that is permanently changing – but with a lot of new forms of communication and a lot of new friends, and a lot of new ways of thinking about the work that you do and the outcomes of that work.

So, Rebecca Solnit's piece landed on me like an anvil, because it expressed something that I felt to be absolutely true but hadn't really tried to articulate for myself. It is a call to arms, really, for making art differently, and living life differently. It started my journey – dramaturgically, ethically, and philosophically – and I hope that these three realms will always be interconnected in the work that I do and the ways in which I do it.

GC – Just in parenthesis: Rebecca Solnit wrote this for a catalogue for Ann Hamilton, who is an artist I greatly admire. Hamilton, as far as I know, only once made the scenography for a dance piece, which was a piece by Meg Stuart.

It was Meg's lightest piece, not as dark as much of her other work, and also one of her pieces that I personally most enjoyed. What Ann Hamilton did was to cover the entire stage with a very thin layer of clay. They needed a crew of twenty people two hours before the performance to roll out the clay, and then, through the heat of the lights, the clay dried and there was this dynamic of transformation throughout the piece.

The theatre technicians hated it, because it was so much work and also because there was the danger of dust for the dancers.

RL – Of course they did. Akram has worked with clay many times, and all kinds of versions of dust as well – for example at the beginning of *Vertical Road*. To me it is an incredibly profound material to use in art and especially in dance, where you give it movement.

The piece, at the beginning, has a large company of dancers wearing traditional costumes of some kind, but you don't know what kind. They were modelled essentially on Chinese warriors. I happened to be reading the writer Annie Dillard at the time, another really important influence in terms of focusing on the small and the value of the small, and Annie was writing about going to see the terracotta Chinese warrior sculptures for the first time, describing their hands and body parts emerging from the clay. She then goes into this fantastic riff on dust, and the little known fact that a ton of micro-meteorite dust falls on us every hour. It is happening now, there is this constant gentle little rain of silt, made up of meteorite dust – and also mostly spiders' legs, apparently, which are one of the most commonly blown about bits of things. It is just falling on us all the time. So I came into rehearsals one day, absolutely fired up by this idea that the reason that we sweep houses is that without really knowing it we are trying to stop ourselves being buried in this dust. The reason that we move is so we don't become buried in it.

And Akram, because he is a genius and a thief, grabbed that idea and gave it to Kimie (Nakano), the designer. Together they created this astonishingly powerful image at the beginning of the piece, with the dancers pounding the dust. He then stole the idea again for the opening ceremony of the Olympics.

Artists using clay often really specifically emphasise fragility, change and transformation. It is a beautiful material but a really difficult one – it's true – for dancers to work with.

GC – You have worked on two of Akram's group pieces, *Vertical Road* and *iTMOi*, and then two solo pieces. One of them was *Gnosis*, one of his classical Kathak pieces...

RL – ... which wasn't quite a solo piece, there was a duet in it as well...

GC – ... and then *Desh*, which is a contemporary, more theatrical, dance theatre piece. Let's talk a little bit about *Desh*. The starting point for it was a sophisticated and in-depth research process that doesn't happen often in performing arts, especially in dance.

RL – It was a great privilege, actually, though I wouldn't say it was too sophisticated. What was exceptional about it – and expensive, of course – was that the whole creative team made that journey. *Desh* would not have been *Desh* without it, because it brought together all those languages of performance: the visual, the design, the music, the lighting and the movement, and all of us seeking to bring them all together.

What was interesting about *Desh* to begin with was that Akram didn't know exactly why he was making it. He knew that he wanted to create a solo work called *Desh*, and he knew that *Desh* has many meanings. As far as I understand it, *Desh* works at many levels of scale, because it began as a personal piece, but inevitably it became a very political piece as well. Sometimes, giving yourself the anchorage of a single world can be a valuable thing, especially if that word is ambiguous. 'Desh' can mean country in terms of nationality, as in Bangladesh, but it also means country in a more indigenous sense and in the way that aboriginal people use it in Australia, meaning *my* country, *my* place, the place where I have the strongest affinity and affiliation with my material environment. It raised all sorts of issues around belonging, and of course, if you have seen Akram's work you know that this is predominantly what it is about. That is not to simplify it; it is to say that it is immense, because surely that is what we are all doing all our lives in one way or another. He comes out and says it: 'I don't know where I belong'; 'I'm going to try a series of experiments in this context to see what produces tension, or a sense of arrival, for me.'

So, over to Bangladesh we went and spent time travelling, recording the travelling, and gathering a great deal of material. Jocelyn Pook, the composer, wandered around the streets with a digital recorder and she gathered ambient sound, and we were then able to use those resources to influence the physical and movement material of the piece, because there was such a richness of language.

We were also partly guided through a series of conversations by the writer Karthika Nair, who created some of the text for *Desh*, along with Akram. In the end far more text was created than was used. I do want to talk a little bit about the *Desh* that wasn't made – or rather the *Desh* that was unmade, after having been made, like knitting that is then unravelled.

GC – Karthika is a poet, and there was also PolarBear, who is a spoken word artist.

RL – There was hardly a word of PolarBear's in the work in the end, but actually his influence is very strong. PolarBear's work is very concentrated and works a lot with silence and held space, so he was part of the unmaking that was a very essential part of the making of the piece, if this makes sense.

Karthika gave us six words, which were: Desh, river, land, memory, cloth, and light. The word 'light' is also interesting because in Bengali the word 'noor' means light, but it was also the first name of a young pro-democracy activist called Noor Hossain, who became a martyr of the independence movement in Bangladesh.

This coupling of concepts, and then holding them in very specific words that had a lot of ambiguity in them, made possible a rather extraordinary associative research route for *Desh*. And it's also why we made so many *Deshes* before Akram chose the final *Desh*. Going to Bangladesh brought all of us to the same place, literally, and allowed us to have conversations that were sometimes very difficult. Akram really resisted the physical experience of being in Bangladesh for quite a long time, because he didn't know what he was learning by being there – except that he wanted to be at home, some of the time, or he didn't want to have to spend a whole evening with his aunties, or he got sick. There were real physical difficulties around being there, as well as the extraordinary opening up of social worlds and realms when we spent time in the poorest parts of Dhaka. Just being in Dhaka itself is an astonishing experience when you are trying to make a solo piece, as it's a city of twenty million people. The weight of society comes down very heavily on you and of course that produces a sense of responsibility: How do I tell the story of so many people when there is only me and my body?

In one sense, the whole of *Desh* was an unplanned discovery. We found the piece by removing layers of supposition and wishful thinking and preconception. That led, I think, to a more truthful and universal account of the contradictory human desire to belong and to determine one's own identity.[3]

GC – You said that a lot of the dramaturgical process on *Desh* was to unmake, or get rid of a lot of material that was created, or allow the material to transform. Is there maybe one particular example that shows this process?

RL – Yes, for me there is. There was a scene in a restaurant. We spent a lot of time rehearsing this scene in the restaurant which involved many people as well as Akram. PolarBear was part of it, Karthika had written a script for it, and I was sitting there chewing my lip thinking, this is getting really complicated because they are asking the dancers to be actors and we are writing dialogue. Akram had to be in this place because he had been a waiter in his father's restaurant when he was growing up, and the experience of resisting what the people in that restaurant wanted from him – which was to be an Indian waiter – was a very significant part of his own resistance. It was part of what took him into classical Indian dance, and out of it as well.

He wanted to explore his experience of being in that restaurant, of being at other people's beck and call, of being looked down on as a young British Bangladeshi, and of not feeling himself to be a young British Bangladeshi. There were all sorts of tensions at play and it was absolutely fascinating, but what came out of this improvisation was a lot of text, which then got quietly snipped away because it was really just illustrating what he was trying to find.

Akram does have a tendency to do this and I'm sure you've had this experience yourself, Guy. I feel he should be here because I'm talking about him in his absence, but I think he would understand and I hope he would agree that in the early days of exploring a subject he grabs at things. He is an absolute snapper-upper of possibilities, many of which get discarded. But you have to hold them and you have to try and put them in relation to each other in order to find where the resonance lies between them. What are the false links that might be being created here? And there were false links being made in this fascinating restaurant scene.

It could be done as a play some time. We had an Israeli character coming in and getting drunk and shouting in Hebrew, we had Bangladeshi waiters – the whole thing was just so mad. But what came out of it was that Akram developed an improvisation of moving around the restaurant, trying to move in a single line while he was being constantly pulled in one direction or another.

One of these pulls came from his father, who was always trying to make him do a little bit of classical Indian dance for the clients. Akram hated doing it, resisted it and pushed back at it, and that is also expressed in *Desh*, but elsewhere. Another pull was the racism that accompanied his working life, and his own frustration that came from that. That was what he was exploring, but the more we asked him about it, and the more he asked himself what that movement meant, the clearer it became that he wasn't really telling a story about Akram as a teenager working in his father's restaurant. Really he was expressing disorientation and frustration, and also a sense of bewilderment at all the cultural influences around him.

In the end there was no more expressive context for that than the traffic in Bangladesh, in Dhaka. Because if you try to cross the road in Dhaka, you encounter thousands of people, and animals, and beggars, and each of those encounters confronts you with another social situation that is very difficult either to just ignore, respond to, or circumvent. Akram's movement across the road became a much more telling account of what it was to be Akram out of his depth than the one in the restaurant. In the end everything fell away, except for his movement. And we also found a place here for Jocelyn's ambient soundtrack, which came back in to show the chaos that was happening in the background. I love seeing it, because there is this whole progression in how it came to that. When you see it as it is now, it is close to perfect.

GC – We have a clip of this section, both in rehearsal and of the actual performance. You have made a wonderful compilation of different fragments, so before we see Akram rehearsing and performing this scene, there is some other material. Can you introduce it and explain why you chose to show it?

RL – Yes, I couldn't really make up my mind about what to bring because there are so many scenes I would like to show. The general concept I wanted to explore in these clips is disorientation. What you'll see are different forms of disorientation as they relate to complex systems.

I am very interested in complexity, and the science of complexity, which I think is a much more accurate way of describing what happens in a live performance than we find in much dramatic theory, particularly Aristotelian approaches of dramatic structure. There are better ways of describing the structure of lived experience than the ones we have inherited – but you have to go to the physical sciences to find them. So the very first clip is just a really simple example of how a complex system works. In other words: very simple causes can lead to incredibly complex outcomes, which is a great relief for makers of theatre or dance to know. Events don't have to follow on from each other in a linear or causal way, because in life they don't.

You'll see a little illustration of that, and then the rest is Akram. (*Guy Cools shows the compilation of video fragments.*)

One of the things that Akram does very brilliantly is that he takes an idea or a concept or an object and then re-orientates it, or re-orientates himself in relation to it. The sky-forest is what we called the piece of set that you just saw, and it came out of the physical experience of being in Bangladesh and going to some of the river communities with their rice paddies and the reeds that grow there. But it also came out of the idea of transformation. So all of that material is anchored in the core rule of the piece that Akram set and that we tried to adhere to, which was that things must transform.

It is an unusual way of thinking about things, to say that nothing must stay the same, everything must become something else. That is the experience of many Bangladeshi, because they live in a country that is constantly being washed away. Even a concept such as 'land', which has such solidity for us, doesn't have that solidity there. Bangladesh is the world's biggest river delta, so a large percentage of the population is always being moved. The concept of property is actually different in those rural regions. If your land moves and appears in another place, you go and occupy it there. It is almost incomprehensible to us, because we are so rigid in our understanding of land and place.

Again, there was a lot of made and then un-made material around the river, and the transformations that the river makes possible, or inevitable. Akram looked at a whole sequence of himself in water, there was a boat design, as well as all sorts of things which in the end were absorbed into the final shape of the piece. When I look at it now, it feels like none of that depth of exploration has been sacrificed, it has just been absorbed. Of course it is not for an audience to be able to pick all these things out, but I think that something special happened in *Desh*, which was that we were true to the deeper idea of the piece. And in that truth is a concentration of possibilities that makes it open in its interpretation.

GC – I've worked with choreographers for almost twenty years as a dramaturg, and one of the things I still struggle with – in a good sense, because it is part of my creative process – is the balance between being there as a witness of the process and then interfering with it at certain moments. Ideally, when I have a thought and it already happens on the floor so I don't have to intervene – these are the best moments because it feels like we are on the right track.

How do you deal with this yourself? How much of your work is just being there to perceive what is happening, and how do you find the moments to contribute yourself?

RL – Well, I think that varies from project to project, it inevitably does. You've probably had that experience, too, but even in the years that I have worked with Akram my process in relation to him has changed. Relationships should grow and it would be wrong to just continue in the same way. My dramaturgical relationship with him – and that is what dramaturgy is; it is a relationship, or a set of relationships, not so much a role that you can just take and apply from one process to another – is emergent, in the sense that it comes into being as a result of that relationship. Akram has immense curiosity and that is perhaps one of the risks of the ways in which he makes work. It is an energy-intensive process because there is so much being trialled and discarded or shifted around. So part of the dramaturgical role has been for me to try and create some distance between him and the material that is being trialled. I can stand back much more effectively than he can, especially when he is both directing and dancing, and that standing back is offering an interpretation. That is all I can do, but obviously it is based on trust – he has to believe that what I see and what I experience is of some value to him and may, in some way, stand for an audience experience.

I think it has to do with confidence, too. When I started working in dance I had no right to say anything,

I was literary manager at the Royal Court and I knew how to commission and develop a play, but suddenly to take away language from me was very disorientating and I knew I had an awful lot to learn. I have now become more comfortable in my dialogue with him because we know how to balance the dialogue: I am the one with the words; he is the one with the movement. What is the most effective marriage of these two sets of experience?

Usually it comes down to breakfast. We have really good breakfasts together. It's annoying because he gets up much earlier than I do so I am usually a bit dishevelled, but that is the time, interestingly, when what has happened the day before has been unconsciously processed. Sometimes it is a very difficult and complicated dialogue, but that dialogue doesn't happen so much in the space. The rehearsal space is where the piece has to be made, and has to be trialled.

GC – Dramaturgy is a young profession, especially dance dramaturgy, and in the literature on it from about ten years ago the emphasis is very much on distance, staying away, and being an 'outside eye' – which I think is a really bad description of it. But in recent literature it has become much more about intimacy, and the interplay between intimacy and distance.

I have the same experience as you, that in the studio I am really just there, watching. I don't interfere because I don't want my voice to complicate the dialogue that is going on. And then we always meet before and after. Finding the right moment is important, and depends on the context. When we were making *bahok* in Beijing, we also used to meet for breakfast in the hotel, and I think that mornings are good, because it is better to give feedback when you have slept on it.

RL – Yes, because we are dealing with human psychology. We should all really have degrees in psychology to work in theatre and dance, because human beings are fragile things. For all our apparent resilience, it is difficult to listen to and acknowledge and live with something that feels uneasy, but doesn't necessarily have a logic behind it.

That is why for example Liz Lerman has developed her method of Critical Response Process (CRP), which is an entire methodology for communicating criticism. The word 'criticism' itself is problematic, but to try to move a process forward in such a way that nobody falls away from it, we have to learn certain skills and techniques.

A work is constantly becoming itself – the process is the most important thing, not the piece itself. I love something that Jonathan Miller said in relation to working with a German dramaturg, who asked him: 'What is your concept?' Miller said, 'I've got some ideas about the piece, but I don't have a concept', and the dramaturg said, 'Without a concept you will have great problems with your praxis.' I thought, yes, that sums up the worst of dramaturgy – that you come along with a preconceived theory of what a performance piece is and how it works. If you adhere to the idea of complexity you can't do that, because the development of the piece will show you what the piece is going to be. You cannot come in with a set of expectations of where the process will take you, but have to be prepared to make mistakes and then recover the form of the thing, and continue to make mistakes.

David Lan at the Young Vic says that making theatre is 'a series of approximations to the truth', and I think that's true also of science, of art, and of life itself. If you're lucky enough, you make enough approximations to be able to rest with the history of those approximations. It is a perpetual series of discovering and unmaking.

GC – You've put together a very eclectic collection of clips to illustrate what dance dramaturgy could be, or how to work with movement and create meaning out of movement, not going back necessarily to text. Can you say something about this?

RL – I was really just following a movement hunch, because I was thinking about some of the movement qualities that I respond to and that I find fascinating, or complicated, or beautiful, or perplexing. One of them is synchrony, which has been described as one of the most pervasive forces in the universe, and yet it's incomprehensible in a sense, because it's a fine and beautiful pattern that is created out of seeming chaos. When it appears and when it is used most effectively in dance, it has a particular quality, because it's unexpected. There is something very unexpected about seeing people respond so intimately to one another's presence, and it's a lovely thing to watch.

I wanted to put together some clips around the idea of synchrony, and to put that in context with something that to me is much more important, which is influence. You and I have talked a little bit about the kind of work that we do and the work that we are interested in, and at its heart, really, is influence – the multiple ways in which our bodies, minds, experiences and societies are influenced by their contexts. We come into being through our relationships. This idea of man being an island is rubbish, because even an island is not an island. It's connected in so many ways, it has a porous border and it is connected to so many energetic and material flows, and so are we.

GC – It's one of the reasons why I always prefer to talk about contamination, rather than influence. I know that contamination has negative connotations, but for me it is about being porous yourself. There is this whole history of how our skin was originally a porous border and a site for exchange, and then it became more and more about keeping outside influences out and ourselves separate. I think that there is a necessary practice of allowing yourself to become contaminated by the environment and by other bodies. Influence for me sounds more like manipulation – I try to influence you.

RL – Yes, but I think that's important, too, because I think we are constantly in negotiation with each other. Harold Pinter argued that life is a series of negotiations for advantage in which everything is brought into play. We don't speak and we don't move innocently in relation to one another, because we are trying to bring about change. It is a really helpful insight to have if you are a playwright, or a dancer or a choreographer. The ways in which we move are intended to influence, to sway, to have an impact on other people. Have a look at these clips.

(*Guy Cools shows a selection of video clips, including the free-style ice skaters Le Patin Libre and Turf Feinz* RIP RichD Dancing in the Rain Oakland Street.[4])

What I love about this last one is the context, the fact that this extraordinary lyricism and joy comes out of that bleak Californian roadside experience. And the fact that they are dancing for a friend who was killed on that corner in a car accident. The re-making of that situation in the piece is incredibly profound, and also fantastic to watch and to listen to. Look it up, they are called Turf Feinz and they are amazing.

So meaning is, in effect, found not in the pattern itself, but in its disturbance, and the creation of new patterns. Knowledge lies at thresholds and edges of experience, and this is the place where dramaturgy happens.[5]

GC – You said before that dramaturgy is about working with complexity, and bringing live dynamics on stage. Another principle that you have been referring to a lot is that in order to be able to deal with such complexity, we have to look for patterns. It seems that this is something innate to us as human beings. Playing with these patterns, and disturbing them, is something that is important in our work.

RL – Really important. It's a really important tool that we are all born with. We all have a dramaturgical brain. Our brains are perpetually at work trying to assess the meaning of movement – that's the primary function of the brain. Most of our neural activity is aimed at the recognition of pattern. A pattern is something that forms itself out of the flow of experience, the immense amount of information that we are being bombarded with through the senses all the time. The brain, in order not to go into meltdown, has become astonishingly adept at being able to recognise when a pattern comes into being, or when a pattern is broken. It's the edges of both of those things that are the most important from a dramaturgical point of view. Meaning arises out of the creation or the destruction of patterns.

A really simple example of this is the fact that in order to recognise a still object, the brain needs about five megabytes of information, which is a lot. So if we're in Bangladesh in the Sundarbans and we're wandering through the mangroves in the stripy shadowed light and we see a completely still tiger, we need five megabytes of tiger-information before we are able to recognise it. If that tiger moves, we only need fifty kilobytes of information. We are absolutely programmed not to make a mistake about a moving tiger – you know what to do without knowing how or why. It's the same at every level of scale. We are brilliant at reading and interpreting shift, and change, but we need to create patterns so that we don't have to keep analysing things all the time. As soon as a thing becomes a pattern the brain can switch off to an extent, so the pattern itself isn't the interesting thing – it's the breaking of the pattern, or the creation of a new one.

Shakespeare is also a really good example of this, because all his plays are about the disruption of patterns and the creation of new patterns. The end of a Shakespeare history play, for example, always involves the establishment of a new social pattern, a new ruler, or a new set of ethics. Something gets broken and something new is put in its place. During the plays themselves you get another real approximation of a complex system, this constant shift between order and disorder. It's a really useful way of thinking about how very powerful and effective large performances can be structured.

The coming into being of a pattern – like the synchrony of the skaters that we saw in the clip – draws our attention. If they continued to skate in that synchronised form, then we would very quickly lose interest in it. In fact, in the rehearsal it came out of a section where they were moving in a much more fluid, chaotic way, and so the sudden creation of a pattern grabs our attention by contrast.

What I try to do in my own work is to be very sensitive to pattern formation and disruption, because it is in those moments that meaning is communicated. They are the places to really focus our attention, which is why choreographers such as, for example, Jonathan Burrows say that the choreography itself can be considered to exist *between* scenes or sequences. It's the thing that happens on the edge. The edge, physicists will tell you, is the most interesting place in the universe.

The practice of dramaturgy, like meteorology, is a study of process and pattern, which explores the changing behaviour of systems.[6]

GC – This is why, for me, the active part of working as a dramaturg lies in the transitions. I compare myself to a film editor, and the longer I am doing this work the more I understand that what I am trying to help the choreographer edit is the rhythm of the piece. The visual rhythm and the auditory rhythm are like separate tracks – you have to play them separately and together. And with rhythm it's the same thing: the in-between moments define the rhythm.

The natural phenomenon that best combines this complexity with regular patterns and their disruption is the weather system. You have said that dramaturgy is a form of meteorology, of trying to understand, and play with, weather systems.

RL – It has been for me a really helpful pathway to go down. First of all I was interested in storms in plays, because there are a lot of them. If you read a Chekhov play, there is always a storm: the wind is howling in the fireplace, or the lake is being whipped up into a frenzy.

As an experience of light, sound and feeling that suffused our awareness, the weather is not so much an object of perception as what we perceive *in*, underwriting our very capacities to see, to hear and to touch.[7]

We are in the weather, and it is in us. It is very much in us, because we are subject to the same patterns of turbulence. Our hearts, for example, are very turbulent things. We think of them as having a simple and singular beat, but actually it's a chaotic structure because that gives us more adaptive capacity. A heartbeat isn't in fact regular; it allows us to respond to all kinds of stresses and pressures on the heart. Doctors say that a heartbeat that is very regular is often a signal that something catastrophic is about to happen.

I decided to look at storms in plays, and then I realised that actually I was looking at plays *as* storms. The point is that weather patterns, and particularly weather patterns that culminate in a storm, have a very clear structure. It's just that it is a very unpredictable structure. Chaotic systems, or complex systems, are described as being sensitive to their initial conditions. This is a really useful thing for me to remember when I work with makers, because the initial conditions of a piece will determine what that piece becomes. If you make a tiny shift in one direction or another, you will end up with a completely different piece. So it is important to have convictions about the origins, about where you begin, and then to follow the tendency of the work as closely as you possibly can.

Tennessee Williams said that he liked to look at people in the thundercloud of a common human crisis, and a number of writers and makers have expressed the value of storms and of storm structure in their work. You can have a storm in a teacup – it doesn't have to be a big, cataclysmic thing, and in fact it's often a very concentrated form of expression that can signal the biggest shift. The tension between the immense and the minute is often where drama resides, and where our strongest emotional responses are generated.

GC – Looking for the edges is also the reason why interdisciplinary approaches are so important. We have already talked about this in the context of our profession: as dramaturgs we are constantly referencing nature and science as well as art. You have selected a clip from another piece to illustrate this. Could you introduce it?

RL – Yes, this is a selection of fragments from a film that was released by the choreographer Siobhan Davies with the filmmaker David Hinton. It's called *All This Can Happen*. I think it's a work of genius.

As with so many things that strike you peripherally, it doesn't tell you anything directly about dance, and yet for me it communicates more about the relationship between the human body and human experience in context than virtually any other work that I've seen for a very long time. This is partly because a choreographer is making a piece that is not about dance, and doesn't reference dance. She is working across boundaries, with a filmmaker and a film editor, creating a piece in a two-dimensional form, using multiple frames, which is very different from choreography itself. The piece is based on a text written in 1917 by Robert Walser. It's a prose piece about going for a walk. Siobhan Davies has been absolutely true to that text and she has expressed aspects of it by drawing on archival footage from many sources, most of it shot before, during or shortly after the First World War.

I'd like to show you two things: one is how other expressive forms can teach you about your own form, and the second is how powerfully the grotesque, or grotesque uses of the body, can illustrate the psychological effects of the First World War on those who experienced it and on our society, which was industrialising so heavily at the same time. It is a piece about everything that went wrong in the twentieth century, but it does this at a pedestrian pace and with great intimacy. This is where I think its epic quality comes from. (*Guy Cools shows a compilation of clips from the film.*)

GC – I want to talk about the importance of walking. You started off with a quote by Rebecca Solnit, whose most iconic book is called *Wanderlust*, about the history of walking from antiquity to today. We have been talking a lot about the importance of reconnecting the body to its environment, and walking seems to be the ideal practice for that. There are also a lot of contemporary artists, especially visual artists, who have been reconnecting with such practices. Can you comment on that? Maybe it is also a moment to bring in the second part of your quote.

RL – I will bring in the second part. I went for a walk with Rebecca Solnit not long ago – it is how she communicates, and it suits me perfectly. I think she describes it as 'stitching' the body back into relation to place, and it is something that we are losing the capacity to do. Particularly dramaturgs, who spend their lives sitting in dark theatre spaces watching other people's work!

Walking is not just a necessary activity; it is a metaphor for reducing the pace with which we accumulate information about the world, and the scale of that information. It is also about redeveloping our sensory capacities in space, and it has implications for the ways in which we make art. The argument that Rebecca Solnit makes, and that Tim Ingold and Robert Walser communicate, is about renewing our sense of context and about creating rich contexts for one another to work within, rather than blank spaces of possibility. It is also about developing our understanding of process and our capacity to stay with process, even though it involves a certain amount of not knowing and insecurity. And it requires of artistic practice that it becomes more socially engaged than some strands of art have been since Romanticism, when the image of the artist as hiding away in isolation became so prominent.

From my point of view I want to work with art that interweaves itself more fully and more insistently into the world, because the world is in such a state of crisis and pre-calamity. In Bangladesh, calamity is already well and truly underway. I'm not talking about instrumental art, except in the sense of a musical instrument: art that you play upon, that you take into different situations, and that you invigorate through the nature of its connections. This is summed up far better than I can do it by Rebecca Solnit in that same piece about Hamilton, written twenty years ago as a plea to all of us.

Think about the possibility of the work of art shifting allegiance – embodying rather than representing the cyclical, embracing labor, mortality, change, process; becoming more deeply part of the mutable world rather than a monument on its banks. Reconnect the act of making to its sister acts of laboring, consuming, attending, the acts that make the world, over and over again. Shift from the new to the renewed; recognise the world has no lack of things, only of attending to things; shift then from production to maintenance.[8]

I have been thinking recently, in another context, about some of the words that underpin the things I believe in and the ways in which I want to work, and I have been looking at their etymology. Maintenance is one of them: 'to maintain' comes from the French 'main-tenir', which means to hold in the hand. It is a really important thing for all of us who work in the embodied arts – for those of us who have bodies, actually – to understand the role of maintenance, of holding in our hands the work, the creative process, and the relationships with those we work with. 'To entertain' is another of those words, which comes from the French 'entre-tenir' – to hold between. To hold in between what is and what might be, and to allow for ambiguity and a sense of suspension and not knowing. A third one is 'to sustain', which means literally 'to lift up'. I like the multiple meanings of these words, and the possibilities that they offer in artistic practice.

GC – We have been circling around this notion of belonging to a place and reconnecting with the environment – being receptive, which I think lies at the heart of our practice as dramaturgs. It is therefore maybe inevitable that we end up in contemporary eco art practices, because that seems to be the field where all of this is now being developed. Most of it out of necessity.

Parallel to your work as a theatre and dance dramaturg, you have also been involved with a big project, Cape Farewell, which takes place mainly on boats. Can you talk about how this is connected with your dramaturgical practice?

RL – I don't really see any distinction between the work that I do as a dramaturg and the work that I do with Cape Farewell, because they are both interdisciplinary, they both work across borders and boundaries, and they are both absolutely based in ideas of embodied learning and embodied knowledge.

Cape Farewell is an organisation that works with artists and scientists in the context of climate change, developing other ways of communicating both the science of climate change and the ethics around change itself in ways that the scientific community, by its own admission, has been unable to do. Nobody has the answer, but artists are able to perhaps formulate the questions in ways that are more emotive and affective – and learn a little bit more about the world that we live in. We really need to learn as much as we can about its patterns and processes, because we are right on the edge of chaos. The systems that we are part of, including our economic systems, are so complex that what economists tell us does not suffice. We have the responsibility to develop our knowledge and understanding of complexity.

Cape Farewell runs a series of expeditions on sailing boats in the High Arctic, and I have been running a project in Scotland for the last three years. The principle of that project is to explore the relationship between people, place, and resources – the ways in which we connect to the places in which we live and work and function and dream; the resources that we draw on to do that, and where those resources come from. We are trying to generate a bigger narrative. As Rebecca Solnit says, where energy and matter come from is now 'no better known than nowhere'; well, we wanted to go to those places. So we've been to Orkney, where a renaissance has been taking place in renewable energy extraction, and where they are stealing energy from the sea with wave and tidal technologies. There is now immense interest in this tiny cluster of islands in the North Sea on the edge of the Atlantic, because they may hold the key to some of the energy technologies of the future. But because we're imposing our existing economic model on that, there is pressure to scale it up and produce these huge installations and arrays of technology. Nobody is talking to the local communities, who are the custodians and the stewards of those costal environments and whose seas are going to be profoundly affected by the industrialisation of the marine environment.

These are the sort of questions that we are inviting artists to get their heads into, and it does mean having to learn about things such as the EU Common Fisheries Policy and marine spatial planning and things that most of us know nothing about. This is our world, and the decisions that are being made by our governments are the things that put fish on my table, for example, if I choose to eat fish. I am not eating farmed fish at the moment, because I've seen it, and unless it is done on a humane and intimate scale, forget it! We are industrialising our resources right through the oceans and it is the most profound and catastrophic act of vandalism that humankind has ever undertaken. But there is time for us to get involved, to learn more about it, and to participate in some of these decisions.

That's why I feel that my art practice has to have an ethical underpinning. It doesn't necessarily have to be about ecology, but it has to be made with an ecological frame of mind, and that means thinking in terms of complex systems and dynamic processes, and change.

Working with Cape Farewell has been fantastic for me because it has brought me into contact with artists and people from many different fields and forms of practice. I have witnessed the fact that artists are becoming much more fully and enthusiastically engaged with scientists and research organisations and new forms of knowledge. It is enriching their work, throwing them into some complex moral and ethical situations, and it is producing new forms – particularly new collaborative forms that are probably the forms of the future.

GC – One of the many things that we found out during the preparations for this talk is that we are both collaborating on books with a similar subject...

RL – ... *Art and Ethics*! Yes, we have both been involved in completely separate books with the titles *Art and Ethics*, or *Ethics and Art* – there's convergence for you! It is the pattern or the system expressing itself, and we're just in the current of this thing. I do think we are all part of a movement that is asking for more forms of engagement, and recognising that that brings us into more places of uncertainty and confusion.

GC – I think this is a nice moment to conclude.

Notes

1. Ruth Little. Speech at Kenneth Tynan Award ceremony (unpublished, 2012).
2. Rebecca Solnit, 'Landscapes of Emergency', in Chris Bruce, Rebecca Solnit and Buzz Spector, *Ann Hamilton: Sao Paulo and Seattle: A Document of Two Installations* (Seattle: Henry Art Gallery, University of Washington, 1992), p. 43.
3. Ruth Little, unpublished notes on *Desh.*
4. www.youtube.com/watch?v=JQRRnAhmB58.
5. Ruth Little, speech at Kenneth Tynan Award ceremony (unpublished, 2012).
6. Ibid.
7. Tim Ingold, *Being Alive: Essays on Movement, Knowledge and Description* (Abingdon: Routledge, 2011), p. 130.
8. Solnit, 'Landscapes of Emergency', p. 50.

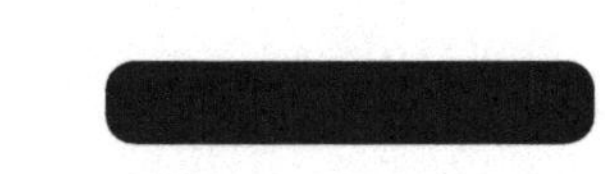

The Energetic Body
A Conversation with Antony Gormley

In trying to deal with the basic conditions of human survival, I began to examine the containers as well as the contents of the human body.[1]

Guy Cools – I clearly remember meeting Antony for the first time during a 'Catalytic Conversions' seminar at the Royal Opera House, in 2000. We were co-sharing a session to inspire the next generation of choreographers and dance leaders. Then we collaborated on *zero degrees*, the piece by Akram Khan and Sidi Larbi Cherkaoui, which I am sure we will talk more about during our conversation.

Antony is very articulate about the body and the body's relationship to space, so he has been on my shortlist for this series from the very beginning. I invited him to participate every single season, but up to now it has not been possible. I am therefore very happy to conclude the series with him, and to finally welcome Antony as our guest.

Antony Gormley – Sadler's Wells is a wonderful place full of energy and bravery, and it has become a generating location for new thoughts about the engagement with the body in movement. And that means the *living* body in space.

I have always loved dance. It is less about finding visual inspiration than perhaps about literally being energised by that feeling of life itself being used as the primary material in an interpretation of life. There cannot be a purer form, in my view, than the idea of lived time shared *in* time between bodies, where somehow intelligence is expressed through movement – through action without purpose, or, in other words, action that is not directed at a cause-and-effect relationship. That is what dance is for me: a liberation of the body to a freedom of expression before words, before interpretation, that can be transmitted and received without the hermeneutics of language. That is why places like Sadler's Wells, where new paradigms of understanding the body in time can be engendered, are so important.

GC – You're right. You said that this series links body and language, but actually, before language there is the body in space. It is a relationship that you have been researching throughout your career, and choreography, too, as an art form that is about the body in space. It is maybe strange – and we will talk more about this later – that choreographers such as William Forsythe have arrived at the same point as you from a different direction, creating spaces that give people a choreographic experience. It is part of the journey I want to make with you tonight, a point to arrive at perhaps. So let's go back to this fundamental relationship between body and space. You have said that you resist the notion of objects or sculptures occupying space, and you want to create sculptures that activate, rather than occupy, space.

AG – This has to do with the semantics of sculpture, and how the body has been put to work in sculpture. If we think of the trajectory – we could start with the Pisano works in Pisa in the thirteenth century and go right through to Rodin – the body was always used as a protagonist within some narrative structure, be it mythological, religious, or political. This notion of using the body as an actor obscures something much more important, which is that the body does not have to be representational at all, it can be something else – it can be reflexive.

I think this applies to the art form of dance as well. The liberation that Merce Cunningham and his generation went through after the Jungian moment of Martha Graham was all about looking again at the syntax of the body in space: waking, sitting, standing, and looking at it as an intrinsic emotional language without the need to carry any narrative. For me this was the key question, how to begin to treat the body otherwise – not through the understanding of the relationship of bone to muscle to skin. Anatomy was such a vital prerequisite of sculptural excellence. In those days you couldn't really tell the world that you were a sculptor unless you understood anatomy, and then put that knowledge to work by making believable bodies, either in three dimensions or in two.

What do we replace that with? I think we begin to look at the body as a space, not as a thing. The body is the place that each of us, in our own way, is dwelling within. The collective subjective of the human condition is that we occupy a body. I think we spend a lot of our lives trying to escape from it, but I want to get back to that place. You could call it the darkness of the body, because it is so obscure to us. But we can begin to mine it, begin to recognise it, to give it some presence. This means dealing with the body in terms of *being* rather than *doing*, which is a very important distinction.

GC – I remember you saying that for you, the ideal sculpture is just a simple stone that is put there in nature to mark time and space.

AG – Yes, I think the primal sculptural gesture is taking a found stone that might be lying in the river or at the bottom of a cliff, and standing it upright. Immediately it becomes a marker. Immediately it becomes a point of reference in space at large, against which your movement and your time are measured.

I use Buddhist meditation in becoming very still. When you agree to give up your freedom of movement and you dispense with desire and aversion, something happens: a kind of concentration of energy.[2]

GC – In your own work you have been searching for stillness for a long time, using your own body. Did that come as a result of this? Is it a discovery that has autobiographical roots?

AG – I think I probably wouldn't have gone on this journey without having had a very strong childhood experience of feeling the space of the body. I was a child of the fifties and was sent up after lunch for an enforced rest – which wasn't really a rest for me, it was more like torture. But I was a good catholic boy and did as I was told. I was six years old, I went upstairs and lay down. The experience was of being completely still in this tiny, claustrophobic bed. The bedroom was an old balcony that had been glazed in, so it was very bright and very hot, and somehow the heat and brightness were right there behind my eyes in this absolutely burning, claustrophobic, matchbox space. I had been told that I had to lie there for half an hour or an hour, and the strange thing was that as I lay there, this tight, tiny, hot space became cooler, and darker, and bigger. The experience of going from imprisonment to release – being released into an almost cosmic space, the endlessness of a night sky – was something that I later re-discovered in India, through studying Vipassana meditation.

I had had a fairly classical education where articulation was highly prized and where being articulate and being able to remember things that you had learned out of books was of high value, but suddenly, through meeting this very straightforward ex-businessman from Burma called Goenka, I learned that high value could actually come from different sources, and that you learned things simply by looking at what *is* when you sit still and concentrate on being itself. That gave me the key. I had to decide whether I was to become a Buddhist full-time meditator, a monk, or try to make something out of that realisation – in other words, make an objective correlative of what it feels like to inhabit a body. And I think that's what I have been doing ever since.

GC – A lot of your iconic work started out with your own body: making moulds, or casts, and putting them in different spaces – inhabiting these spaces, activating them, relating to them. You selected a work that you created in Cologne, which is called *Total Strangers*. Maybe we can look at some images of it and you can comment on them?

AG – I think that is a good idea. The piece was a commission from Udo Kittelmann for the Kunstverein, which is a museum space in a low building on the Cäcilienstraße in Cologne. It usually has a number of rooms, and I simply decided to remove all of the walls that created the rooms and open the space up. I made six copies of myself that were solid iron casts from a plaster mould, so that when you came into the space there was just this one body, but then there were also others outside. It was about reflexivity – taking this place of display and turning it into a hide from which you might look out at the real world, where there were more of these things. You might ask, what are they? What is the status of these multiply-produced objects?

They identify a space where a human being once was and could be again. The interaction between the still time of these industrial fossils and the moving time of life on the street was really the subject of this piece. People were invited to go into the museum and encounter this singular body – to touch it, to feel it – and then look at its reproduction, or its copies outside.

I guess I am trying to admit that this is the time of industrial production; these bodies are mass-produced, they are not unique, wonderful hand-crafted objects, but are simply indexical traces of the place that a particular body once stood and that anybody could stand in again. They are being released, as it were, back into the world, in a place of display where you have to begin to think about everything to do with your position in space and indeed, the ongoing life in the street.

You may say, 'well, he is overegging this particular cake', but for me this was a really important moment of trying to interrogate time as lived and time as represented. You look out through this square window (that could be the size of a painting!) at the real world. None of these slides show those moments when the old lady on her way to the shops stops because her dog has a pee on the feet of the sculpture, but there was a way in which the accommodation of life around these empty, meaningless, nameless total strangers – or strange things – became a choreography. It became a thing that we were invited to look at, something very quiet and supremely inexpressive, that was also using the space of art not to explain, but to investigate or re-examine the conditions of life. It did this from the position of display, but also from behind it.

GC – You started off with a beautiful defence of dance, saying that dance offers an experience of time in real time. *zero degrees* was the first time that you contributed to a dance piece, making the scenography for this work by Akram Khan and Sidi Larbi Cherkaoui. Do you remember how you got invited into the project?

AG – Akram just rang me up and we agreed to meet on the South Bank. He told me the story of him going to Bangladesh. At that point he wanted me to make him a tree that he was going to hang upside down, but things evolved from there...

GC – ... when you were working together on the piece, you made other proposals – more than one.

AG – Yes, I think we realised that the idea of doing scenography wasn't really the most challenging thing from my point of view. We ended up making copies of Akram and Larbi as rubber dummies.

I took Akram as a rubber dummy on the Eurostar (in the luggage rack) and delivered it to Akram and Larbi, who were rehearsing in Antwerp. I had cut into its elbows and shoulders and knees so they were only held together by a rope connector. When Larbi picked up this very floppy object, it was just a fantastic moment. He started playing with it as you would with a doll, except that this was Akram, and it was Akram's size. Immediately something very rich and interesting came out of it – about body doubles, I suppose, but also about how something falls, and about the acknowledgement that the lifeless body has its own syntax that isn't meaningless. You could spin this thing around in a centrifuge and it would take one position, and if you threw it into a corner it would take another.

I think at first it was Larbi, rather than Akram, who saw the possibility of a choreography that had to do with the living and the dead, or to do with a highly animated and intelligent body relating to one that was very evidently made of rubber. And then, as a result of this very first experience, we decided that the second dummy, which was a copy of Larbi's body, should actually be able to stand. It had floppy arms, but its body could stand up. In a way there was already a lot built into that, so it was then only a matter of clearing the stage and making sure that there weren't too many unnecessary distractions.

For all my distrust of narratives, particularly grand ones, Akram took us on a journey, and interestingly it was Larbi who was the Virgil in this: Larbi gave Akram the mission to begin to reflect on this particular story of going to Bangladesh as a Bangladeshi born in Britain, and to do it in a variety of ways. One of the interesting things was that we made a double of rubber out of a living body, but what Larbi did was to make a double of Akram, out of his personal story, by copying every hand gesture and every phrase of this story as it was told for the first time. I have no idea how Larbi did this. He is quite a magpie, very good at pinching things, but he is also very clever at structures. He managed to record Akram the first time he told his story of going to Dhaka and experiencing a culture that was completely his own, but that he had hitherto been separated from. This very personal story became a universal one about our present state of multinational displacement. What is an identity and from where do we derive it? The dummies became useful in a similar way: by making a copy you can look at the original in a new way.

GC – I worked on this production as a dramaturg, and you are right in what you said earlier, that Larbi, with his inquisitive nature, started to experiment and play with the dummies the moment you introduced them in the studio. But my memory of it is that they then got left aside, as there was movement material to develop. We rediscovered the dummies in the last days of rehearsal, when we moved from the studio theatre on to the big stage and Akram and Larbi felt lost in the space – especially during solo moments, when the other one just had to sit on stage. They remembered the dummies as a way of relating and as a way of grounding themselves in the space, and this is where they rediscovered the playfulness. The dummies became a very important part of the process, because we needed an emotional counterpoint to the lamentation in the second part of the piece.

We can actually look at some of it. I prepared two video clips: One is a clip of the making-of, where you see how the dummies are being made in Antony's loft, and then I selected the last five or six minutes of the piece, where you see how the bodies and the dummies and the space relate. (*He shows two video clips, of* zero degrees *and of* zero degrees, Infinity,[3] *the documentary of the making-of.*)

Looking at it again, it seems that it is about emptying the space.

AG – Yes, it is a sad scene. I haven't seen this film, and I hadn't seen the scene of Larbi being cast in plaster. That moment when you are enclosed in a shell is really very frightening. I am impressed with Larbi's complete composure while he is being turned into an object.

In all these works the body has become a place in which mass has been released from its stable condensed form into a field of energy.[4]

GC – There is another line in your work in which you create spaces where you want the audience, or the spectator, to have a particular experience for themselves.

AG – I think there have been two trajectories in the work. It doesn't look like *Total Strangers* anymore. I have begun to use the language of the built world that shelters the body to articulate what it feels like to inhabit the body. You could say that it is a revision of Cubism, but we are looking at building bodies in the same way that you might build a high rise.

GC – Sort of like cell structures.

AG – Yes. We have moved from physical pixels through to bigger and bigger volumes of mass. It is one side of the work that continues in its own way, using different forms of structural mapping of the body as a space.

And then parallel to that I think I am trying to make devices or structures that actually allow the viewer to experience this for themselves. They are proprioceptive devices – devices for reconsidering what it means to inhabit a body, for example by making a room full of light and cloud, or by re-articulating architecture through multiple frames. My last real attempt at this was to make a platform of fifty by twenty-five metres that hangs seven and a half metres from the ground and can take a hundred people at a time. There is no containing fence, but anybody's movement is immediately transmitted to everybody else's movement. In a way it is a dynamic model of the ideal democratic relationship between individual freedom and the collective body.

GC – I have brought in some images of this strand of your work. (*He shows images of* Blind Light.)

AG – Ah yes, this image is of a piece I made for a show at the Hayward Gallery in 2007, *Blind Light*. It is a room that is about twelve by twelve metres and contains 7000 lux of light and very dense cloud that is ten times denser than any natural cloud. The threshold is permanently open, so that you walk across it and you disappear. You disappear not only to others but also to yourself. You can't see your feet or your hands. You are conscious that you are alive, but you are disembodied. You enter another kind of space. This was a luminous version of what I was trying to describe within the meditative space of Vipassana, where you have allied consciousness within the body with an experience of space as infinite extension. This was exactly the same, but with light. Your eyes were open, but you could see nothing. You were awake and you were moving, but you had no objects in your vision. You were inside a space that had qualities – you could hear voices and you were aware that it was wet, that there was precipitation, and that you were walking on a kind of rainy pavement – but it allowed you to think about the relationship between embodiment and consciousness.

GC – This is an image of another piece, *Horizon Field Hamburg*.

AG – Yes, this is the last instrument for collective proprioception. It is a 67-tonne structure that is capable of carrying a hundred people at the same time. But it also swings. It has an oscillation of about 0.18 Hertz, so it can move almost two metres. It has five tonnes of black polyurethane on it, on a very thin surface that is almost like a mirror. Edmund Burke said this wonderful thing, 'there is no beauty without some terror', and there is an important amount of terror here: you could fall off.

The interesting thing for me is the relationship between viewers and the viewed – viewers becoming the viewed. The sound of the people on the platform is transmitted to the people below, and you have a feeling of being in control but at the same time also losing control. The children are very much the teachers of the adults in how to negotiate this new experience of instability. You could say that it is a big black monochrome painting on which the public are allowed to walk. I did get people to take their shoes and socks off as they came in, and that was very important so that you could receive impressions through the bare soles of your feet. Everybody walking on that surface transmitted a vibration that was picked up by others and that you could hear underneath the platform.

Instead of a fence, we had a net that was one-and-a-half metres within the edge. You could say that there is not a lot going on here, but I think it was also an invitation to look out at the city. We removed all of the obscure windows from around the roof lights at eye level, and from that unstable platform you could look out at Hamburg. There were wonderful scenes of people pointing out to each other where they worked, or where they came from, or a scene on the street.

This idea of inverting the function of a museum, where usually items of unique beauty or miraculous craftsmanship are shared as objects of virtue, allows it to become a place that is in the world but not of it, from which you look back at the world and reconsider it, almost as if it were a representation of itself. It is a way of thinking of the space of art reflexively, rather than representationally.

GC – It is this aspect of your work that really makes me think of a lot of William Forsythe's recent work. He calls his pieces 'choreographic objects', and they are basically installations that give the audience a choreographic experience in the space. Again, you both seem to have arrived at the same point, although the journey has been a different one.

After *zero degrees*, you continued to work with Larbi. Is this one of the nice parts of the dialogue between the two of you – creating a space that is like a breathing room and then inviting the audience into it to have an experience? What Larbi seems to be able to offer you, is to bring that space into movement.

AG – Yes, it is fantastic and it is like that with Larbi. You seem to throw him a few toys and he will say, 'Well, I like this one and that one.' A lot of the things I gave him to play with during *zero degrees* actually ended up in *Babel.*

I did make him a little aluminium room to sit in, and he tried it out and we could see that there was potential there, but in the end we had enough with the dummies. Equally, the idea of translating a human body into a box that could be interpreted in multiple ways first came up during *zero degrees*, and we later used it in *Sutra*.

It is very lovely to work with somebody who naturally wants to see what affordances a stick or a hat or a piece of rope can give him in terms of interrogating how a body can move in space. And it has been very fruitful. I think that Larbi's whole life has been an investigation of what is possible. Unlike Akram, who in a sense was born through the ingestion of a long tradition, Larbi is completely uninterested in forms for themselves; he is only interested in how he can mutate them to his own purpose. That is excellent for somebody like me, who wants to make diagnostic instruments with which you can interrogate the context, and the body, and everything in between.

Gormley's preoccupation with encasing things places great significance on the skin as the boundary between the internal space of the object and the external space in which it exists.[5]

GC – Shall we have a look at a fragment of *Babel*? (*He shows a clip from the production.*)

AG – A bit too much moving of the furniture! It is strange to look at it now. I want to say, 'just hang on a minute'. We have an image here that requires a degree of stillness, but we are allowing these mutable things to take over.

One of the things I am very aware of is that we live behind our skins, but then we cover our skins with clothes, and we further protect ourselves in rooms, which become buildings, which become towns and cities. The piece was a meditation on this idea, and on the way in which individuals and groups cohere in something that we call the urban grid. It is an affordance, but it is also our frame. Now all these choreographed unfoldings are very beautiful, but I would have liked to have had pauses.

It is exactly the same as what happened with *Sutra*. I made boxes; every one of the dancers had a box and I thought, well, there are lots of things we can do with these boxes but let's just try and find four arrangements that are going to become the landscape through which the movement will somehow be framed, or focused, or contained. But that isn't Larbi's way! (*Laughter*). It is wonderful, and I can't then come along and say, 'cut this'. Larbi has this incredibly fluid intelligence and wants to keep everything in, and everything that I do is about trying to keep a lot of stuff out. But I think that this tension between us has been very good.

I also have some trouble with this plangent music that kind of anaesthetises you. It is very beautiful, but I would actually want to be completely attentive, on the edge of my seat, because the relationship between body and space is being explored in such a precise way through the agency of the geometrical frame. I don't want to be in a lovely, soft, warm bath of a place while I am watching this. I have the same kind of trouble with the darkness. I didn't want the darkness. It is a very precious material, and darkness used as a form of anaesthetising the audience into a kind of hypnosis is not of interest to me. I think that dance, when it is really good, gets you absolutely to the edge of your seat, wanting to attend to levels of detail that you would never ever notice on the street.

GC – Would you say that what Larbi doesn't offer you, you have created yourself?

AG – Yes, that is right. And the fun of collaboration is that you get taken to places where you wouldn't go on your own.

GC – Last year, you had an amazing show in the White Cube Gallery, *Model*, which brought the two strands of your work together. You looked at the body from the inside, and also created spaces where people had proprioceptive experiences themselves. It was essentially an oversized body that filled the entire gallery.

AG – I think of architecture as being a second body. We live in a body that is always going to break down – our physical body – and then we put that fragile, unreliable thing into a second body that is super reliable. Architecture is supposed to make you feel secure. I wanted to make architecture that made you feel exactly the opposite. It is a hundred tons of steel making a body, which in this installation you could never see, but could refer to in a model room. You could explore it, and suddenly this condition of being inside architecture was revealed as a series of volumes that actually kept you out – in a way it was like abstracting the notion of the interior and making it into an object that you could move around in. The right-hand foot was also a threshold that you could walk across and enter through. At the end of that first tunnel, which was the foot, you saw yourself as a silhouette in relation to the reflected light. You were then forced to modify the way in which you normally behave in relation to architecture, where you are able to articulate your own movement in the space because everything is visible and you understand the spatial syntax of where you are. Here this was replaced with absolute uncertainty. You had to use your ears and your hands and your sense of movement to negotiate spaces that were completely unpredictable. How these different spaces related to each other and how they related to light was something that you had to discover. Whole areas that you could take to be a wall were actually a threshold, and things that looked like a threshold were actually a wall.

Wherever you were in this body, you were aware of other bodies moving through it, because it had a resonance to it. It was a very responsive environment and the acoustic qualities of the spaces encouraged you to be like a bat, sensing your environment through your acoustic ability.

The whole thing was derived from a lying form – a fallen body, me lying on the floor – but you would never be able to see that, unless it could be outside and you saw it from high above.

GC – You have also collaborated with Hofesh Shechter on a Barbican project, *Survivor*, which was very different to working with Larbi. It was a one-off event, and it was really about exploring the space together from different angles.

AG – Yes. It was a kind of sketchbook of possibilities of bridging the intimate and the shared. There are aspects of it, mainly to do with spatial experience, that I would still like to recover. It was the first time that I or Hofesh had integrated real-time filmmaking and archive footage into a production. (*Guy Cools shows an image from the production.*) This was a bath that I bought for my house but that ended up in the production. It had a wonderful feeling of being a solid object that was also a place, and that obviously referred to the body. We used it as a kind of confessional, where Bruno [Guillore] here in the image is talking to God via the plughole. He becomes incredibly animated, but you can't see him because he is actually invisible in the bath, which is filled with light. There is a camera above him filming in real time, which lets you see what you otherwise would not be able to see.

The movement of shoals and herds and flocks was also part of what we were exploring. Rupert Sheldrake calls it 'morphic resonance', and I think we want to believe that there is something like a collective mind. Animals have it already, and the internet is a sort of objective correlative of it. The way in which the big murmurings of starlings have a meniscus, an edge, at the point when every bird turns – it is not possible that it is communicated by signal. It is literally an expression of a collective body, the same as with shoals of fish. Suddenly they will turn, and suddenly this thing that was a black silhouette becomes a reflective silver cloud. I was very interested in this as a demonstration of the kind of bodily intelligence that exists before words. As far as I am concerned, it is pure intelligence. In choreographic terms the flight of starlings is one of the most moving, extraordinary things.

I just threw a lot of things at Hofesh and he was very kind and accepted them. I didn't accept his five Ikea three-seater white sofas, but he accepted my eight 15-kilo cannon balls! At a certain point they dropped from the fly-tower and landed on iron plates, becoming other bodies involved in the dance. This is a central theme in my involvement in dance: you give the body either a frame or an object that in some way modifies its behaviour. There is a lovely moment in this piece where the dancers move like centrifuges on an old self-regulating diesel engine, and they are holding these 15-kilos of iron hand-forged ball. Spinning around, the ball and the body become one thing.

The idea of vertigo, of changing perceptions of body and space either by putting the body in relation to an inert object of high mass, or allowing the body itself to be an object in space that has its own inertia, in a way takes us back to the dummies in *zero degrees*.

GC – It feels to me that in a way you have been offering your art to Larbi to play with, and maybe Hofesh has here returned the service, offering his dancers for you to play with.

AG – Yes, it's true, and I didn't quite take it on. The principle that I work to in the studio is that I don't ask other people to do things that I can't do myself, and it became very apparent to me that a lot of the things that I was interested in doing, I could not do myself. It was a very strange feeling of detachment from the subject. I didn't want to take that responsibility of using bodies as surrogate bits of paint, using other people's lives to illustrate my ideas.

But I still love everything about the extraordinary agreement that happens in a theatre, when the audience accepts that they will give an hour of their lives to this collective space and that together they are going to go on a journey. The potential of that is infinite, and maybe we are only just beginning to scratch at the real potential of the space of theatre – not as a space of demonstration, but of exploration. In the end it is the energy of the audience that is reflected in the energy of the dancers. Dancers *need* your time and your attention. It is an incredibly open field of human experience that I think is full, full, full of potential!

GC – I think that's a great way to end. I want to thank Antony for finally being here...

AG – No, not finally...

GC – ... I had to wait for five years!

Notes

1 Antony Gormley in Michael Mack, ed., *Antony Gormley* (Göttingen, SteidlMack, 2007), p. 61.
2 Antony Gormley in Richard Noble, 'The Utopian Body', in ibid., p. 24.
3 *zero degrees, infinity*. Directed by Gilles Delmas (Paris: Lardux Films, 2016), available on DVD.
4 Noble, 'The Utopian Body', p. 45.
5 Ibid., p. 21.

Coda
The Backpack of the Dramaturg

Piet Defraeye in Conversation with Guy Cools

One of the essential axes on which the practice of dramaturgy turns is the accumulation of a reservoir of material – amassing knowledge in all fields: reading, listening to music, viewing exhibitions, watching performances, travelling, encountering people and ideas, living and experiencing and reflecting on all this. Being continuously occupied with the building up of a stock which may be drawn from at any time. Remembering at the right moment what you have in your stockroom.[1]

Piet Defraeye – The opening question: You are a professional dramaturg. I teach dramaturgy here (the theatre department of the University of Alberta, in Edmonton, Canada) and the first term we usually spend on definitions of dramaturgy. What is dramaturgy? What is your definition of a dramaturg or the activity you call dramaturgy?

Guy Cools – If you do your work well as a dramaturg, there is an ambivalence that you stay invisible in the final result, because you don't have an actual, concrete contribution to the process. But my own way, how I am thinking about this today – and this is an ongoing evolution that still changes – is that I am there to support the artists to better articulate themselves in whatever formal language they have chosen, And with that kind of broad definition, I feel that dramaturgy or a dramaturgical reflection or support can be realised in any art form. It is not limited to the theatre or the performing arts. The dramaturgical reflection and support are always already provided, to a certain degree, by people who are around the artist, without there being a professional dramaturg present. As an artist you need dramaturgy but you don't need a dramaturg. That is just a choice.

PD – In one of your articles, and I found this intriguing, you talked about feminine and masculine dramaturgy. Can you elaborate on that a bit?

GC – In continental Europe, the contemporary practice of the dramaturg, both in theatre and dance, originated in Germany and is still most powerfully developed there on all levels, also on the level of support to the profession. Historically, contemporary theatre dramaturgy starts with Brecht. As far as contemporary dance dramaturgy is concerned, the first choreographer to work with a dramaturg was Pina Bausch and this was in the late seventies.

These two lines developed really different approaches. In theatre dramaturgy, which is also often called conceptual dramaturgy, the dramaturg is often an intellectual sparring partner who, together with the director, defines an interpretation of the text or the concept of the actual work the theatre makers want to create and then the whole rehearsal process becomes a way to bring that concept alive in an actual performance.

The line that comes out of the dance current, which is often called 'open dramaturgy', is different in the sense that the concept or the meaning or the structure are not defined in advance but they are the very last thing in the process that is put together, often during the last days of rehearsals. It is a much more process-oriented approach, and the way choreographers generally work. They have different sources to work with. They have text, visual images. They have the bodies of their dancers and they play with all that material and little by little out of that playing, small sections become more defined and only at the end, these sections come together and a certain coherent structure or narrative emerges.

The masculine-feminine is just a metaphor to talk about that.

PD – What is your take on dramaturgy in Canada?

GC – In the twentieth-century history of dance, there are two main currents. One that is historically continentally European dance-theatre, which from the beginning mixed movement with more theatrical aspects and often also integrated voice. And there is an Anglo-Saxon, North American current of abstract, pure dance. So it is kind of logical from that historical perspective that the European, continental dance tradition was the one to introduce dramaturgy into the dance practice. While in the North American tradition it was a more alien concept, and choreographers would often work more with rehearsal directors.

My background was in theatre and I grew into dance little by little, but even today as a dramaturg I never interfere with the movement vocabulary because I think that is the task of the choreographer. If he or she needs assistance with that aspect, which happened quite often with the productions I worked on, there is usually another choreographic assistant or rehearsal director to work specifically on the movement vocabulary. So this position of the rehearsal director is much more acknowledged in

North America. Some of the good rehearsal directors – and I have a couple of close friends among them – are, in my opinion, dramaturgs as well, in the way they often expand their relationship with the choreographer and they are not only shaping or rehearsing the movements. But they also enter into dialogue with the choreographer about other aspects of the work.

So when I arrived here in Canada, there was a huge interest in the profession, but there was very little history of it. But it is happening. Personally, I regularly work in Montréal with Danièle Desnoyers. Meanwhile, I also started to work in Toronto with Toronto Dance Theatre. Dancemakers, the other main contemporary dance company in Toronto, has hired a dance dramaturg Jacob Zimmer on a full-time basis. He also comes from theatre. York University has initiated a course in dance dramaturgy. The Arts Council has added 'dance dramaturg' to the boxes you have to tick when you make a grant application to define yourself.

PD – Do you see a difference – it might be too early to speculate on this – between French speaking and English speaking Canada with regards to this particular practice?

GC – No. Canada always had a kind of mid-position between the States and Europe, between these two currents of abstract dance and theatre dance. So Canadian dance is quite unique, both on the level of aesthetics and how to create. Maybe there is a paradox that for instance in Montréal in particular, aesthetically they are more linked to Europe, while the way they produce, their modes of production, are more North American.

PD – One of the things that has struck me in the days you have been here in Edmonton and in the many conversations that we had, is how important books are for you. Books, dramaturgy and performance. Can you talk about that?

GC – The godmother of the profession is Belgian. She is called Marianne Van Kerkhoven. She was a theatre dramaturg. She came out of the politically oriented theatre of the sixties. And she continued to work in theatre but also more and more in dance. Her definition of the dramaturg is that of a backpack of useful and non-useful things that you pull out whenever the director or the group of people you are working with needs them.

In a recent issue of *Performance Research*,[2] the magazine that is published by the University of Aberystwyth in Wales, which is completely dedicated to dramaturgy, another dramaturg uses a similar metaphor: 'You are a magpie; you look for all these shiny pieces that are everywhere. You collect them.'

In that kind of backpack, at least for me personally, books are a big and heavy part. But it is as much about going to see exhibitions, or listening to music. It remains so unpredictable what a particular process will need as input.

There is a shift in this, as with the two choreographers I have been working with most, Sidi Larbi Cherkaoui and Akram Khan, of which I will show a fragment later. They are in their early thirties and that generation, all their sources come from the internet, such as YouTube clips. They challenge me to go and look there as well. And I challenge them to read a book from time to time. It is a generational thing; how you grew up. I have this attitude. I can walk into a bookshop and within seconds always find out if the shop has something I can use for the projects I am working on. It takes me a couple of seconds to find out and I trust my intuition in that. Even more than looking up on Amazon what is available about a subject I am working on. I also use an intuitive approach to that.

PD – Anything you are reading now that you want to talk about?

GC – I just finished two creations in Toronto, one with Toronto Dance Theatre and another with Andrea Nann. And she gave me a beautiful book as a present. It was her own copy that had been passed on from hand to hand. It is Joan Acocella's (who is a critic for *The New Yorker)* book *Twenty-eight Artists and Two Saints.*[3] Little portraits of mostly twentieth-century artists in theatre, dance, writing and visual arts. And they are amazing: these short autobiographies, each framed around a particular theme.

PD – So that is in your backpack now.

GC – Yes. With many other books. Each time I travel from Canada back to Europe, I spend a lot on overweight.

PD – One of my experiences in the rehearsal hall is that sometimes actors or directors roll their eyes: 'there is the bookish fellow'. Is that part of your experience too?

GC – This schism between the director being more the practitioner and the dramaturg being more the theoretician. I reject that. Maybe for some of my colleagues it is more valuable. But personally, I love to engage in the process itself. I also reject the idea of being an 'outside eye' because of the eye just representing the rational element.

I defined myself once, and I keep doing that, as an 'outside body'. In the early stages, when the rehearsal process allows it, I often jump in and improvise with the performers, the dancers. Because I also want to understand physically what they are researching. And it is also a good way for them to accept my presence in the space. Later when it becomes too virtuosic and my untrained body doesn't allow me to follow anymore, then I play intuitively with being close to the process, proximity and then moving away and having some distance and with the distance also having a different perspective.

PD – I call it the privilege of the dramaturg to actually have that freedom and liberty that the director and the actors don't have, because they are up to their eyeballs in it. As a dramaturg you also published a lot. Writing is quite a different mode, is it not, from being involved in a production?

GC – Writing for me is also a physical activity. I need to write by hand. Often I compose the frame of a text or a lecture by walking. If I sit behind a desk my brain doesn't seem to function. Or with all the texts I have written, there is a long incubation period where the physical practice nourishes the ideas. Then I have to find a time and a space where I can isolate myself a bit more in order to write down the ideas that have been growing in my mind over a longer period. To put them on paper. That sometimes requires a separate time and space.

I was very fortunate last year, in 2009, to get a Canada Council grant to take some time off from the practice and to have some time to reflect and write and then I deliberately chose a particular place to do so. I was on Cortes Island in north British Columbia, just to do that. But even then I needed to go for a walk and at the end of the walk, I would sit down and write down my thoughts.

PD – When you do dance dramaturgy, you know whom you would do it for. When you write, whom do you write for?

GC – Some articles are commissioned for specific publications or specific events but I write mostly to pass on whatever I experienced, whatever knowledge I have to the larger community with a focus on the fellow professional arts community.

PD – Do you feel it has an impact? That it dialogues with the practice? That is one of my frustrations. Who bloody well cares and who bloody well reads this?

GC – It is the frustration of every writer. It is a very lonely profession. And even if you are successful, if your book gets published, you don't know your audience and there are very few people that get back to you. It is one of the qualities of performing arts that your audience is in front of you and that often after the show – if the environment allows it – people are able to come and talk to you.

PD – In one of your articles you talk about writing and about a performance by TG Hollandia, a major Dutch theatre company...

GC – ... which doesn't exist anymore because the director Johan Simons first moved to Belgium, and now he is in Munich.

PD – You said something which I found fascinating. You were talking about the performance of *Leonce and Lena* by Georg Büchner. You said: 'The latter is a textbook case of how the rhythm of a performance can be the key element to its interpretation.' Obviously there is a dance mind at work here. A dance mind writing. And I thought it was a fascinating approach to any kind of performativity. I even thought of painting when I read this. Rhythm of a performance as a base of interpretation. Can you talk a bit more about that and perhaps we can look at one of your examples at some point?

GC – For me it is the key element that makes a performance successful in the end. It is how it has been rhythmically shaped. I learned that from the people I worked with. Even in theatre, one of the big evolutions in Europe in the eighties was this generation of theatre directors like Simons, who founded the company with Paul Koek, a composer and musician. From the very beginning, they started to explore, even when they were doing text-based theatre, not to interpret the text psychologically, but to play with the musicality of it and then, eventually, meaning and psychology would be discovered. But the original approach would be much more formal. And that is the generation of directors I grew up with and I saw the amazing results of that.

When I work in dance, the way choreographers work – there are exceptions – most of the time they create these little units of five or six minutes that have a shape in themselves and then, towards the end of the process, they start to combine these units. I do feel that if I am actively involved, I work like an editor, more like a film editor – and then it is very much about the overall rhythm of the piece. Which comes also from spending a lot of time on the transitions. If there is not enough production time, then people always tend to choose automatically to do transitions in the same kind of way, going from one section to the next and then the whole thing becomes extremely flat. You need to shape each transition. Certain transitions can be sharp and others become little scenes in themselves and every two scenes, what you put in between needs a unique solution. Then you get a rhythmically more varied pattern that engages an audience.

PD – The rhythm in design elements too? Do you talk to the designers as well?

GC – The scenography often is part of that, in the sense that in a lot of productions I worked on, the discussion would also be, in order to have this variation in rhythm, this can also be supported by having a change in scenography that is not just dictated by the meaning but that can be a surprise in itself. To play with the change in space can become an element. For sure. all choreographers would also consider that space has as much rhythm as time has.

PD – Any examples of that?

GC – The fragment I want to show is from the piece I am most proud of. It is called *zero degrees* and it was created in the summer of 2005 by these two choreographers I already mentioned, Akram Khan and Sidi Larbi Cherkaoui, who are amazing personalities in the dance world today, although they are still very young. The piece was about exchange between the two of them. They had known each other for three years and seen each other's work and talked about it and they wanted to exchange their knowledge about dance when they went into the rehearsal process. Again, this open process without things being defined too much in advance. But one thing we would often do, if we did use narrative, the stories would be generated by the performers themselves. So in this case Larbi asked Akram to tell a story, which was the story of his journey back to India as a second generation immigrant in London. The narrative of that train journey became the skeleton of the piece. We kept that story and just edited it. We chose the fragments we found most powerful and put them in their original chronological order. The dance sections were more abstract. They were created out of a desire to explore particular forms of movement. Each of these dance sections founds its place in relationship with the narrative. Sometimes very concrete. Sometimes more associative.

So we had shaped that piece and the structure was there, but there was still an element missing. The set design was made by Antony Gormley. He had never done set design before. There was a whole process of him integrating himself into a more collective process. Antony had made a very simple proposal after a long process of trial and error, which was a huge white box with two dummies.

In his own visual art work, he often makes casts of his own body, which he puts in different landscapes, all over London or on a huge beach, with these bodies buried in the sand. So he had made two real casts of the two dancers. And we called them 'dummies'. They had been in the studio, but we hadn't actually explored working with them. And when we went from the studio to the set, which was huge and was created for Sadler's Wells, a 1500 seats theatre, Akram and Larbi felt completely lost, especially when they were going into solo moments. When they were doing something together, they had each other. The suggestion was made: 'If you do feel lost and you don't have your partner to support you, there is still your dummy.' So at the very last moment, we started to make these transition scenes with the dummies which were also very funny and kind of cruel. You can do much more with a dummy than with a real body. They became the element that made the overall rhythm of the piece so successful.

I am a big believer in counterpoint, also in this piece, which became a very tragic, sad piece towards the end, because it becomes a lamentation for a dead body on a train. That is where the narrative takes us. It is the fragment I would like to show you. But inside this tragic build-up, there are these comic interludes, which bring a bit of relief. When you build up this sad emotion, you have this comic relief and then you go back to the original emotion and you pitch higher than where you left it because of the emotional counterpoint you built into the rhythm. So the fragment I selected is halfway into the piece and it is the last part of the narrative of this train journey and the confrontation with this dead body. There is another third part of the performance where the whole piece becomes a really powerful lamentation with music, with dance, with singing for this dead body.

What made it so personal and emotional is that we had created this piece. The opening night was July 12th, 2005. But we had two public try-outs, the first one on July 8th and then, the day before, the London bombings took place. We had created a piece which was a lamentation for a dead body on a train. The two choreographers both had Muslim backgrounds, although they have a mixed identity as immigrants. In the end we decided: 'Let's present it.' There was this synchronicity and the first audience that saw the piece was very emotional and that original, emotional energy that was exchanged, was kept with the piece throughout its whole tour until its very last performance in New York. Which also felt like coming full circle.

PD – Perhaps we can look at it now. (*He shows fragment of* zero degrees.)

Interesting. This might be a good occasion if there are any questions or responses to what we have just seen. Anybody wants to raise something?

Beau Coleman – At the beginning, when they are doing the gestures with the hands, they were mirroring each other and then very shortly after that, they went into a different pattern: when he is raising this hand, I am raising that one. So I am wondering how that decision came about?

GC – The particular kind of vocabulary of the hand movements is part of Sidi Larbi's language. He has been using it in almost all of his pieces. He got it from Fernand Schirren, who was a very important rhythm teacher at Mudra, the school of Béjart in Brussels and afterwards also at PARTS, the dance school that Anne Teresa De Keersmaeker founded. Schirren is now dead, sadly. But he would say that the basis of all choreography are the hand movements that we use when we are speaking to underline our words. So Larbi took this idea literally and in a lot of his pieces he would ask his dancers to tell personal stories that relate to the subject of the piece or whatever he wants to research. He would film them and then he would choose these sections that he found most interesting or most expressive and ask the performers to exactly learn and repeat their original improvisation or talk. Which looks very easy but takes hours and hours to get all the details right. And then he would mirror it as well. In the learning process the rhythm would slightly change. Often it would speed up and it would become a bit more formal, more artificial which also would often create a comic effect, just by its form. Often the subjects were quite hard, but the form would make it lighter.

So in this particular case, through the whole piece, there are three of these dialogues or mirrored monologues. For sure they wanted to find variation in it. In the beginning of the piece, they both walk on stage. They sit down next to each other and they do, as Larbi had done in other pieces, just talk, but completely synchronised. Then it was a challenge to find a different way for the second and the third section. The first thing that was discovered, was this new sitting position on top of each other, which came out of the tiredness.

There is something similar with the dummies. One is stiff and rigid and always in a vertical position. The other dummy is literally cut up so that it is more lose and it is in a horizontal position all the time.

A lot of the ideas that were developed during the process came out of the theme of mirroring: the twin identity.

We have these hand movements. We find a position and by rehearsing it, it would become eventually more and more detailed, with more and more variation inside the same concept.

BC – I was just wondering about that change of actually mirroring to doing the opposite gesture.

GC – That is probably an intuitive choice that grew out of the rehearsal process.

Lin Snelling – I would like to talk about this notion of the dramaturg as a witness, and when you choose to intervene and how long that process goes on. I am sure it changes with each person, but I would like you to talk a bit about that.

GC – The creative process has two important poles, which are perception and articulation. As an artist, in order to improve your language, you have to improve your perception and improve your articulation.

As a dramaturg, a big part of my work is just being present as a witness. That is the receptive side. The articulated side is then to get involved in the editing process of the work. But the witness function is very powerful because already your presence and attention influence the dialogue between director and actors, between choreographer and dancers.

In this case, Larbi and Akram co-directed the piece and they explicitly asked me as a witness and later towards the end of the process, they allowed me to direct them a bit. They wanted a go-between that would moderate between them.

Playing between this witness role, which is only seemingly passive, and the actual interfering in the process, there lies my creativity. Where I shift from one to the other? I follow my intuition or it can be that I am invited to do so by the choreographer or that we talked about it, outside of rehearsals and that we decided it would be a good moment to interfere. So there are all these variations and again, as you mentioned yourself, it also depends so much on the particular process, its needs and the dialogue and relationship you have with a particular person.

PD – Where or what kind of comment do you have on the pedagogical side of drama, performance, being here in a theatre department? The dramaturgical activities that you engage in, is there a responsibility in a drama department to respond to that, to take that up? Or do you think everything is fine as it is? You, yourself did theatre studies at university level, more a dramaturgical training than a practical, conservatory training.

GC – My main physical practice is a yoga practice. I did integrate a more practical training, but much later. And the essence of yoga philosophy is that as humans we have different bodies – a physical body, an emotional one, an intellectual one, and, if you wish, also a spiritual one and an energetic one. And 'yoga' is etymologically related to 'yoke'. It means that through the practice you learn how these bodies are connected with each other and how you can access the other bodies from one body .

So for me, it is always about connectedness and integration. In my own biography for a long time only my head was developed and it is through the work I did with dancers that I started to go down from the head into the body and access other centres of knowledge. That is one journey. You can also do the journey in the other direction.

In the end intelligent thinking nurtures a creative practice. A creative practice nurtures intelligent thinking.

In the same way, on a more technical level, you can separate voice and movement. And it is important to do so, but then you have to find moments to reintegrate them in an intuitive, creative way.

PD – Can dramaturgy be taught? Or does it just have to be done?

GC – There are many tools that can be taught and methodologies too. And at the same time, you have to be able to practice as much as possible and find your own particular way of approaching things, using all the information you have. My own practice is changing with every production I do because my experience has changed.

I was formed theoretically and then I made this long, curved journey doing a lot of other professions in the field to eventually arrive back at my training as a dramaturg. And I am very happy that I made that long journey because all of it is informing the practice.

PD – It takes some time for a magpie to find the right silver.

Notes

1 Marianne Van Kerkhoven,'Looking without pencil in the hand', in 'On Dramaturgy',ed. Marianne Van Kerkhoven,special issue *Theaterschrift 5-6*, p. 146.
2 'On Dramaturgy', ed. Karoline Gritzner, Patrick Primavesi and Heike Roms, special issue. *Performance Research* 14, no. 3 (2009).
3 Joan Acocella, *Twenty-eight Artists and Two Saints* (New York: Pantheon Books, 2007).

Index

Acknowledgements

Imaginative Bodies, Dialogues in Performance Practices is the written record of a series of public talks that took place at Sadler's Wells in London between 2008 and 2013 under the title *Body:Language Talks*. The idea for the *Body:Language Talks* came out of a number of conversations with Emma Gladstone, one of the producers and dance curators at Sadler's Wells London. Emma eventually produced the whole series and she was also pivotal in having the first seven talks published. As such, she is the commissioning editor of this book. I am very grateful to her, to Eva Martinez who took over for the last series of talks and to the staff at Sadler's Wells who worked on their realisation, providing them with ideal conditions and a great first audience. The idea for the talks was to have an in-depth conversation with an artist/ choreographer that was not linked to a particular performance, like conventional pre- or post-performance talks, but that would stand on its own and would raise a public interest for an audience willing to buy a ticket for it. We decided on an hour-and-a-half format, always on a Monday evening at 7 pm. The talk would be illustrated with video fragments from the 'body of work' of the artists, or from sources that inspired them, and I would also pre-select a number of quotes that I would bring in at random, depending on the direction the talk would take, illustrating or further nurturing it and bringing the oral conversation into a dialogue with a corpus of written texts.

The talks were presented on the stage of the Lilian Baylis Studio in a simple, yet staged, scenography. We also consciously decided not to hold a Q&A session with the audience afterwards, but instead to always offer the opportunity to join us on stage at the end and to address the artist in a more personal and intimate way. Thanks to the support from the Jerwood Foundation, there was always a lot of research time to prepare the talks and to meet with the artists in the weeks leading up to each talk.

The first series of talks took place in November and December 2008, when I was on a month-long residency at the October Gallery in London as part of a six-month sabbatical. The residence was supported by Sadler's Wells and a grant from the Canada Council for the Arts. The success of this first season, both in terms of quality of content and audience attendance, prompted Sadler's Wells to decide to continue the series. A second season took place in the autumn of 2010.

All the talks had been recorded, originally, only in order to archive them, but after the continuing success of the second series, the desire grew to also publish them. Both Sadler's Wells and the Jerwood Foundation, with the support of the Research Institute *Arts in Society* of the Fontys School of Fine and Performing Arts, raised the money to make a beautiful, bibliophile edition of the first seven talks. Meanwhile, a third season had already been planned for the autumn of 2012, continuing to expand the range of artist and subjects. The final season of talks took place in the autumn of 2013.

This publication would not have been possible without the financial support of Akram Khan Company, Concertgebouw Brugge, Eastman, Fontys Dance Academy, les ballets C de la B and Sadler's Wells. But even more important than the financial are the human resources. Lisa Marie Bowler has been the dedicated editor of these talks, who has accompanied every stage of their realisation with both her insightful knowledge of its subjects and her superb language skills. In the final stages, she was joined by the staff of publishing house Valiz, in particular Astrid Vorstermans, Pia Pol and copy editor Leo Reijnen. They turn the publication of a book into an art form itself. I am extremely grateful to all of them.

Last but not least, I am very grateful to all the artists who participated in the talks for allowing an almost private conversation between colleagues or friends to go public, without losing any of its intimacy. After their first public reception at Sadler's Wells, this book now opens them up to a larger audience of readers, who we hope will benefit from the unique insights offered by some of the twenty-first century's most important choreographers and artists into their creative process and the thinking that accompanies it.

Guy Cools

Contributors

Lisa Marie Bowler is a London-based writer, translator, and dramaturg specialising in dance. She worked at Sadler's Wells for several years before completing her PhD on the phenomenology of theatre architecture.

Sue Buckmaster is the co-founder and artistic director of Theatre-Rites, which creates boundary-pushing, contemporary theatre work for children and young people, combining puppetry with dance, installation and digital media. The 2007 Theatre-Rites production *Mischief*, directed by Buckmaster, won the 2008 TMA Achievement in Dance Award and toured throughout the UK, as well as to Barcelona and New York City. In 2015 she directed a re-imagined version of Akram Khans *Desh* as *ChottoDesh*, suitable for children, which is currently touring and has won the Family Arts Award 2016. A specialist in puppetry, she has worked with companies including the RSC, National Theatre, Young Vic and Lyric Hammersmith, as well as engaging with puppetry on a theoretical level (her MA thesis explores the power of the puppet from a psychoanalytical point of view). She has been instrumental in raising the standards of puppetry and children's theatre in the UK.

Former Royal Ballet soloist and choreographer **Jonathan Burrows** and composer **Matteo Fargion** began collaborating in 1989. Very soon the separation between their respective roles dissolved, and since 2002, they have collaboratively choreographed a series of duets which they have performed all over the world. *Both Sitting Duet* won a 2004 New York Dance and Performance Bessie Award, and *Cheap Lecture* was chosen for the prestigious 2009 Het Theaterfestival in Belgium. While continuing to work together, Burrows and Fargion both maintain separate careers, collaborating with other artists as well as writing, lecturing and teaching at universities and performing arts schools, among them Anne Teresa De Keersmaeker's school P.A.R.T.S. in Brussels.

For more than three decades, **Rosemary Butcher** (1947–2016) has been the UK's most consistently radical and innovative choreographer. Profoundly influenced by her time in New York, 1970–1972, she encountered the work of the Judson Group at its height, subsequently introducing those ideas to Britain at her 1976 ground-breaking concert in London's Serpentine Gallery. Since then, Butcher developed her own movement language and choreographic structure. By her determination to remain an independent artist, her use of cross arts collaboration within the choreographic process and her frequent choice of non-theatrical spaces to present her work, she forged her own place within the European contemporary dance scene.

Dana Caspersen is a performing artist and conflict mediator. Born in the United States, she has worked in Frankfurt in Germany since 1988 as a member of the Ballet Frankfurt and The Forsythe Company. Caspersen has contributed to and created numerous works for the stage as a dancer, actor, choreographer and text author. For her work, she has received a Bessie Award for Outstanding Creative Achievement and has been nominated for a Laurence Olivier Award for Outstanding Achievement in Dance. In recent years, her research into the dynamics of conflict situations has led her to develop projects that explore how persistent structures and systems that produce destructive conflict can be transformed by the people living inside them.

Sidi Larbi Cherkaoui began his choreographic career in 1999. He has since created a vast array of dance works, ranging from intimate duets to large-scale opera and film projects, collaborating with artists and musicians including Antony Gormley, Nitin Sawhney and Akram Khan, as well as the artist collective les ballets C de la B. A Sadler's Wells Associate Artist since 2006, he launched his own company in 2010. Named *Eastman*, a literal translation of his Arabic surname, it is based at deSingel International Arts Campus in Antwerp. Cherkaoui was twice named Choreographer of the Year by the magazine *Tanz* and was awarded – among many other prizes – the 2011 Laurence Olivier Award for Best New Dance Production.

Guy Cools is a dance dramaturg. Recent positions include Associate Research Professor at the research institute Arts in Society of the Fontys School of Fine and Performing Arts in Tilburg, and Postdoctoral Researcher at Ghent University, where he finished a practice-based PhD on the relationship between dance and writing. He has worked as a dance critic, curator and policymaker for dance in Flanders. He now dedicates himself to production dramaturgy, contributing to work by choreographers all over Europe and Canada, including Koen Augustijnen (BE), Sidi Larbi Cherkaoui (BE), Danièle Desnoyers (CA), Lia Haraki (CY), Christopher House (CA), Akram Khan (UK), Arno Schuitemaker (NL), and Stephanie Thiersch (DE). With the Canadian choreographer Lin Snelling he developed an improvised performance practice *Rewriting Distance* that focuses on the integration of movement, voice, and writing. His most recent publications include *The Ethics of Art: Ecological Turns in the Performing Arts*, co-edited with Pascal Gielen (Valiz, 2014) and *In-between Dance Cultures: On the Migratory Artistic Identity of Sidi Larbi Cherkaoui and Akram Khan* (Valiz, 2015).

Jonzi D and **Soweto Kinch** are regular collaborators and have performed, emceed, and created shows together, among them *Markus the Sadist* in 2009. Kinch – lyricist, emcee, alto-saxophonist, producer, composer, mentor and curator – crosses between the genres of jazz and hip hop. He received two MOBO awards for Best Jazz Act and his first album was nominated for a Mercury Music Prize in 2003. Jonzi D trained at the London Contemporary Dance School and became an Associate Artist at The Place before founding his own production company and moving to Sadler's Wells as Associate Artist and Artistic Director of the annual festival *Breakin' Convention*. He has been involved in the British hip hop scene from its inception in the eighties – rapping, b-boying, and eventually synthesising all these art forms into the genre of 'Lyrikal Fearta', or hip hop Dance Theatre. His productions, including *Aeroplane Man*, *TAG ... Just Writing My Name* and *The Letter*, have toured all over the world.

Piet Defraeye is a drama theorist, critic and director. He taught and directed in Belgium, Dublin, Toronto, and Fredericton before coming to the University of Alberta, where he is now Professor and Associate Chair (Grad. Studies). Trained as a literature and theatre scholar, he has published extensively on contemporary performance. He has embarked on a larger research project that focuses on the representation of the Rwandan genocide in cultural discourse, and on the representation of the figure of Patrice Lumumba. He recently directed De la Chenelière's *Bashir Lazhar* (2009–2011), Federman's *The Voice in the Closet* (2012), and Van Leeuwen's *White Bread* (2014–2016).

Tim Etchells' work is diverse, spanning performance, visual art and fiction. Based in Sheffield, he is Artistic Director of the theatre company Forced Entertainment, which has developed more than forty theatre and performance pieces in a distinct style since 1984. Besides writing and directing for Forced Entertainment, and occasionally performing with them, Etchells has collaborated with artists from all around the world to create performance- and text-based work, installations and dance pieces. In addition to his three volumes of fiction, *Endland Stories*, *Dream Dictionary* and *The Broken World*, he has published *Certain Fragments*, an academic book about the work of Forced Entertainment. He is also Professor of Performance at Sheffield University.

Few people within the contemporary art scene have been as influential both in their work and its accompanying discourse as **Antony Gormley**. The body lies at the heart of his artistic practice and he is best known for the life-sized casts of his own body in bronze or iron that inhabit a variety of landscapes, beaches and cities across the world. Passionate about dance, Gormley has put his own creativity to the service of choreographers Sidi Larbi Cherkaoui and Hofesh Shechter, creating stage environments for pieces such as *zero degrees*, *Sutra*, *Babel (words)*, and *Survivor*. For his own work, which has been exhibited in all the most important museums and galleries throughout the UK and internationally, he has received a Turner Prize, a South Bank Prize for Visual Art, an Obayashi Prize and the Praemium Imperiale. He continues to investigate the relationship of the human body to its surrounding space through sculpture.

Akram Khan is a dancer, choreographer and Artistic Director of the Akram Khan Company. He was born in London into a family of Bangladeshi origin and started to train in the classical Indian dance form of Kathak at seven. Throughout his career he has maintained his commitment to classical Kathak, while developing contemporary work for his own company as well as collaborating on duets with Sidi Larbi Cherkaoui, Sylvie Guillem and Juliette Binoche. An Associate Artist at both Sadler's Wells and MC2: Grenoble, Khan has received numerous awards for his work, including a Laurence Olivier Award and a South Bank Sky Arts Award. He was awarded an MBE for services to dance in 2005.

Ruth Little is a theatre and dance dramaturg, a teacher and a writer. She lectured in English literature at the University of Sydney and was Literary Manager at Out of Joint, Soho Theatre, the Young Vic and the Royal Court. She is now Akram Khan's regular collaborator, also working with choreographers Sidi Larbi Cherkaoui and Siobhan Davies, as well as with English National Ballet, Sadler's Wells, Northern Ballet, and the freestyle ice skaters Le Patin Libre. Thinking about theatre and dance pieces in terms of live, chaotic systems has led to an expansion of her practice into environmental projects. She is Associate Director at Cape Farewell, curating and producing the artistic and environmental research programme *Sea Change*. Little is among the first generation of dance dramaturgs and an influential voice in the field of bodily, non-literary dramaturgy.

Choreographer **Russell Maliphant** and lighting designer **Michael Hulls** have been collaborating for more than twenty years, creating a unique and distinctive artistic signature in which the dancers interact with the light that enwraps them. Both trained in dance. Maliphant left a career in classical ballet to develop his own choreographic language out of elements of ballet, contact improvisation, yoga, capoeira and tai chi, while Hulls switched to lighting design after college, receiving a bursary to attend dance lighting workshops with Jennifer Tipton in New York. Working together as well as separately, they have collaborated with renowned artists including Sylvie Guillem, Isaac Julien and Robert Lepage, and have received numerous awards including a South Bank Show Dance Award, two Critics' Circle awards, and an Olivier Award for Best New Dance

Production. Hulls holds two Knights of Illumination awards and has recently created his first stage production for light without any dancers.

Alain Platel trained as an orthopaedic therapist and maintains that his career as a theatre director and choreographer happened accidentally. In 1984 he set up a small performance collective with a number of friends and relatives in Ghent in Belgium. With *Iets op Bach*, 1998, the group – by now called les ballets C de la B – gained international recognition and acclaim, which has continued to this day. As well as creating dance and theatre pieces, Platel has collaborated with the British film director Sophie Fiennes on *Because I Sing*, 2001, *Ramallah! Ramallah! Ramallah!*, 2005, and *VSPRS Show and Tell*, 2007. He has won several international awards, including the prestigious Prix Nouvelle Réalités Théâtrales in 2001 from the European Union.

A former drummer in a rock band, **Hofesh Shechter** is known for creating all the music for his own dance pieces. While still a dancer with the Israeli dance company Batsheva. he began studying percussion in Tel Aviv and Paris. He then moved to London and in 2003 made his choreographic debut with the duet *Fragments* at The Place. Shechter's work soon translated to the large scale, with the double bill *Uprising/ In your rooms* being performed both at the Southbank Centre and Sadler's Wells Theatre in 2007. *In your rooms* won the Critics Circle Award for Best Choreography 2008. Since founding his own company in 2008, Shechter has created and toured a range of new works for his own dancers and initiated a comprehensive education programme, as well as creating works for other dance and ballet companies all over the world. He is an Associate Artist at Sadler's Wells and Hofesh Shechter Company is Resident Company at Brighton Dome.

Partners

Akram Khan Company

Co-founded in 2000 by award-winning choreographer Akram Khan and producer Farooq Chaudhry, Akram Khan Company has established itself as one of the foremost innovative dance companies, performing to sell-out audiences in leading festivals and venues around the world. Embracing Khan's artistic vision that both respects and challenges tradition and modernity, the Company has become renowned for its intercultural, interdisciplinary collaborations and has developed a significant range of works from classical kathak and modern solos to artist-to-artist duets and ensemble pieces, with imaginative and highly accessible productions such as *Until the Lions*, *Kaash*, iTMOi (*in the mind of igor*), *DESH*, *Vertical Road*, *Gnosis* and *zero degrees*. Khan's work is recognised as being profoundly moving, and his intelligently crafted storytelling is effortlessly both intimate and epic. A milestone in the Company's journey was the creation of a section of the London Olympic Games Opening Ceremony in 2012. The Company has been showered with prestigious honours including an Olivier Award for *DESH* and a record-breaking six Critics' Circle National Dance Awards.

www.akramkhancompany.net

Concertgebouw Brugge

Concertgebouw Brugge is an international music and performing arts centre devoted to the development and presentation of world-class art. It focuses on music and contemporary dance and plays a leading role in the contemporary dance world, both in Flanders and abroad. Concertgebouw Brugge's wide range of dance offerings always brims with renowned (inter)national companies and choreographers. But there is also plenty of room for young up-and-coming talent. They also offer young choreographers a chance to present their work.

Within the programming, particular attention is paid to dance performances to live music (facilitated by the outstanding acoustics of the Concert Hall). Cultural diversity is another priority. And all of this is backed up by a wealth of context activities and art-educational projects. Since 2009, Anne Teresa De Keersmaeker and her company Rosas have been resident artists. From 2017, their works will be complemented by those of new resident choreographers Claire Croizé and Etienne Guilloteau.

Each year the December Dance Festival brings the cream of the world's contemporary dance to Flanders. In uneven years an internationally renowned choreographer is invited to be its guest curator. Sidi Larbi Cherkauoi, Anne Teresa De Keersmaeker, Akram Khan, Wim Vandekeybus and Jan Fabre have already done the honours. In even years the festival has a geographic focus. Quebec/Montreal, the Nordic Countries, Central Europe and Asia have previously been featured. December Dance 2016 will focus exclusively on the UK dance scene.

www.concertgebouw.be
www.decemberdance.be

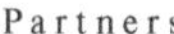

Eastman

Founded in January 2010, Eastman was set up to produce and spread the work of artistic director/choreographer Sidi Larbi Cherkaoui. Cherkaoui's work provides the audience with a vast array of projects and collaborations; ranging from contemporary dance, theatre, ballet, opera, musical and other forms of performance. His non-hierarchical thinking on movement, body language and culture is the basis of his artistic approach. Set in his native harbor city of Antwerp (Belgium), Eastman forms the central point for all of Cherkaoui's work. Eastman is resident at deSingel International Art Campus (Antwerp). Sidi Larbi Cherkaoui is associate artist at Sadler's Wells (London, UK).

Since Eastman's foundation in 2010, under its wings Cherkaoui has created, among others, *Babel* (*words*), *Play*, *Rein*, *TeZukA*, *Puz/zle*, *4D*, and *生长genesis*. Eastman also coordinates all the work of Cherkaoui for other organisations. International partners of Eastman include Les Théâtres de la Ville de Luxembourg, Grande Halle de La Villette Paris, Theaterfestival Boulevard 's-Hertogenbosch, Festspielhaus Sankt-Pölten, Fondazione Musica per Roma, Sadler's Wells London, De Munt Brussels.

Eastman is supported by the Flemish authorities and BNP Paribas Foundation. Eastman is European Cultural Ambassador 2013.

www.east-man.be

Fontys Dance Academy

The Fontys Dance Academy offers authentic, inquisitive and distinctive dance artists an inclusive learning environment; a clear focus on individual growth and cooperative exploration; diverse training and research in performance and movement practices. Our students are the creators and performers of their own work. We specifically appreciate students who challenge our ideas of what a dance artist is. We invite dancers with different backgrounds with an urgent interest in creative, playful and conceptual dance training.

Next to the profile 'Dance Arts in Context' Fontys offers the unique profile 'Contemporary Urban' with a clear style addition of hip hop. In both profiles students are challenged to collaborate with other art disciplines on different locations inside and outside the theatre through different kind of projects. This is made possible in and around the beautiful building of Fontys School of Fine and Performing Arts, in the heart of Tilburg. The building is shared with fourteen other art educations ranging from Circus and Architecture to Visual Arts and Music.

Based on the acknowledgement of the growing multiplicity in future dance careers an educational dance programme was created that encourages students to shift embodied skills into different situations to be able to connect their artistry more with society. An international Erasmus+ Project *Inclusive Dance and Movement Practice, the transferable skills of the dance artist*, will support this further with a co-created online platform for dance professionals.

https://fontys.edu/Bachelors-masters/Bachelors/Dance-Academy/
www.inclusivedance.eu

les ballets C de la B

In 1984, les ballets C de la B (Ghent-Belgium) was founded by Alain Platel, together with his friends and members of his family. Since then it has become a company that enjoys great success at home and abroad. Over the years it developed into an artistic platform for a variety of choreographers, remaining faithful to the will to share. They include Christine De Smedt, Hans Van den Broeck, Sidi Larbi Cherkaoui, Koen Augustijnen, Lisi Estaras, Kaori Ito. The company still keeps to its principle of enabling artists from various disciplines and backgrounds to take part in this dynamic creative process. As a result of its 'unique mixture of artistic visions', les ballets C de la B is not easy to classify. It is nevertheless possible to discern a house style (popular, anarchic, eclectic, committed), and its motto is 'this dance is for the world and the world is for everyone'.

www.lesballetscdela.be

Sadler's Wells

Sadler's Wells is a world-leading dance house, committed to producing, commissioning and presenting new works and to bringing the best international and UK dance to London and worldwide audiences. Its acclaimed year-round programme spans dance of every kind, from contemporary to flamenco, Bollywood, ballet, salsa, street dance and tango. Since 2005, it has helped to bring over a hundred new dance works to the stage and its award-winning commissions and collaborative productions regularly tour in the UK and overseas.

Sadler's Wells supports sixteen Associate Artists, three Resident Companies, an Associate Company and two International Associate Companies. It also nurtures the next generation of talent through research and development, running the National Youth Dance Company and a range of programmes including Wild Card, New Wave Associates, Open Art Surgery and Summer University. Located in Islington, north London, the current theatre is the sixth to have stood on the site since it was first built by Richard Sadler in 1683. The venue has played an illustrious role in the history of theatre ever since, with The Royal Ballet, Birmingham Royal Ballet and English National Opera all having started at Sadler's Wells.

Sadler's Wells is a National Portfolio Organisation and receives 9 per cent of its revenue from Arts Council England.

www.sadlerswells.com

Colophon

Colophon

Imaginative Bodies
Dialogues in Performance Practices

Author
Guy Cools

Editing
Lisa Marie Bowler

Antennae Series n° 22
by Valiz, Amsterdam

Part of the Series
'Arts *in* Society'

Copy Editing
Leo Reijnen

Proof Check
Els Brinkman

Index
Ingrid Oosterheerd
Elke Stevens

Design
Metahaven

Paper Inside
Munken Print 100 gr 1.5

Paper Cover
Bioset 240 gr

Printing and Binding
Ten Brink, Meppel
POD: Scanlaser, Zaandam

Publisher
Valiz, Amsterdam, 2016
Second print, POD, 2024
www.valiz.nl

ISBN 978-94-92095-20-6

This publication was made possible through the generous support of Akram Khan Company, London (UK); Concertgebouw Brugge (BE); Eastman, Antwerp (BE); Fontys Dance Academy, Tilburg (NL); les Ballets C de la B, Brussels (BE); Sadler's Wells, London (UK).

Distribution:
USA /Canada/Latin America: D.A.P., www.artbook.com
GB/IE: Anagram Books, www.anagrambooks.com
NL/BE/LU: Coen Sligting, www.coensligtingbookimport.nl
Europe/Asia/Australia: Idea Books, www.ideabooks.nl
Australia: Perimeter Books, www.perimeterdistribution.com

ISBN 978-94-92095-20-6
NUR 675

Printed and bound in the Netherlands

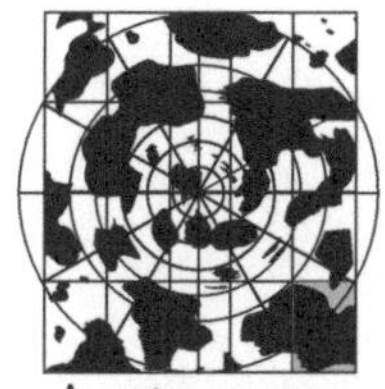

Antennae Series

Antennae N° 1
The Fall of the Studio
Artists at Work
edited by Wouter Davidts
& Kim Paice
Amsterdam: Valiz, 2009
(2nd ed.: 2010),
ISBN 978-90-78088-29-5

Antennae N° 2
Take Place
Photography and Place from Multiple Perspectives
edited by Helen Westgeest
Amsterdam: Valiz, 2009,
ISBN 978-90-78088-35-6

Antennae N° 3
The Murmuring of the Artistic Multitude
Global Art, Memory and Post-Fordism
Pascal Gielen (author)
Arts *in* Society
Amsterdam: Valiz, 2009
(2nd ed.: 2011),
ISBN 978-90-78088-34-9

Antennae N° 4
Locating the Producers
Durational Approaches to Public Art
edited by Paul O'Neill
& Claire Doherty
Amsterdam: Valiz, 2011,
ISBN 978-90-78088-51-6

Antennae N° 5
Community Art
The Politics of Trespassing
edited by Paul De Bruyne &
Pascal Gielen
Arts *in* Society
Amsterdam: Valiz, 2011 (2nd ed.: 2013),
ISBN 978-90-78088-50-9

Antennae N° 6
See it Again, Say it Again
The Artist as Researcher
edited by Janneke Wesseling
Amsterdam: Valiz, 2011,
ISBN 978-90-78088-53-0

Antennae N° 7
Teaching Art in the Neoliberal Realm
Realism versus Cynicism
edited by Pascal Gielen &
Paul De Bruyne
Arts *in* Society
Amsterdam: Valiz, 2012
(2nd ed.: 2013),
ISBN 978-90-78088-57-8

Antennae N° 8
Institutional Attitudes
Instituting Art in a Flat World
edited by Pascal Gielen
Arts *in* Society
Amsterdam: Valiz, 2013,
ISBN 978-90-78088-68-4

Antennae N° 9
Dread
The Dizziness of Freedom
edited by Juha van 't Zelfde
Amsterdam: Valiz, 2013,
ISBN 978-90-78088-81-3

Antennae N° 10
Participation Is Risky
Approaches to Joint Creative Processes
edited by Liesbeth Huybrechts
Amsterdam: Valiz, 2014,
ISBN 978-90-78088-77-6

Antennae N° 11
The Ethics of Art
Ecological Turns in the Performing Arts
edited by Guy Cools & Pascal Gielen
Arts *in* Society
Amsterdam: Valiz, 2014,
ISBN 978-90-78088-87-5

Antennae N° 12
Alternative Mainstream
Making Choices in Pop Music
Gert Keunen (author)
Arts *in* Society
Amsterdam: Valiz, 2014,
ISBN 978-90-78088-95-0

Antennae N° 13
The Murmuring of the Artistic Multitude
Global Art, Politics and Post-Fordism
Pascal Gielen (author)
Completely revised and enlarged
edition of Antennae N° 3
Arts *in* Society
Amsterdam: Valiz, 2015,
ISBN 978-94-92095-04-6

Antennae N° 14
Aesthetic Justice
Intersecting Artistic and Moral Perspectives
edited by Pascal Gielen &
Niels Van Tomme
Arts *in* Society
Amsterdam: Valiz, 2015,
ISBN 978-90-78088-86-8

Antennae N° 15
No Culture, No Europe
On the Foundation of Politics
edited by Pascal Gielen
Arts *in* Society
Amsterdam: Valiz, 2015,
ISBN 978-94-92095-03-9

Antennae N° 16
Arts Education Beyond Art
Teaching Art in Times of Change
edited by Barend van Heusden &
Pascal Gielen
Arts *in* Society
Amsterdam: Valiz, 2015,
ISBN 978-90-78088-85-1

Antennae N° 17
Mobile Autonomy
Exercises in Artists' Self-Organization
edited by Nico Dockx &
Pascal Gielen
Arts *in* Society
Amsterdam: Valiz, 2015,
ISBN 978-94-92095-10-7

Antennae N° 18
Moving Together
Theorizing and Making Contemporary Dance
Rudi Laermans (author)
Arts *in* Society
Amsterdam: Valiz, 2015,
ISBN 978-90-78088-52-3

Antennae N° 19
Spaces for Criticism
Shifts in Contemporary Art Discourses
edited by Thijs Lijster, Suzana Milevska, Pascal Gielen,
Ruth Sonderegger
Arts *in* Society
Amsterdam: Valiz, 2015,
ISBN 978-90-78088-75-2

Antennae N° 20
Interrupting the City
Artistic Constitutions of the Public Sphere
edited by Sander Bax, Pascal Gielen
& Bram Ieven
Arts *in* Society
Amsterdam: Valiz, 2015,
ISBN 978-94-92095-02-2

Antennae N° 21
In-between Dance Cultures
On the Migratory Artistic Identity of Sidi Larbi Cherkaoui and Akram Khan
Guy Cools (author)
Arts *in* Society
Amsterdam: Valiz, 2015,
ISBN 978-94-92095-11-4